WINNING THROUGH
PLATFORMS

WINNING THROUGH PLATFORMS

How to Succeed When Every Competitor Has One

BY

TED MOSER

CHARLOTTE BLOOM

OMAR AKHTAR

United Kingdom – North America – Japan – India
Malaysia – China

Emerald Publishing Limited

Emerald Publishing, Floor 5, Northspring, 21-23 Wellington Street, Leeds LS1 4DL.

First edition 2024

British Library Cataloguing in Publication Data
A catalogue record for this book is available from the British Library

ISBN: 978-1-80455-301-5 (Print)
ISBN: 978-1-80455-298-8 (Online)
ISBN: 978-1-80455-300-8 (Epub)

INVESTOR IN PEOPLE

To our families, for their infinite inspiration, encouragement, and love

CONTENTS

Part 3 Demand Plays

Part 4 Innovation Plays

Part 5 Interaction Plays

Part 6 Transformation Plays

LEADING A PLATFORM BUSINESS

Part 7 Culture Shifts

Part 8 Transformative Leadership

AMA INTRODUCTION TO BOOK SERIES

Welcome to marketing in the 21st century – the age of data, social, mobile, automation, and globalization. The field is changing so quickly; it's difficult to keep up. There is increasing uncertainty about the profession's mission and responsibilities. Meantime, the demands marketers face are ever more complex and critical.

This is why the American Marketing Association (AMA) has engaged some of the world's most innovative professionals, academics, and thought leaders to create The Seven Problems of Marketing – a seven-book series that introduces and explores a new set of organizing and actionable principles for the 21st-century marketer.

Each book in the series takes a deep dive into one problem, offering expertise, direction, and case studies while striking a balance between theory and application. The goal is to provide a contemporary framework for marketers as they navigate the unique challenges and vast opportunities of today's dynamic global marketplace.

Here are the seven problems addressed in the series:

Problem 1: Effectively targeting high-value sources of growth.
Problem 2: Defining the role of marketing in the firm and C-suite.
Problem 3: Managing the digital transformation of the modern corporation.
Problem 4: Generating and using insight to shape marketing practice.
Problem 5: Dealing with an omni-channel world.
Problem 6: Competing in dynamic, global markets.
Problem 7: Balancing incremental and radical innovation.

Importantly, the books in this series are written by and for marketers and marketing scholars. All of the conceptual and analytical frameworks offered are born from practice. The authors have applied their tools and methods in client settings, allowing them to test and refine their ideas in the face of real-world challenges. You'll read true stories about how marketers have used innovative thinking and practices to overcome seemingly impossible dilemmas and bring about game-changing success. Theories are explored in a way that busy marketers can understand viscerally. Client stories have been incorporated to illustrate how to apply the analysis frames as well as deal with application and practice-based issues.

Our fundamental aim with this series is to hone the practice of marketing for the 21st century. The AMA has asserted that there is a critical tension within every enterprise between "best" and "next" practices. Marketers often choose best practices because they are safe and proven. Next practices, which push boundaries and challenge conventions, can be riskier. Few enterprises, however, transform themselves and achieve breakout performance with best practices alone. The next practices discussed in this series are often responsible for driving outperformance. The books in this series are designed to engage you on two levels: individually, by increasing your knowledge and "bench strength," and organizationally, by improving the application of marketing concepts within your firm. When you finish each book, we are confident you will feel energized and think differently about the field of marketing and its organizing principles. Through the explanation of theory and compelling examples of its application, you will be empowered to help your organization quickly identify and maximize opportunities. After all, the opportunity to innovate and make an impact is what attracted most of us to the field of marketing in the first place.

Bennie F. Johnson, CEO
American Marketing Association

BOOK SERIES OVERVIEW

In 2016, the AMA established its first-ever intellectual agenda. This intellectual agenda focused on complex, challenging, and difficult-to-solve problems that would be of interest to both academics and practitioners. A working team of scholars and practitioners, selected by AMA leadership, identified seven big problems of marketing as the foundation of the agenda. These problems were ranked from a much longer list of challenges. These seven big problems shared three attributes: they were pressing issues that confronted every organization, they were C-suite level in scope, and they could not be solved by one article or book. Indeed, the team felt that each problem could trigger a decade-long research agenda. A key purpose of the AMA intellectual agenda was thus to stimulate research, dialogue, and debate among the entire AMA membership.

The purpose of the AMA book series is to shed a deeper light on each of the seven problems. In particular, the aim of the series is to enable readers to think differently and take action with regard to these big problems. Thus, the book series operates at two levels: individually, increasing your knowledge and bench strength, and at the organization level, improving the application of marketing concepts within your firm.

Given the nature of these problems, no single book or article can fully address the problem. By their very nature, these problems are significant, nuanced, and approachable from multiple vantage points. As such, each of the books provides a single perspective on the issue. This single perspective is intended to both advance knowledge and spark debate. While the books may emerge from academic literature and/or managerial application, their fundamental aim is to improve the practice of marketing. Books selected for the series are evaluated on six criteria.

1. *Seven Big Problems Focus*
   Each book is focused on one of the seven big problems of marketing. These problems identify key conceptual issues in the field of marketing that are the focus of emerging academic research and that practitioners are actively confronting today.

2. *Audience*
   The book is written primarily for an audience of thoughtful practitioners. Thoughtful in this context means that the practitioner is an active reader of both professional articles and books, is dedicated to enhancing his/her marketing knowledge and skills, and is committed to upgrading the organization's marketing culture, capabilities, and results. A secondary audience is academics (and students) and consultants.

3. *Integrative Framework*
   The book provides an integrated framework that frames the problem and offers a detailed approach for addressing it.

4. *Field-based Approach*
   The authors have applied their frameworks in client settings. These client settings enable authors to test and refine their frameworks. Conceptual and analysis frameworks are enlivened via practice and case examples that demonstrate application in the field. Named and/or disguised client stories illustrate how to apply the analysis frames, how to deal with application issues, and other practice-based issues.

5. *Academic Literature*
   The integrative frameworks should be new to the marketplace. The conceptual frameworks should extend existing thinking and the analysis frameworks should provide new ways to conduct marketing-related analysis.

6. *Readability*
   The book should be intelligible to the average reader. The concepts should be clearly defined and explained, and cases written

so that a reader can understand the content on a first read. On behalf of the AMA, I am excited to bring these books to market. I am anxious to hear your feedback – both positive and challenging – as we move the field forward.

Bernie Jaworski
AMA Book Series Editor

FOREWORD
David Aaker

David Aaker is the author of 18 books and over 100 articles on business strategy, marketing strategy, and branding. A member of the NY AMA Marketing Hall of Fame, he is often called the father of modern branding. He is Professor Emeritus at UC Berkeley and Vice Chair of Prophet, a global growth consultancy.

Dear reader,

This book is a tour de force, providing a comprehensive road-map for platform-based digital strategies. It is astonishingly broad in scope, organized with a rich conceptual model, and full of deep insights that lead to actionable strategic options. This book is also incredibly timely in the way it addresses topics like Artificial Intelligence and Extended Reality. Every executive, manager, and rising professional who needs to cut through confusion around intelligent platforms and then identify business risks and opportunities will benefit greatly by reading and applying Winning Through Platforms.

Let me highlight four specific reasons why I am impressed.

First, the central concept of this book – the digital platform – provides readers an expansive look at recent trends in digital strategy. It reveals many different ways that platform data sensing, software code, and computing power enable you to observe, interact with, and provide value to customers as they use what it is they have accessed from your company. The authors show how the customer's use journey — formerly inaccessible but now visible through platforms — holds the most value.

This book explains how a wide range of companies have creatively used their platforms to beat competitors and create new avenues for growth. It explains the strategic evolution of companies you might naturally think of as platform owners – Uber, Zillow,

Airbnb, Salesforce, and Netflix for example. It also explains strategic innovations by companies you might not think of as platform owners – Nike, Haier, Autodesk, Disney, and SleepNumber to name a few. Each company has innovated through platforms to shift what their customers buy and use, opening huge growth opportunities. In all, this book distills winning moves of over 50 companies into principles you can use.

Second, the methods and tools of the platform age are explained in action, from Internet of Things to different branches of Artificial Intelligence (machine learning, natural language processing, computer vision, and generative intelligence). The book demonstrates how they can be applied in a competitive context to win the customer.

In the same vein, this book helps me better understand why Artificial Intelligence and Extended Reality have been on such a sharp rise when their underlying technologies have been advancing for at least two decades. The authors' depiction of recent widespread platform adoption makes clear that there is much more customer "use journey" data now to access, analyze, and act on than before. Because this book also shows how innovative user journey experiences can drive customer relationship, loyalty, and expansion, the case for company investment is made, including strategic value at a level not seen in the past.

Third, I value how this book organizes winning moves into an amazingly comprehensive playbook. The playbook covers – with equal intensity – platform plays for strategic advantage (business portfolio and platform design), in-market advantage (demand acceleration and ongoing innovation), and organizational execution (operations and transformation). Each of 24 "plays" falls into a way of winning that can drive growth.

To give you a taste:

- A play called "Optimal Platform Roles" provides a thought-provoking set of options for platform business strategy. Including a strategy used by Netflix to build a competitive advantage by creating synergies between its platform (streaming media distribution) and physical business (A-list actor movie production).

- A play called "Success to Momentum" illustrates why and how Amazon Prime and Salesforce Trailhead take different approaches to achieve the same customer momentum goal.

- A play called "Full Journey Engagement" shows how Nike engages customers through a full journey of platform touch-points to achieve a 4X higher customer lifetime value.

- Other plays explain how Haier and the World Expo differenti-ate globally through high-impact innovation using platform-enhanced experiences.

By addressing topics from strategy through execution, this book ensures that every reader will find insights that helps them advance today. Additional insights they don't use immediately will serve them tomorrow as their needs change.

Finally, I like the writing style that the authors use. The 24 plays are not introduced in the abstract but are illustrated by one, two, or more case studies. I also enjoy the diverting historical metaphors that explain needed culture shifts. You'll enjoy the read as you learn; so will your teams.

To summarize, this book is a guide to transforming in a way that every business needs. By providing critical stepping stones for win-ning in a platform world, this book can be a real difference maker for every reader, at a key moment of risk and opportunity.

David Aaker

THE SEARCH FOR PLATFORM ADVANTAGE

COMPETING IN THE PLATFORM ERA

We're living and leading in a fast evolving business era – the platform era.

The 2010s were the takeoff years for platforms, when simply having one could bring differentiation.

In the mainstream 2020s, platforms are becoming a must-have. This means markets will be platform crowded, customers platform expectant, and investors platform impatient.

It's time to move beyond simply heralding platform business, to focus on how companies can win at platforms when every competitor has one. Enough experiments have occurred that we can glean success patterns. Enough technologies are emerging that we can see new opportunities.

What's missing is a how-to-win playbook, focused on ways to earn customer choice and energize customer use for advantaged growth and economics.

This book is that playbook. We believe you should learn it. Because when business eras change, the rules of winning change too. Those who learn, apply, and scale the new rules of platform success are those who will prosper.

Introduction

LIGHT THE DARK

When humanity took its first big space adventure in 1969, our most gripping moment didn't come during the rocket's voyage to the moon and back. It didn't happen during astronaut Neil Armstrong's descent to the surface, walk on the moonscape, or ascent to redock. No, when we really grabbed our chairs and held our breath was when astronaut Michael Collins flew the spaceship Columbia around the "dark side" of the moon, the half that never faces Earth.

It lasted 47 agonizing minutes. No radio contact, no visual sighting, no way to know what was happening. If the ship had crashed or escaped lunar gravity for a long drift toward the sun, we could have only guessed – with a sick feeling in our stomachs – at what had gone wrong. All we would know is that they never came back. We collectively exhaled when Collins and Columbia reemerged into view.

Fast forward to 2019. What a difference 50 years of learning and innovation make! China's Yutu-2 rover landed – on purpose – on what we once called the "dark side" of the moon. We called this new visit a trip to the moon's "far side," no longer dark because we learned the sun shines there and new communication satellites keep us constantly connected.

Yet far bigger than a new name was a change in our perspective. Geological moon samples taught us that the far side of the moon is the most valuable side – by far. Economically it has valuable minerals like titanium and platinum. Existentially it has Helium-3, the most promising material for clean, non-radioactive

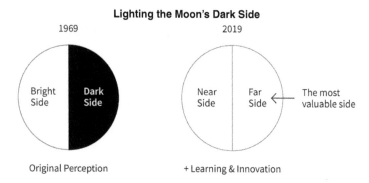

Lighting the Moon's Dark Side

Int.1.1

nuclear fusion energy. Experts estimate that fewer than a dozen space shuttle cargos of Helium-3 annually could provide enough fuel to sustain all human beings on the planet for 10,000 years.[1,2] In short, the side of the moon that we couldn't see for so long is the side that can change our future for the better.

Now, the race is on to realize the full value of our discovery. The world's major powers have all reprioritized lunar mining exploration.[3] Tech incubators are developing infrastructure for the far side.[4] Experts in geology, robotics, and energy work cross functionally to solve new problems. And futurists remind everyone that success depends on global collaboration. Our fate is too interconnected to work in siloes.

LIGHTING THE CUSTOMER JOURNEY

The most important business story of our lifetime runs remarkably parallel to our story of lunar discovery. This story is about the digital lighting of the customer journey. It's particularly about how platforms enable your company to light the dark side of your customer's journey – the post-purchase "Use" journey. Platforms are the technologies that enable your company to observe, interact with, and provide value to customers as they use what they have accessed through you. This story is about how you can shine the light of platforms for advantage. Your customer's advantage, your company's advantage, and your competitive advantage. As you do, you'll discover that the side of your customer's journey that had always been dark is in fact the most valuable side.

The digital lighting of the customer journey launched in 1969, the same year as our lunar rocket. A new startup named Intel designed a microchip that would change everything – the microprocessor that powered mass market computing.[5] The rising customer visibility that resulted over 50 years is represented by three customer journey "moons" in three different years.

Each journey moon has two sides – the customer's *Choose journey and Use journey*. In the Choose journey, customers explore their needs and options, assess their final choices, and transact. In the Use journey, customers use the products and services they have accessed, then eventually decide whether to access them again – and if so, from who.

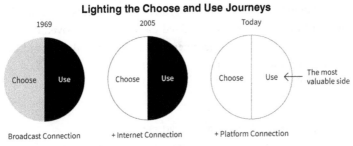

Lighting the Choose and Use Journeys

1969   2005   Today

Choose   Use   Choose   Use   Choose   Use ← The most valuable side

Broadcast Connection   + Internet Connection   + Platform Connection

Int.1.2

Two major lightings got us to where we are today.

Lighting the Choose Journey: 1969–2005

In 1969, the customer's Choose journey was murky to companies, and the Use journey was pitch dark. Customers would emerge from shadow into light as shoppers, perhaps lured by an analog broadcast advertisement – no one knew for sure. The shopper would expose their needs and identity, make their purchase, and then disappear into the dark.

When shoppers became users, companies lost their line of sight and communication. If a customer drifted away, there was no way for a company to know if they had learned how to use what they bought, if they had become stuck, or if they turned sour on a purchase and bad-mouthed the brand to friends. All that a business would know is that the customer never came back.

From 1969 to 2005, the computing revolution started by Intel and other innovators shined new light on the customer's Choose journey. First companies used computers to analytically personalize messages for segmented mailing and phone lists, raising customer response rates. Then networked personal computers enabled direct communication to shoppers, with real-time stimulus-response adjustments.

The Choose journey shone brightest with the Internet revolution. Internet search engines and websites transformed one-way company communication at customers into a two-way dialogue with customers, inbound and outbound, as they were in the act of choosing.

By contrast, in 2005, the customer's Use journey was still dark to companies. True, most companies had improved new purchase onboarding and had set up call centers for moments of need. Yet the real-time user journey remained dark – an undiscovered land, an untapped source of customer and company value, a hidden treasure waiting to be mined.

Until platforms arrived.

Lighting the Use Journey: 2005 to Present

A platform runs on customer sensing data linked to cloud-hosted software code and computing power. It is the act of cloud hosting that enables your company to observe, interact with, and provide connected value to customers during their Use journey, for mutual gain and growth. Regardless of whether you're swiping a cell phone, tapping a keyboard, accelerating your car, working out, cooking a meal, or lying in your bed – Use journey darkness between customer and company has come to an end.

A platform isn't experienced directly by the customer, but is expressed to the customer through one or more experience hubs. These experience hubs may take on many names: apps, super apps, clouds, suites, consoles, exchanges, displays, dashboards, and more. The moniker doesn't matter – the job of an experience hub is to convert platform functionality into valued customer experiences of interface, interaction, and performance.

Today's tech titans pioneered platforms for themselves around 2005. Then in a burst of creativity from 2005 to 2010 several titans created the infrastructure that the world's entrepreneurs would need to get into the platform game. Apple (iOS) and Samsung/HTC (Android OS) invented smartphones with app stores, paving the route to market for platform app developers. Titans also began renting their data center infrastructure and know-how to every company, creating a business model that today we call Cloud Service Providers. Those titans were Amazon Web Services, Google Cloud Platform, and Microsoft Azure. Thanks to every titan's lowering of investment barriers, platform innovation took off.

During the takeoff years of 2010–2019 more than 16,000 platform companies started up,[6] backed by risk capital and hoping for Initial Public Offerings (IPOs). Platform companies who filled business headlines in the early 2010s included Uber, Zillow, AirBnB, MasterClass, Netflix, Tesla, and OneTrust, to name just a few. These early disruptors proved what a difference a platform can make. By turning the customer's darkened use journey into a zone of visibility and interaction, disruptors created new markets, took market share from incumbent leaders, and raised customer expectations for what a modern brand could deliver.

Progressive incumbents didn't stand still. Inspired by disruptors, they added platforms to their businesses, most in the later years of the 2010s. Firms like Adobe, Disney, Autodesk, Progressive, Nike, Haier, Thompson Reuters, Zebra, and Sleep Number all began or completed transformations to become platform companies.

And the innovations kept coming. Platforms can now be found across the economy, spanning agriculture, construction, banking, cosmetics, medical devices, fitness, media, eyeglasses, transportation, home appliances, mattresses, apparel, investment management, cybersecurity, real estate, insurance, hospitality, accounting, and global poverty alleviation. Businesses in every corner of the economy are being made stronger through platforms.

Fueled by mounting evidence of success and turbocharged by the pandemic, platforms have gone from being a novelty to being top of the list of every management team's agenda. In other words, the platform era's takeoff years have evolved into its mainstream years.

The implication for business is profound. Just as no major company thrives today without a website to interact with buyers on their Choose journey, in 5–10 years no major company will thrive without a platform that enables them to interact with customers on their Use journey.

That's why business leaders need to raise their competitive game to make experience hub and platform advantage a critical new means of achieving business advantage. Through this book, we'll introduce a playbook for winning through platforms.

But before we do, we'll provide three important answers you can give your leadership team if they question the business imperative behind platform excellence and advantage. Managed well, platforms will redefine your company's relevance to customers; they will give investors confidence in your future; and they will equip you to compete in convergent competitive markets. Managed poorly, the opposite will be true.

PLATFORMS REDEFINE YOUR RELEVANCE

Platforms redefine – by elevating – a company's relevance to its customers. They add a new value proposition – infinite connection throughout the customer's Use journey – to the company's traditional value proposition. This higher relevance is reflected through the customer's view of the company's brand. One fact-based proof point is found in the results of an annual Brand Relevance Index (BRI) survey carried out since 2014 by the growth consulting firm Prophet.[7] The survey asks tens of thousands of consumers annually about the relevance of hundreds of brands in their lives. The Prophet survey also captures and correlates the underlying drivers of that relevance. Brand relevance is the business equivalent of the canary in the coal mine. It is existential, because it indicates whether customers want to be in a forward-looking relationship with your company.

We averaged the BRI scores of brands who were tested a minimum of three years during this time. The results are revealing. From 2014 to 2022, brands with higher and lower relevance scores are highly correlated to whether a platform does or doesn't play a key role in their value proposition to customers. The top 10 brands are 80% platform businesses; the next 10 brands are 50% platform;

the next 30 brands are 33% platform. These all contrast with the middle-scoring 150 brands which are 26% platform, and the bottom 50 brands, which are 16% platform.

These percentages drive home how platform Use journey connections redefine brand relevance. They also remind us that having a platform is not a guarantee of brand relevance – it's what you do with it. Platform brands in the middle- and low-scoring cohort tend to have functionality of a utility (certain social media channels, news aggregators, and online banks, for example).

Platform Businesses and BRI Rankings

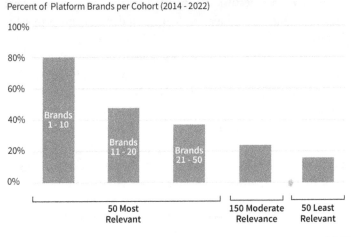

Percent of Platform Brands per Cohort (2014 - 2022)

Int.1.3

By contrast, platform brands in the high-scoring cohorts deliver more vibrant and valued customer benefits. Rather than tell now many of the stories we'll tell throughout this book, we'll simply mention that high relevance brands score strongly on four clustered benefit attributes:

- *Pervasively innovative* in approach and benefits.

- *Personally critical* to the customer's aspirations.

- *Ruthlessly pragmatic* in solving customer problems.

- *Distinctively inspiring* to the customer's sense of values and purpose.

Keep in mind these relevant drivers as you read what platforms can do for customers. You'll see the connection.

Here's our customer takeaway – it will be hard for your company to remain relevant, and therefore thrive, without developing a platform valued by your customers. Renewing your brand relevance through platforms is an opportunity to renew your long-term business vitality.

PLATFORMS GIVE INVESTORS CONFIDENCE

During the 2010s, investors voted overwhelmingly in favor of the structural advantages of platform-related businesses. The investment community's perspective is visualized in the stock index chart below. The Morgan Stanley technology index, a good proxy for platform sentiment during the decade, rose 16% annually from 2010 to 2019, compared to 8% growth in the general world index.[8] Investors supported platform-enabled companies, believing they were gaining significant competitive advantages over companies without. Platform pioneers rewarded investors with financial proof that digitally interacting with customers throughout their use journey was a powerful growth enabler. Here's an investor takeaway – if your competitors are establishing platforms and you aren't, you're likely to lose investor confidence over time.

Investor Perspective: Internet and Platform Eras

The Internet Era		The Platform Era		
Takeoff	**Mainstream**	**Seeding**	**Takeoff**	**Mainstream**
Startups	Incumbents	Cloud Services	Startups	Incumbents
Risk Capital	Adjacents	Smartphones	Risk Capital	Adjacents
IPOs	New Disruptors	Pioneers	IPOs	New Disruptors

US$ rebased to 100 in 1994 ——— MSCI World Technology ——— MSCI World

Int.1.4

The gap between the two stock indices grew even stronger from 2020 to 2022, during the COVID pandemic, when major segments of the population embraced digital life to avoid exposure. The pandemic certainly boosted digital consumer and workforce behavior and – as a ripple effect – boosted platform business models. A return to physical behaviors is slowing some platform company growth and bringing some highflyer valuations down. But the early 2020s didn't *make* the platform revolution. They only *intensified* and *accelerated* what had already become unstoppable business performance and investor confidence from the 2010s.

PLATFORMS EQUIP YOU TO COMPETE

When platforms appear in a market, the competitive ground shakes beneath everyone's feet. Five types of competitors converge (because data easily crosses market boundaries), each bringing unique angles of value rather than simpler like-for-like competition. The strength of your platform position will determine your competitiveness.

- Category innovators bring a new platform value proposition to customers, highly valued stock for acquisition currency, and a strong talent base via founders and venture capital network recruits.

- Incumbent leaders either incubate or acquire a platform, then eventually integrate the platform into their core business to exploit their strategic assets – often triggering internal battles between old and new business practices.

- Adjacent market platform winners "category jump" into the market seeking new revenue.

- Niche players invest to own particularly valuable customer journey steps or assets, then add partnerships to establish defensible positions.

- Next wave disrupters, backed by new risk capital, either fill gaps or further challenge the status quo.

As mainstream competition heats up, customers respond in new and challenging ways. They take for granted and come to require platform approaches and associated benefits that they once considered novel. Customers learn how to evaluate platforms, and third-party services emerge to help customers compare them before selecting one. Customers also learn how to switch from one platform to another; attackers and third-party services will help them do that, too.

And if this isn't enough, mainstream investors watch convergent competition with shrinking patience for each company's strategy. They no longer have time for the promise of future platform launches, revenue and profit. They will ask for proof that companies have their platform strategy and execution in place and working. If they don't see it, they will sell stock.

Our takeaway – mainstream platform markets are more complex than any in business history. They are competitively crowded, customer expectant, and investor impatient. Your platform must equip you to compete as the challenge of becoming a platform winner moves only in one direction.

Up.

A MAINSTREAM MARKET IN FULL VIEW

To illustrate mainstream platform competition, we'll choose a platform market that operates in every reader's full view – streaming video. Consider the complexity and intensity of platform competition that goes into the movie or TV show you may watch Friday night.

The Innovator Scales

In 2007, Netflix's streaming video distribution system became a showcase for platform innovation. With an all-you-can-watch subscription plus analytics that translated into real-time customer experience, Netflix promoted to the top of each viewer's screen the movies and TV shows they were likeliest to want to watch next.

In 2013, Netflix the distributor became Netflix the movie maker. It used the lure of its large captive audience to attract A-list actors and directors, then used their star power to add subscrib-ers. In the 2010s, Netflix built a subscriber base of 222 million and became the strongest performing S&P 500 stock, boasting a 4,150% return.[9,10]

But along the way, a growing number of competitors attacked, creating new value propositions that overlapped with the one Net-flix had led. Each proposition was designed to peel a part of the customer-base away from the takeoff era's platform winner.[11]

Mainstream Market Competition: Streaming Video

Innovators scale...	Competitors respond...				Innovators evolve...
Innovator	*Incumbents*	*Adjacents*	*Niche*	*Next Gen*	*Innovator*
All-you-can-watch tailored to you **Netflix**	Characters your *family loves* **Disney+**	Free streaming *and free deliveries* Amazon Prime Video	Discover what's *next* in streaming IMDb		*Broadest* catalog at the *best price for you* **Netflix**
	Stream *live* sports **ESPN+**	Create and watch *video entertainment* YouTube	Your *own* AI movie studio Curious Refuge		
		Free with your *best* tech products Apple TV+			

Int.1.5

Incumbents Use Strategic Assets

From 2017 to 2019, the incumbent media conglomerates used their unique content assets to strike back, in some cases pulling inventory back from Netflix. New streaming services from Disney, HBO, Para-mount, and Peacock collectively added over 380 million subscribers by 2023.[12,13]

Disney was the star among incumbents, gaining the most on the back of its family-friendly bundle of Disney+, Hulu, and ESPN. Disney+ differentiated through strategic assets like like Disney and Marvel characters, plus live sports programming. Yet even Disney faced internal challenges of platform transformation. Its stock-holders debated heavy streaming growth investment versus the rich media dividends they expected. Creative studio units and the streaming distribution team wrestled over optimal theater versus home streaming release mix. Disney's former CEO had to be called out of retirement to re-lead the company, in large part to ensure that Disney's platform transformation succeeded.

Adjacents Jump Categories
Amazon, Apple TV+ and YouTube all category-jumped to attack Netflix' market from their respective empires. Amazon, an early entrant with Netflix, made streaming video free for its 200 million e-commerce Prime loyalty subscribers.[14] Apple, a late entrant with far fewer viewers,[15] used its beloved consumer products and brand for streaming media cross-promotion and distribution. Both companies used their deep corporate pockets to launch first-run media production houses to compete with Netflix for A-list movie and TV stars.

The least glitzy but perhaps most potent adjacent attacker was YouTube. Its stronghold category is creator-generated content. YouTube boasts 800 million videos on 37 million channels that grow ever-more sophisticated,[16] while Netflix "only" has 17,000 distributed videos and 1,500 self-produced titles.[17] And within its "amateur" channel, YouTube embeds a wide range of Hollywood-to-Bollywood offers: free ad-based movies, à la carte payment movies, and Google TV subscriptions. It also mimics short-format TikTok via YouTube shorts.

Niche Players Create Strongholds
IMDb, a niche player, carved out an ownable platform. The company began pre-Internet (1990) as a simple database of actors, actresses, and movies. IMDb's platform is now the go-to platform for over 300 million visitors seeking streaming entertainment information (ad-funded) and new media launch promotion (subscription-funded). Here's a twist: Although IMDb has independent management rights, it sold to Amazon in 1998 and partners regularly with the company.[18]

Next Generation Disruptor
Can AI make a movie? Can savvy consumers use an AI platform to get into the movie making business? Curious Refuge believes that AI is the future of moviemaking, The startup offers platform tools, training, and AI movie trailers to make its case. From idea generation to scriptwriting, from scene creation to editing and animation,

from voice over to distribution, Curious Refuge is angling to bring a fresh approach to the streaming media market.[19]

The Innovator Stalls, Then Evolves

Netflix's stock value growth flattened in 2018 as competition rose. COVID gave Netflix a boost, but that wore off when most returned to the office. In April 2022, intensified mainstream competition led Netflix to report its first drop in subscribers in over a decade, leading to a plunge in stock value.[20]

Yet Netflix' story didn't stop there, because the mainstream years are a time of agile competitive adaptation. Netflix is now fighting back through lower priced, ad-funded subscriber options that reframe the company as a superior value while still growing revenue per customer. Netflix' initial adjustments helped it return to audience and revenue growth in early 2023.[21]

There Are Countless Mainstream Markets

Streaming media is just one example of a convergent mainstream platform market; there are countless others. In the personal mobility market, platform competition is underway between ride-sharing services, car makers, scooter and bike makers, consumer electronics makers, public transportation systems, and digital service companies. In financial services markets, platform battles are playing out through embedded finance apps, verified-behavior insurance pricing, neobanks built on third-party platforms, and robo-investment advisors.

HOW WILL YOU WIN?

When platforms become existential for every business, knowing how to win through platforms – at scale and through your people – becomes existential for your professional success. Business competition of the future will feel like The Platform Games, where winning at business means winning through platforms. When you hear "The Platform Games," you might be inspired to think of The Olympic Games and envision your company climbing the podium

to receive a bronze, silver, or gold medal. You might also think of
the survival movie *The Hunger Games*, and its rule that losers are
eliminated. You'd be right on both counts.

Every player in The Platform Games will need to know how to
win through platforms when every competitor has one. This starts
with the leadership team, but it extends throughout the organization to all teams. And here's the catch. Business school and work
experience have taught most professionals how to win through
product lines. Winning through platforms is different. The rules of
success aren't the same. Leaders and their teams need to learn new
rules to succeed.

This book will help you succeed by drawing lessons from over
50 platform firms in diverse industries to codify and share plat-
form-specific ways to win. Rather than describing a product line
game where one product is developed for one target customer, we
describe a platform game where a shape-shifting kaleidoscope of
modular platform value is designed to serve an entire coalition of
customers. Rather than describing a product line journey where
the sale is the end goal, we describe a platform journey where the
sale is just the start of an infinite customer connection. Rather than
describing a product line culture where leaders advance by controlling siloed product line assets, we describe a platform culture where
leaders advance by contributing in sync to shared platform assets.

The result is a playbook that can both help your company build
a successful platform for the first time, and a playbook that can
help your existing platform company elevate its game to the next
competitive level. The time is right for such a playbook. The rules
of success from the platform era's takeoff years have become clear
enough that they be codified as platform best practices and winning competitive plays. New playbook rules can be learned, taught
to teams, and practiced throughout your company to raise your
odds of success.

We wrote this book to help you do just that.

LEARN THE PLAYBOOK,
FIND YOUR PLAYS

The heart of this book is a win-through-platforms playbook. There are 24 winning "platform plays." Each play is a move you can make to build your platform business. You don't need every play immediately. You don't need to use plays in the order they appear. Rather, after learning the playbook, you can flexibly use the plays that create the impact you need now, then use additional plays as your needs and opportunities arise.

This book dedicates one chapter to each play. Each chapter defines a play, provides examples of companies who use the play, explains a key-step framework for you to use the play, and challenges you to answer key questions to apply that play to your business.

The 24 platform plays are grouped into *6 types of plays*, described as *6 parts of the playbook*. These parts of the playbook work in pairs to give you *3 advantages*. The following graphic displays our 24 plays in a playbook format, showing which types of plays and types of advantages they support.

The Platform Playbook

Learn the Playbook,
Find Your Plays

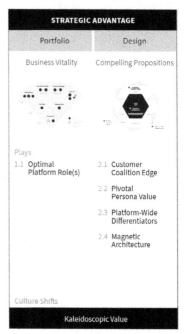

Int.1.6

Here are the platform advantages that our playbook provides, and the types of plays that support each platform advantage. We won't describe specific plays here – that's the job of the book.

- *Achieve Strategic Advantage*: you'll bring something structural to market that the competition doesn't have in order to achieve a competitive advantage.

    o *Portfolio Plays (Part 1)* help you choose the best platform role(s) for your business.

    o *Design Plays (Part 2)* help you develop a differentiated platform and experience hubs.

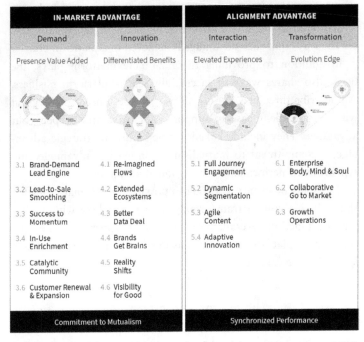

IN-MARKET ADVANTAGE		ALIGNMENT ADVANTAGE	
Demand	Innovation	Interaction	Transformation
Presence Value Added	Differentiated Benefits	Elevated Experiences	Evolution Edge
3.1 Brand-Demand Lead Engine	4.1 Re-Imagined Flows	5.1 Full Journey Engagement	6.1 Enterprise Body, Mind & Soul
3.2 Lead-to-Sale Smoothing	4.2 Extended Ecosystems	5.2 Dynamic Segmentation	6.2 Collaborative Go to Market
3.3 Success to Momentum	4.3 Better Data Deal	5.3 Agile Content	6.3 Growth Operations
3.4 In-Use Enrichment	4.4 Brands Get Brains	5.4 Adaptive Innovation	
3.5 Catalytic Community	4.5 Reality Shifts		
3.6 Customer Renewal & Expansion	4.6 Visibility for Good		
Commitment to Mutualism		Synchronized Performance	

Int.1.7

- *Achieve In-Market Advantage*: you'll grow at higher-than-market rates through better-than-competitor growth moves.

  o *Demand Plays (Part 3)* help you accelerate growth through full-journey demand creation.

  o *Innovation Plays (Part 4)* help you provide new and distinctive benefits.

- *Achieve Alignment Advantage*: you'll translate better internal alignment and collaboration into stronger customer engagement and superior organizational performance.

  o *Interaction Plays (Part 5)* help you create strong journey-wide customer engagement.

  o *Transformation Plays (Part 6)* help you evolve into a high-performing platform company.

The business objectives that our playbook addresses – strategic, in-market, and alignment advantages – are timeless. What's new are the ways that each advantage is achieved in a platform era.

In addition to providing these 24 new platform plays, the book also shares ways to successfully lead a platform business. We describe three new culture shifts that you'll need to carry out within your talent base to support your plays and deepen your advantage. They include kaleidoscopic value for strategic advantage, a commitment to mutualism for in-market advantage, and synchronized performance for alignment advantage.

We finally describe ways you can provide transformative leadership, whether you are transforming company-wide or within a key business function. Overall, these leadership chapters remind us that becoming a platform business is as much a human endeavor as it is a technological one.

THIS PLAYBOOK IS FOR YOU

The playbook can be a vital resource to you, no matter where you are in your career.

- If you seek to advance professionally by learning what's next, the playbook can help you become the next-generation talent that employers seek.

- If you are a go-to-market leader (Chief Marketing Officer, Chief Sales Officer, or Chief Customer Success Officer), it can help you build an innovation and transformation agenda that boosts your company's growth and makes your team more essential to your company's success than ever.

- If you are an executive responsible for moving the company's entire go-to-market system forward or growing a business unit, you can use these ideas to modernize and make the customer-facing portion of your business more effective. You can accelerate customer-base growth and increase new customer acquisition effectiveness.

- If you are a CEO, you can use high-level platform ideas to describe a paradigm shift in the way your business gets done, repositioning your firm to board members, customers, talent, analysts, and investors. You can help them all see more value in your company than ever before.

- If you are a business school professor or student who seeks a modern curriculum, you can find value in the book's educational content and the playbook's modular format.

There's one other way that this playbook is for everyone. The customer-centric platform can have a profound impact on the short- and long-term health of companies in every sector of the economy. The presence value and customer benefits of platforms can help companies improve the lives of people around the planet. While platforms raise major societal issues along the way – particularly around the intimate use of customer data – our approach is to address these issues head-on and to consider how to create win-win outcomes. The opportunity to improve both your company and your society through the playbook make it well worth your effort.

NEW MINDSETS FOR NEW RULES

If you have deep experience in a platform business, you may want to skip this chapter and go straight to the playbook. The thought process we describe here might feel familiar, and therefore not as valuable to you as the action orientation of each play to come.

But if you are new to platform thinking, you'll find great benefit in reflecting on ways that platforms will challenge your assumptions about how business works. These mindsets are shifts you'll need to make best use of the playbook. You will also benefit from a broad overview of the playbook's content before diving in, so you can see how one play relates to another.

This chapter supports you in both ways. It describes two new rules and mindsets needed to use each part of the playbook to its fullest – twelve new rules and mindsets across the six-part playbook. This chapter also previews key diagrams that depict plays within each part of the playbook.

Orient yourself to platform thinking and begin your immersion. You'll be better equipped to turn the new rules described throughout the book into new success.

PORTFOLIO PLAYS

In Part 1, "Portfolio Plays," you'll choose the optimal role(s) that a platform can play in your business portfolio.

New Rule: Choosing the best platform role(s) for your business is an opportunity for strategic creativity. Becoming a platform company is not a one-size-fits-all business design task. Part 1 provides options for the way a platform can enhance your business portfolio. It then helps you choose the role that best fits your business needs.

New Mindset: Drop narrow ideas about what a platform company is so that you can think freely about what your platform company could be. By opening your mind, you'll be better able to creatively map potential platform role(s) against your strategic intent, opportunities, and risk tolerance and then make best choices.

––––––––––––

New Rule: Leadership teams need better defined platform concepts and communications to win. Multiple technology, business, and customer teams use the word "platform" but mean different things. Confusion can lead teams to strategize and communicate poorly. Part 1 recommends ways that leadership teams can better communicate and collaborate.

New Mindset: Question whether your management team is at the top of its game when developing platform strategies. Advocate for improvement if it isn't. Develop a clearer language and visualization to clarify intent and tactics. Include customer-centric functions (marketing, sales, success, insight) during strategy formation, not after the fact.

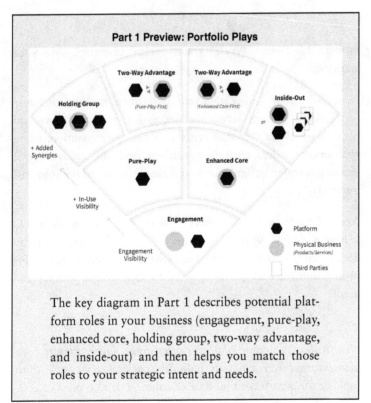

Part 1 Preview: Portfolio Plays

The key diagram in Part 1 describes potential platform roles in your business (engagement, pure-play, enhanced core, holding group, two-way advantage, and inside-out) and then helps you match those roles to your strategic intent and needs.

Int.1.8

DESIGN PLAYS

In Part 2, "Design Plays," you'll design advantage into your platform.

New Rule: Your design approach shifts from product customer to platform customer coalition. Successful platforms serve and connect up to six customer types in a customer coalition: users, sponsors, providers, creators, advertisers, and rule makers. Part 2 challenges you to design your advantage through and for your customer coalition.

New Mindset: Shift your mindset from product line design to platform design. With a customer coalition in mind, you can design platform features and benefits that create a compelling value proposition for each persona, tuned to their unique journey and needs.

New Rule: A winning platform offer architecture attracts complementary buyer types. It pulls in specificity buyers – those looking for a perfect-fit module or solution. It also pulls in commonality buyers – those looking for platform-wide capabilities that help all users or use cases. Part 2 helps you configure different offers and value propositions to different customer targets.

New Mindset: Imagine how the modularity of platform and experience hub design can provide you with new offer levels that attract new customers and empower new growth. Pair them with new go to market channels and capabilities. Your offer architecture choices can broaden your market access, create new growth move options, and reduce the risk of a single-source growth slowdown.

Part 2 Preview: Design Plays

The key diagram in Part 2 illustrates the plays you can use to design in advantage. These include shaping your customer coalition edge, delivering pivotal value to key customer personas at pivotal journey moments, creating platform-wide differentiators, and presenting your design to the market through magnetic architecture.

Int.1.8

DEMAND PLAYS

In Part 3, "Demand Plays," you'll acquire new customers more effi-ciently and grow the value of current customers more effectively for in-market growth advantage.

New Rule: Through platforms, you can raise your efficiency of new customer acquisition. Part 3 explains how platforms can structur-ally accelerate customer acquisition. They build stronger brands, make demand generation more agile, and improve conversion of leads to revenue.

New Mindset: You should be skeptical that your current acquisi-tion motion is achieving all it can. Be ready to shift your brand portfolio to platform brands, customize demand generation for platform modularity, and help prospects say "yes" to platform by removing key obstacles.

New Rule: Your interaction with customers during their Use journey is your largest untapped resource for growth. Part 3 describes how with a platform you can create customer momentum for expansion, enrich the customer's experience of value in-use, and build communi-ties that become growth catalysts.

New Mindset: You should bring an investor's orientation and a continuous learning spirit to platform Use journey opportunities. You probably don't currently take full advantage of your plat-form's power to grow customer lifetime value. Your new steps will create user expansion energy and next-best offers insights that will yield high return on investment.

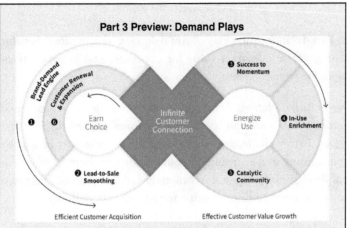

Part 3 Preview: Demand Plays

Brand-Demand Lead Engine

Customer Renewal & Expansion

❸ Success to Momentum

❶ ❻ Earn Choice

Infinite Customer Connection

Energize Use

❹ In-Use Enrichment

❷ Lead-to-Sale Smoothing

❺ Catalytic Community

Efficient Customer Acquisition   Effective Customer Value Growth

The key diagram in Part 3 defines the plays that accelerate your in-market growth. The left circle of the loop represents your customer's Choose journey, while the right circle represents their Use journey. The center "X" represents the infinite customer connection that the platform helps complete between your customer, your company, and others. The six plays cover actions you can take to raise platform demand.

Int.1.9

INNOVATION PLAYS

In Part 4, "Innovation Plays," you'll develop new platform benefits that generate in-market value for customers and growth advantages for your company.

New Rule: Platform innovation should help your customers travel better paths in work and personal life, through better flows. Part 4 challenges you to unlock new customer benefit by reimagining and rearranging your customer's digital and physical flows, linking those flows to extended ecosystems, and offering customers additional value for added data visibility.

New Mindset: Commit to knowing your customer at a flow level. Learn their current workflows and life flows, discover how your platforms can change their flows for the better, and understand how their new flows translate into new benefits. Then watch innovation grow.

New Rule: Platform innovation gives your customers broader powers than ever before. Part 4 challenges you to make your users feel like superhumans through mind-blowing intelligence and the ability to change realities. Make them part of a movement (your customer coalition) that changes the world for good. Continuously improve these innovative experiences to stay distinctive.

New Mindset: Think bold and make sure the user power you deliver has a clear benefit. Customers will value the innovative powers you provide if they can use them to gain identifiable and relevant benefits that matter.

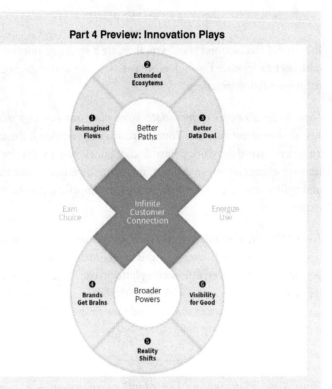

Part 4 Preview: Innovation Plays

The key diagram in Part 4 illustrates platform-powered innovations. Better Path innovations create reimagined customer flows, extended ecosystems, and greater value for data sharing. Broader Power innovations deliver intelligent assistance, new forms of reality, and impact for good that aligns with customer values.

Int.1.10

INTERACTION PLAYS

In Part 5, "Interaction Plays," you'll create a stronger journey-wide customer experience through more personalized and engaging platform interaction practices.

New Rule: You can differentiate your platform through distinctive customer interaction. Your platform's experience hubs create an interactive user world. Part 5 challenges you to develop full journey engagement capabilities, including dynamic segmentation and agile content management, to create compelling platform user experiences.

New Mindset: Commit to making interactive excellence one of the ways you win. Don't overlook this lever in the face of functional performance pressures. Interactive platform excellence means knowing who you're interacting with, what they're trying to achieve, what content to share, when to share it, and how to share it. You'll become a preferred platform by doing so.

New Rule: Platforms enable adaptive innovation – a form of interaction that can improve both your users' experience and your new offer success. Part 5 outlines how customer usage signals can launch a virtuous cycle of hypotheses, research, new offer concepting, new application development, and new offer launch.

New Mindset: Treat your customer's use data as a rich source of innovation insight deserving of its own innovation process. It will supplement your long-term innovation processes through a more-agile process powered by an in-market perspective. The right observations can reveal pain points to eliminate, existing features to upgrade and new features to add.

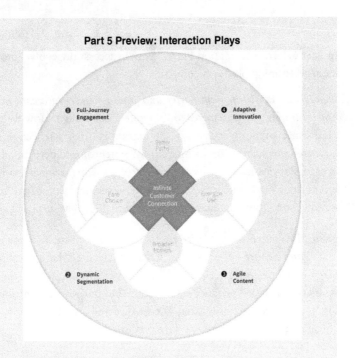

Part 5 Preview: Interaction Plays

The key diagram in Part 5 depicts four forms of customer interaction. Each is a platform play that delivers enhanced customer experience (full-journey engagement, dynamic segmentation, agile content, and adaptive innovation). The result is higher quality engagement and personalization, leading to customer preference for your brand.

Int.1.11

TRANSFORMATION PLAYS

In Part 6, "Transformation Plays," you'll successfully evolve into a high-performing platform company.

New Rule: Platform modularity and interdependence create new opportunities and challenges for alignment advantage. How well a platform company performs in the market is often a reflection of how well it synchronizes its operations. Synchronized performance is hard. Part 6 encourages you to use three transformational change levers to achieve synchronization: body (structures that organize), mind (know-how that enables), and soul (beliefs that inspire).

New Mindset: Expect platforms to create more interdependence and require more collaboration. Create a culture where synchronized collaboration is celebrated as high performance. Help those who control siloed product assets today find purpose in contributing to a shared platform asset. The quality and speed of your synchronization achievement will create your advantage.

New Rule: Collaboration and coordination by go to market teams unlock platform growth. Part 6 encourages you to implement two transformations. One creates new go to market roles that impower cross-functional collaboration. The other creates a growth operations team that enables coordination and identifies growth opportunities free from organizational siloes.

New Mindset: Stop viewing your go-to-market teams as separate functions; start viewing them instead as coordinated parts of an integrated system. The quality of your growth operations insights, and the pace of your coordinated response to those insights, will drive your advantage.

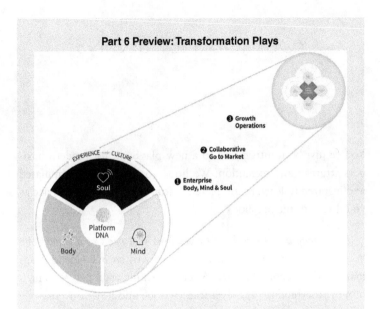

Part 6 Preview: Transformation Plays

The key diagram in Part 6 outlines three key transformation plays that enable you to achieve synchronized performance. One is at the enterprise level (applying body, mind, and soul concepts), one at the go-to-market team level (implementing cross-functional workflows), and one at the operations support level (creating a growth ops team).

Int.1.12

YOUR JOURNEY BEGINS

You've just been introduced to a new playbook for modern business strategy and execution. We hope you are feeling stimulated and inspired to learn more! Here are four quick words of advice as you dive into the playbook.

First, keep a running list of questions you need to answer. The book provides many answers, as we've written it to blend pragmatic and conceptual advice. After unpacking each play – using a mix of storytelling, play-level frameworks, and how-to steps – we will also ask you key questions. These are meant to challenge you to apply each play.

Second, explore with others to enrich your experience.

- You might huddle around a whiteboard with a team (physical or virtual) to read and discuss key design chapters and then brainstorm how to build a platform.

- You might apply chapter-level insights with a team to understand why your current platform revenue growth is sluggish. You might build new hypotheses around how to accelerate it.

- You might partner with colleagues from other departments, using key alignment chapters to fix operational and leadership disconnects that are preventing your company from realizing full-platform potential.

Third, find ways to keep your spirits high.

- Remember why platforms are a necessity and an opportunity for you.
- Break down problems and solutions – building-block victories can lead to big change.
- Believe in your journey. Your plays will cause customers to root for your platform, motivate modern talent to join and stay, and lead investors to rethink your enterprise value.

Finally, never take your eye off the role of leadership. You'll be leading others on a mental, emotional, and social journey as a transformative leader if you put one, a few, or many of these plays into practice.

If you succeed, you'll create uncommon growth. Uncommon because you will grow faster than your competition. Uncommon because you will grow through transformation rather than incremental change. Uncommon because you will grow in ways that endure competitively and positively impact society. Keep your potential for uncommon growth in mind as you explore and act on ways to win through platforms.

THE PLATFORM
PLAYBOOK

Part 1

PORTFOLIO PLAYS

When we hear the phrase "platform business," we instinctively think of born-in-the-cloud, venture capital-fueled disruptors – and for good reason. Many of the most headline-worthy platform companies originated this way. But now that we're in the mainstream platform era, it's time to think more expansively – to tackle bigger, broader, and bolder questions:

How can a non-platform business win through platforms, no matter its current state?
How can an existing platform business reinvent itself to compete for new value?

Your best answers will emerge from a blend of pattern recognition that identifies commonality in what others are doing, plus strategic creativity that's unique to your business. The market is so full of activity that both themes and variations in platform strategies can be identified. We have distilled seven roles that platforms might play in bringing new vitality to your business portfolio. Each role brings the potential to achieve strategic platform advantage.

Your next platform-powered business portfolio can be developed through a single platform play, described in Chapter 1.1, "Optimal Platform Role(s)." While it is presented as one play, you may need to use the play several times across your enterprise to capture a complete picture of your opportunity, including platform synergies. No matter your industry – no matter if you have several, one, or no platforms in your business portfolio today – use this play to build strategic advantage into your business.

1.1

OPTIMAL PLATFORM ROLE(S)

Ask 10 members of a management team what it means to be a platform business, and you'll likely get 10 different answers (sometimes 11 or 12!). That's because the phrase "platform" is used in different ways today, with different meanings. This is a major problem. If a management team can't have quality conversations about platforms, there's no way they'll win. Let's create clarity before we discuss platform roles.

PLATFORM CLARITY, PLEASE

Fig. 1.1.1 illustrates the multiple ways that "platform" might be used in your next management team's discussion. We'll describe the diagram from the bottom-up:

- The people who *generate the data* that a platform company uses often call themselves an Internet of Things (IOT) platform (creating data from IOT sensors) or a customer telemetry platform (creating data from the customer's smartphone swipes or computer keystrokes).

- *Technology platform* teams make use of the data generated. They store it, process it through computing, and apply software applications code and intelligent algorithms that turn

Better Communication, Better Strategy

"My **platform** for..."
Customers

Strategic Design e.g., customers, differentiators, economics	"We are a **platform** business"	e.g., Management teams
Platform Experience Hubs e.g., apps, clouds, consoles	"Customer **platform** for...."	e.g., Go-to-Market teams
In-house Technology e.g., data, code, analytics, computing	"Our **platform**"	e.g., Technology teams
Outsourced Technology e.g., data, code, analytics, computing	"**Platform**-as-a-service (PaaS)"	e.g., Cloud teams
Data Generation Technology e.g., sensors, customer telemetry	"Our IOT **platform**"	e.g., Product teams

Business Strategy Elements

Fig. 1.1.1

the data into value. This technology platform work is typically divided between two groups:

o Outsourced cloud service providers who provide "Platform as a Service" (PaaS) support, spanning infrastructure and code components to support a company's platform technology needs. Most PaaS providers are generalists, but new PaaS-layer industry specialists are emerging who customize their PaaS for specific industry business models.

o Internal platform teams who build the company's proprietary platform technology. They write application code, build API (application programming interface) connectors, manage data systems, and deploy analytical and artificial intelligence (AI) engines. They build software developer toolkits that empower third-party software developers to write and sell applications on the company's platform.

• Product development, experience design, and go-to-market teams convert platform functionality into *platform experience hubs*: the destinations where customers go to receive platform benefits and experiences. These experience hubs may be called apps, super apps, clouds, exchanges, consoles, marketplaces, or even product displays. No matter the name, the role of an experience hub is the same – it's where the customers experience platform power.

- Go-to-market teams often call their own *company or offer a platform* when they tell customers "We are your platform for ..." as a way to communicate a mission-critical benefit. Customers often mirror this language. When the head of a chemical products company says, "Salesforce.com is our platform for Customer Relationship Management," they are indicating that Salesforce is foundational to the way they do business. Consumers shorten this by simply by saying they are "on" or saying that they "use" a certain platform. The meaning is the same.

- *Business leaders* oversee all of these teams and then tell investors, talent, and customers that the company has a "platform business" and a "platform business model." These claims can mean different things, but they usually focus on how the company creates value for the customer and captures value for itself. The two most common types of platform businesses are *Software-as-a-Service (SaaS) platforms*, with a focus on direct company software value provided to customers, and *ecosystem connector platforms*, with a focus on how a company links members of its platform ecosystem to each other.

Throughout this book, when we speak of a company's "platform," we mean the entire stack as seen in Fig. 1.1.1. When we refer to something more specific, we'll refer to a row name, such as the platform business model, the platform experience hub, or the technology platform.

We suggest you foster this same approach at your company to enable the collaboration that management teams need to produce quality strategies. Don't allow any one group to insist that the word "platform" applies only in the way they use it. Create written definitions. If you're lacking context, insist on a modifier each time someone speaks about the platform so that the speaker's meaning and the listener's understanding are aligned.

OPTIMAL PLATFORM ROLE(S) IN YOUR BUSINESS

With clarity established, let's get onto the big questions. What is the optimal role (or roles) for one or more platforms in your business portfolio? How can it help you achieve your strategic objectives? How will your platform improve your differentiation, shift your customer mix, accelerate growth, raise profit margins, lower asset intensity, and respond to competitor innovation? Fig. 1.1.2 illustrates seven potential platform roles for you to evaluate.

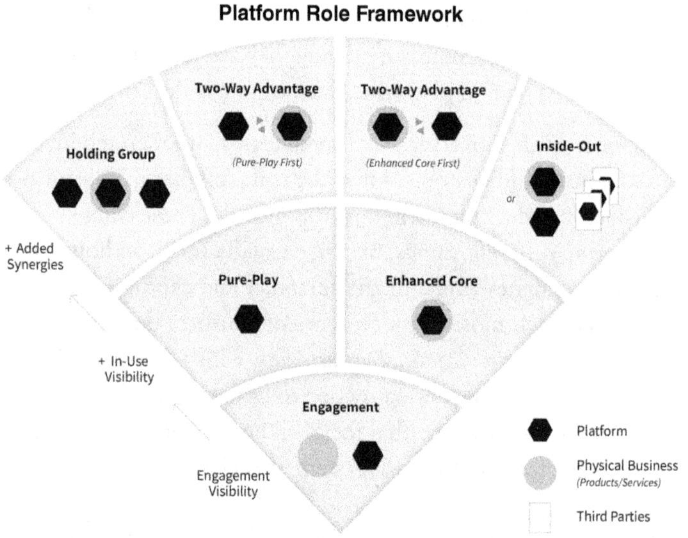

Platform Role Framework

Fig. 1.1.2

Our Platform Role framework is illustrated in the shape of a fan. Starting at the base of the fan is the easiest, but least potent, role that a platform can play for your company – a vehicle for near real-time user *engagement*. In this role, your platform is not connected by sensors to your product or service so you cannot literally "watch" the customer as they use. But if your customer is willing to interact with them – ask a question, give feedback, discuss a topic, log an activity – your platform can give you fuzzy visibility into whether and how the customer uses and likes your offerings and brand.

In the middle layer of the framework are two core platform roles. Each can create significant new value thanks to the data-driven visibility they provide your company during customer use. If the only thing your company operates and monetizes is digital, your platform's role is a *pure-play*. If you sell physical products or services that are connected through sensing to a platform that captures customer use, your platform's role is an *enhanced core*.

In the top layer of the framework, you'll find four more complex roles that platforms can play in your company. These are constructed from *pure-play and enhanced core role combinations* and feature synergies between the roles. The simplest of these is a *holding group* – a collection of pure-play or enhanced core businesses owned by a single company. Next, there are *two two-way advantage* roles – where the same platform takes on a pure-play role in one part of the company and an enhanced core role in another part. There are *two variants* of this *two-way advantage role,* depending on which platform role came first. The final option at this level of the framework is an *inside-out* platform role – one where a company's platform both plays a key role in its own business, then is also licensed to third parties to use (and often embed) in their own business.

Let's profile each of these options in greater depth and consider how other companies have used them. Ask yourself what option best fits your business today, consider whether a second option could support the evolution of your business, and brainstorm whether an innovative option (for your industry context) could help you leapfrog competitors.

Role: Engagement

Physical Business ——— ⬤ ⬢ ——— Platform

The role of an *engagement* platform is to interact with the customer as much as possible during use to observe and enrich their journey, within the limitations of no sensor data flowing from use. Deploying an engagement platform is the next-best thing to being fully connected.

Despite their constraints, when executed creatively engagement platforms have a meaningful impact on customer preference, growth rates, customer lifetime value, and profitability. They also aren't hard to build or integrate into any physical business portfolio. For example:

- *Social media pages as platform:* the 18,000 teaching institutions that grant graduate and postgraduate degrees need an engagement platform to keep alumni energy and connection levels high.[1]

Their graduates span the globe, and many institutions are poor platform developers, so they frequently establish school destinations on a social media platform that alumni already use. Granular data capture is low, but the institutions serve their former students, maintain mindshare, and keep up with alumni career paths – helpful for fundraising.

- *Apps for non-connected product businesses.* Some products just don't lend themselves to being connected – at least not yet. For example, it's challenging for an egg company to put IOT sensors on eggshells. But it's not impossible to ask a consumer to engage with their eggs as they prepare them. Through a QR code on the carton, Vital Farms shows customers video of the hens that laid the eggs they are eating, enjoying their guaranteed pasture-raised life. Customers can feel good, educate their children, and taste the difference the outdoors makes in the flavor of their omelet.

Vital Farms isn't the only example. As we'll share later in this book, Glossier disrupted the skincare business through a community engagement platform. Nike meaningfully improved its customer lifecycle value with the aid of three major engagement platforms.

Still, if you can go beyond an engagement-only platform approach, we encourage you to adopt a more data-rich strategy. Engagement platform energy is hard to keep up and provides the lowest customer use insight. You'll be unlikely to win through platforms if a competitor gets more inventive.

Role: Enhanced Core

If you deploy an *enhanced core* strategy, you'll embed sensors and software into a physical business to enhance the business' total value. Here's where creativity really takes off. Disney turns a guest's theme park visit into an insightful data stream through a magic wristband. SleepNumber's Smart 360 bed collects billions of sleep quality data points per night to improve the sleeper's quality of life. Haier adds a barcode reader to its refrigerator to transform the food inside into highly valued dinner solutions.

You can transform your business by converting your product or service into a platform. You could innovatively generate new customer value, increase market share, support value-based pricing, and access new profit pools. Apple proves each of these points. The company's platform strategy has always lived in the shadows of its heroic product design, engineering, and branding. But every year, it becomes clearer just how much those platforms enhance the core of Apple's consumer electronics.[2] At the end of 2021, Apple had 1.8 billion active devices that used platforms to:

- *Enhance core business value proposition.*[3] Apple's platform-based App Store promises customers 2.2 million seamlessly available apps, world-class media, and financial payment services. This helps uphold Apple's price point and creates barriers to new entrants.

- *Enhance device economics.* A total of 785 million device customers pay for platform-enabled digital services. Apple's platform service revenues (Apps, Media, Payment, Customer Care) rose 20% yearly from 2015 to 2021, while its hardware business (iPhone, Mac, iPad, wearables) grew only 11%.[4]

- *Enhance ecosystem strength.* Since the App Store's launch in 2008, Apple and its community of app makers have divided roughly $400 billion in app revenue.[5,6]

Companies can face two challenges with an enhanced core platform. The first is the struggle to achieve acceptable software economics. Companies with disproportionately high platform ambitions relative to their existing physical businesses may struggle to effectively amortize the cost of platform research and development (R&D) expenditure as they scale. This can lead to companies under-investing in their platform design and launch or risking financial stress on their core business.

The second is the struggle for a company to manage two different profit pools (physical vs platform) that have two different cash flow profiles (one-off product sales vs subscription-based platform sales). The desire for each set of leaders to be in charge of what drives the most profit for a company can easily create a "tug of war" in the boardroom. Navigating internal politics to do what's best for the customer and company is critical.

Role: Pure-Play

 ——— Platform

"Pure-play" describes a straightforward platform role: the platform is the business, and the business is the platform. The objective is to maximize the platform's value. For most pure-play firms, that means becoming the leader of a market category. It can be high reward, high risk. A pure-play strategy isn't restricted to born-as-a-platform startups. Most point-product software companies are transforming into platform pure-plays.

Pure-play platform companies come in two bookended models:

- *Ecosystem Connector Platforms* connect *different ecosystems* of customers with each other. For example, social media companies like Instagram connect users to other users, e-commerce marketplaces like eBay connect buyers with sellers, and digital service companies like Uber connect riders with drivers.

- *Software-as-a-Service (SaaS) Platforms* connect customers to a company's own cloud-hosted software services to deliver *direct value* to users and sponsors. For example, Adobe's Creative Cloud connects users to Adobe's suite of creative software (Adobe Photoshop, Adobe Illustrator). TurboTax helps taxpayers complete their civic duties faster and easier, with lower tax bills and dispute support.

Some think that platform success lies in delivering just one bookend model or the other. Many successful platform companies now blend the two. As a result, pure-play Ecosystem Connectors (one bookend above) should explore how to design-in direct company value, while SaaS platforms (the other bookend) should consider adding ecosystems. Adobe's acquisition of the Behance creative design community – now 30 million members strong – is a great example.[7]

Role: Holding Group

 ——— Multiple Businesses

Some of the world's platform titans (Alphabet, Meta) have chosen to become *platform holding groups*; more mid-sized platform firms may do so going forward to create more flexible growth options. This option involves setting up a separate company (or financial entity) to own and control multiple platform companies in a portfolio. This option is typically pursued to prepare for acquisitions, to incubate new platform ventures without harming mature business results, and to unlock brand or financial synergies.

- *Brand synergies* can often be unlocked by pursuing a *branded house* approach, where all businesses owned by the holding company benefit from the corporate brand name. Each Apple product and platform takes advantage of (and contributes to) Apple's brand equity, making it easier for products and platforms in a portfolio to win, cross-sell, and up-sell customers across the holding group.

- *Financial synergies* are more often unlocked through a *house of brands* approach, where each business owned by the holding group has their own distinct brand. Google achieved this by rolling its portfolio of giant platform brands (i.e., Google, YouTube, Pixel) under a new low-profile investor holding group called Alphabet. This increased investor visibility to the economics of each of each platform brand and unburdened Google from carrying the financial weight of incubator start-ups.[8] The company's share price rose over 5% on the day of the announcement.[9]

The challenge for companies looking to win through holding groups is to identify the right mix of markets to play in. As companies bump up against market share ceilings in their current markets, they'll need to decide whether to squeeze out more growth where they are already present (often by innovating their business model) or grow in new markets (often by applying their platform or business know-how to disrupt adjacent markets).

Role: Two-Way Advantage (Pure-Play First)

Platform ——— ◆ ▶ ⬡ ——— Enhanced Core

In the *first variant of a two-way advantage platform*, a pure-play business extends into a physical business where its addressable market grows, while its platform gives it an edge. The company becomes the owner of *both* a pure-play business *and* an enhanced core business, each designed to strengthen the other.

This strategy is most often pursued by companies that seek to expand their growth potential beyond what their pure-play market size permits. When executed well, this variant helps companies to successfully enter that significantly bigger market and disrupt the incumbent physical businesses who compete there. Two well-known examples include the following:

Zillow began as a pure-play online search engine for US consumers wanting to buy or sell their home. Zillow succeeded, with more people searching "Zillow" than the term "real estate" on Google[10] and with over 60% market share of the online ad revenue from real estate agents.[11] Yet Zillow's success came in an annual real estate ad market capped at $19 billion. To grow, Zillow decided to participate in a blend of digital and physical real estate markets – mortgages, real estate brokerage, title, home repair, and renovation – that had addressable markets totaling over $300 billion.

Zillow's platform model brought a two-way advantage platform because its pure-play search platform acquired new customer relationships that it could then serve through seamless solutions.

Its solutions made it all the more the brand to turn to for a new home search.

Netflix pursued a two-way advantage platform role for different reasons. It had become the leading pure-play platform distributor of others' films before it decided to enter the physical business of filmmaking. Netflix added its new business to give it strategic access to quality content in case other filmmakers decided to get into streaming distribution (which they did). Its two-way advantage was also clear. A massive subscriber audience enabled it to attract A-list media stars for its own productions, which in turn helped it to recruit yet a larger subscriber audience.

The biggest challenge companies face when pursuing a two-way advantage approach is managing two different speeds of business: A fast moving software business (pure-play) that can react to customer needs and competitive threats overnight through code and a slower often labor- or product-based physical business (enhanced core).

Role: Two-way Advantage (Enhanced Core First)

Enhanced Core ———— ⬣ ▸◂ ⬣ ———— Platform

The second variant of a two-way advantage involves companies who start with an Enhanced Core business and then choose to spin out their platform into its own Pure-Play offering. The strategic rationale differs – this two-way model frees platform software to follow current customers – or to gain new ones – free from the constraints of a core physical business.

In 2014, Peloton pioneered the "enhanced core" home exercise equipment market by launching a series of connected home exercise equipment that could deliver streaming instructor content (live and recorded) while capturing user exercise activity. It rolled out its enhanced core model over bikes (2014), treadmills (2018), rowing machines (2022), and free weights (2022).

Peloton's strategy became "two-way" when it spun out its pure-play workout experiences, so they did not require its equipment. It launched a series of bring your own equipment platform experiences in 2018 and branded expansion in 2022. In doing so, Peloton both attracted new users and critically gave its current users a way to count all their exercise toward their motivating Peloton milestone goals, continuity streaks, and leaderboard shout-outs, no matter the sport or equipment they used.[12]

Peloton also encountered the challenge of managing businesses that operated at two different speeds. Peloton's physical supply chain was challenged with supply chain shortages at the height of COVID-induced home exercise demand and then had inventory hangover when COVID subsided.

To overcome two-speed challenges, you should create world-class management capabilities in both the pure-play and enhanced core business. You should also valuate whether your platform is designed with *both* a pure-play and an enhanced core-customer experience in mind. Finally, you should manage with eyes wide open the different agility levels (and potential bottlenecks) of a digital platform and physical business blend.

Role: Inside-Out

When companies develop a platform, they often work with one or more major cloud service providers to determine how much of their desired platform functionality can be outsourced instead of built. An e-commerce shopping cart is a good example – why build a new one when you can plug in proven code from a company whose sole purpose is to design the best e-commerce shopping carts?

This platform element outsourcing unlocks a role of platforms that can sit alongside other roles a company might choose.

Enhanced core or pure-play companies can license parts of their platform to other companies to recoup their investments and unlock new revenue streams while also increasing their reputation for platform expertise in the market. This is an "inside-out" platform role.

Starling Bank in the UK provides a great example. Starling launched one of the first fully digital banks in 2017 after spending three years building an app-first banking tech stack from the ground up with help from AWS[13] and Google.[14] Then Starling went further, fueling a second revenue stream by offering Banking as a Service (BaaS) to other neobanks and fintech companies that needed infrastructure partners to bring their innovations to market (an Inside-Out strategy). Starling branded its BaaS platform "Engine by Starling,"[15] limited its use in the UK to noncompetitors, and began a global revenue expansion drive that provided platform infrastructure to digital disruptors in other geographies.[16]

An inside-out strategy has economic advantages if you're in the right kind of industry. It also has two inherent challenges. First, it's difficult to strike the right balance of priorities when you're investing in and growing your core "inside" platform while also serving third-party customers who require specific features from your "outside" platform. Second, major cloud service players may begin to compete in the same space once they see proof of the market.

HOW TO DETERMINE YOUR OPTIMUM PLATFORM ROLE(S)

What platform roles are best for you? You may have already discovered the best platform role for your business by pattern matching your firm against the stories we've told. But to make it yet easier, Fig. 1.1.3 makes explicit a thought process that may help you decide.

Step 1: Evaluate if you have customer visibility through some form of sensing or device inputs:

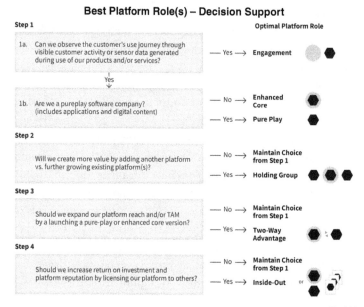

Fig. 1.1.3

- If you *don't have visibility*, a creatively powerful engagement platform is likely your best option. Before accepting that answer, ask yourself if you can create visibility and interaction through some form of innovation.

- If you *do have visibility* and/or you are a software-only company (such as cloud, apps, digital content), then the pure-play option is likely right for you. If you aren't software only, the enhanced core option is likely your best choice.

Step 2: Explore if you could create more value by adding another platform to your portfolio rather than further building out the platform you already own. If so, a Holding Group option is best.

Step 3: Consider if it is possible to gain critical reach or an expanded total addressable market (TAM) by blending both a pure-play platform and enhanced-core use of that same platform. If it is, and if you can manage two-speed complexity, a two-way advantage is your best choice (pure-play first or enhanced core first – depending on your original core business).

Step 4: Research if there is demand in the market by other companies for specific elements of your platform. If there is, and if you have an appetite to increase your return on platform investment and your platform's reputation by licensing your platform to others, an inside-out option may be best for you.

As you step through this decision tree, ask yourself whether the best role of platforms in your portfolio today is also the best decision for their role in three years' time. If your answer does change over time, start planning your platform migration strategy now using the template below (Fig. 1.1.4).

Best Platform Role(s)

	Best Role Today	Best Role in 3 Years	Rationale
Full Business Role			

OR... Roles by Business Segment	Best Role Today	Best Role in 3 Years	Rationale
Business Segment 1 (describe)			
Business Segment 2 (describe)			
Business Segment 3 (describe)			

OPTIONS	Engagement	Enhanced Core	Pure Play
	Two-way Advantage	Inside-Outside	Holding Group

Fig. 1.1.4

If your business is homogeneous, you'll likely have only one answer to the "best platform role" question. But if you own diverse business types, you may need to answer at a business segment level, even before considering the right role of platforms at the full-portfolio level. Segment your business and use the bottom of the template to answer the best platform question for each segment.

The choices you take away from this chapter can fundamentally change your competitive position. As you see competitors enter the market with their own platforms, revisit this play to understand their strategic opportunities and challenges and use it to reinforce your own business vitality.

KEY QUESTIONS FOR CONSIDERATION

1. What's the best role for a platform in your business? What are your leading options? What are the pros and cons of each leading option?

2. What platform roles are your competitors using today? What platform roles do you expect them to use in the future? Consider adjacent competitors, not just direct competitors.

3. How might customers view your leading options?

4. Consider your three-year growth plans. Will your best platform role change over time?

5. If so, how can you take migration into account?

Part 2

DESIGN PLAYS

When customers compare your platform offers to those of your competitors, how often do they choose you? To grow faster than the market, you'll need to win more than your share of these contests.

This requires distinctive platform *design*—to differentiate your company on performance value and customer experience. In today's crowded platform markets, great strategic design is a "need to have," guided by your customer centricity and powered by your competitive strategy. Engineers, business strategists, experience designers, and marketers need to come together to ask how your company's platform can win the customer's heart and mind at "hello," then become something that the customer can't imagine living without.

Your winning platform design can be developed in four plays, illustrated by Fig. 2.0.1. If you're designing a platform for the first time or upgrading broadly, work through all of the plays in order. If you have one platform weak spot, choose your play to improve performance.

Our four design plays are mapped against the backdrop of our Platform Design framework. The white hexagon represents the customer types that use your platform and the value that each one receives. The underlying gray hexagon represents the functionality of your underlying platform. The black hexagon in the middle represents market-facing architecture that communicates to prospects what your platform has to offer.

Chapter 2.1, "Customer Coalition Edge," challenges you to build an advantage through a unique customer coalition – your distinctive blend of customer types and personas. The follow-on choices you

Platform Design Framework – Four Design Plays

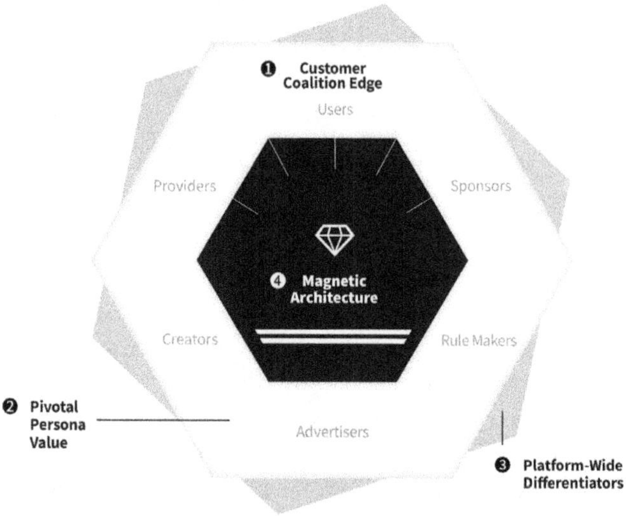

Fig. 2.0.1

make for experience hub offers, platform features, and go-to-market programs should all support your customer coalition strategy.

Chapter 2.2, "Pivotal Persona Value," encourages you to identify one or more pivotal moments in a key customer's platform journey where the customer would be willing to change platform providers (or start using a platform) for the right value proposition. Invest to design a pivotal value proposition at that moment(s). Repeat for influential customer personas in your coalition.

Chapter 2.3, "Platform-wide Differentiators," asks you to identify pervasive platform differentiators that can set yours apart. Some may be patented hero features; others may be combinations of capabilities which, when put together, create distinctive benefits.

Chapter 2.4, "Magnetic Offer Architecture," recommends ways to structure your market-facing offers and value propositions so that they are cohesive yet flexible. With the right architecture you can construct compelling value propositions for every member in your customer coalition.

Any one of these design strategies can bring you an advantage. The more design moves you successfully execute, the more your advantage grows. Taken together, these plays will deliver that touch of design magic that makes customers take notice and choose you.

2.1

CUSTOMER COALITION EDGE

When debating what brings competitive advantage to a business, strategists often debate the importance of business *size* versus business *shape* (often called business design[1]). Imagine a strategy discussion about an airline. The size advocate argues that to be profitable, an airline must be one of the biggest players – yielding a lower cost per passenger. The shape advocate argues that the airline must serve less-contested routes and attract a higher mix of loyal business class flyers – yielding more revenue per passenger. The size strategist relies on cost curves and the shape strategist on customer behavior insights.

This debate has carried over to platform strategy, but with modern digital underpinnings. When platforms were new, all the buzz was about *size* – the platform's network effects and its near-zero incremental costs to scale. Now that platform markets are crowded, it's imperative to think harder about the *shape* of your platform's network – who's in it and whether it can bring an edge to your business. We advocate starting your platform design strategy with shape, intensifying your focus on customer behavior while doing so, for three reasons:

- Every "node" in your network is not just a node; it's a human being. One with roles, pressures, hopes, fears, needs, desires, and choice. Humans aren't locked into your network just because they

---

[1] The concept of Business Design was first outlined by Adrian Slywotzky in his books *Value Migration* and *The Profit Zone*.

belong to it – they often use competitor networks in parallel, turning "relative network size" into a misleading metric of strength.

- Network members are not monolithic. There are six possible types of customers in any platform network: users, providers, creators, sponsors, advertisers, and rule makers. (We'll define these a few pages from now.) Within each type, there are multiple customer personas – e.g., high- and low-end users within the user type. So a single platform network can have dozens of customer personas – each with unique perspectives and needs. The call to "scale your network" should be met with the strategic response "Which personas in my network am I scaling?" "In what mix?" and "Why?"

- Network members often provide value to each other in addition to the value that the company provides. But not every interaction between members is a positive experience, so your network quality and culture counts – not just network size.

In the mainstream platform era, it's time to view platform networks as *customer coalitions* that are multidimensional and deeply human. Your job, as a strategic designer, is to shape your customer coalition in a way that gives you an edge. Then scale that. It's how you'll find the competitive advantage you're seeking.

UBER'S CUSTOMER COALITIONS: SHAPING IN ACTION

The story of Uber provides a rich parable – first about size and then about shape.

Uber's first customer coalition, built from 2010 to 2013,[2] produced global-scale leadership but mixed results. The company aimed to build the leading driver-and-rider coalition in every local market around the world. Uber's CEO was determined to become the kind of category leader whose superior scale beat competitors in country after country. But there were two challenges to this strategy: First, Uber's leadership in local markets did not produce driver or rider loyalty. Both drivers and riders fluidly participated in other ride-sharing platforms, diluting Uber's intended network effect.[3]

This created a second challenge: Profitability did not easily follow from local market scale. Uber's multibillion-dollar deficit grew as the company ramped its global customer coalition. Uber raised and spent tens of billions in private funding rounds, but profitability remained around the corner.[4]

During a new round of strategic design, concentrated from 2014 to 2018, Uber created a customer coalition 2.0, and this time, it produced an edge. In its most challenging markets, it traded its local Uber customer coalition for stock in local competitors: Didi (China),[5] Grab (Southeast Asia), and Yandex (Russia).[6] In the markets where it remained, Uber built a more distinctive Customer Coalition. The company added new customer types and personas to build two new business units: Uber Eats and Uber Freight.

Uber's two Customer Coalitions are visualized in Fig. 2.1.1 (the original customers in black, the second customer additions in gray). Customer types are defined, and Uber coalition members are described after the diagram.

Users: Every platform has at least one user type, and most platforms have multiple user personas. Users may or may not pay for

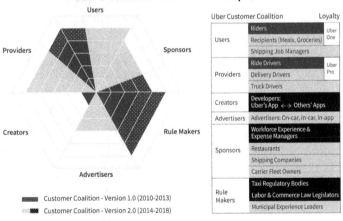

Uber's Customer Coalition Development

Fig. 2.1.1

the platform, but they are the eyes-on-screen and fingers-on-keys-and-buttons actors who receive a functional benefit for platform use. In the case of Uber, users include car riders; recipients of home-delivered restaurant food, groceries, and supplies; and ship-ment managers.

Providers: Providers sell relatively standardized services and/or products to users through the platform. For Uber, providers are car drivers (for Uber Rides and Uber Eats) and truck drivers (for Uber Freight).

Creators: Creators add value through creatively distinctive experiences – performances, services, or products. In the case of Uber, creators are third-party developers whose apps work in con-cert with Uber's apps through open APIs.

Sponsors: Sponsors promote and suggest – and sometimes mandate – the platform's use to others. In Uber's case, these are restaurant owners and shipping companies seeking agile and low-cost product transportation; carrier fleet owners seeking truck driver productivity; and business operations managers seeking to improve workforce business transportation experiences while controlling expenses.

Advertisers: Advertisers want to sell something, buy something, or recruit someone through a platform and are willing to pay for ads that attract their targets. The more pinpointed and qualified a target is, the higher the rate the advertiser is willing to pay. Uber's advertisers may put digital signage on top of or inside Uber cars, as well as integrating advertisements into Uber user applications.

Rule Makers: Rule makers, whether legal or de facto standard setters, can dictate or influence the boundary conditions of what a platform can do. In Uber's case, key rule makers include taxicab regulatory bodies, labor law and commerce legislators, and munici-pality leaders.

Uber's Customer Coalition development illustrates the robust range of creative options available to your company as you design for growth.

UBER'S CUSTOMER COALITION EDGE

Uber's second customer coalition gave the company a new edge – multiple edges, in fact. It set the stage for Uber's more diversified, differentiated, and profitable growth.[7] Uber's story illustrates the various types of edge – diversification edge, differentiation edge, loyalty edge, pricing edge, investment edge, and liquidity edge – that you can gain through thoughtful Customer Coalition design.

Diversification Edge

A robust customer coalition can diversify revenues. Uber's customer coalition did that in dramatic fashion; it probably saved the company. Uber's rideshare business lost more than 70% of its revenue stream overnight at the onset of the COVID-19 pandemic. But Uber Eats and Uber Freight ramped their revenues sharply, reflecting the needs of a new society of people who ordered more products from their homes and wanted delivery to their doorstep. Uber's total revenue activity bounced back less than one year after COVID hit, thanks to a newly diversified customer coalition (see Fig. 2.1.2).

Uber Gross Revenue Level and Mix[8]

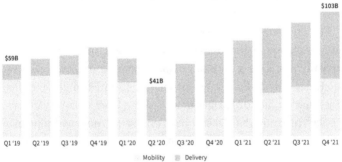

Fig. 2.1.2

Differentiation Edge

A unique customer coalition can lead to unique marketing claims. Uber's multi-line consumer offer became a point of differentiation against its mono-service line competitors in the US (Lyft in rides, Doordash and Grubhub in delivery) who have not matched it.[9] For now, Uber can claim to be the only service that moves the consumer's world in every way they might need. It can also claim to be a driver's most efficient economic opportunity provider, with demand for both rides and deliveries, plus the chance to carry on-car and/or in-car advertising displays.[10]

Loyalty Edge

When a customer coalition delivers multiple platform-powered services to one persona, it creates loyalty program opportunities. Uber built loyalty programs for drivers and consumers.

For drivers, UberPro built on the value proposition of greater economic opportunity. Drivers who drive enough Uber trips (especially at key times) qualify for tiered rewards status, provided they achieve high rider satisfaction and cancel infrequently. UberPro rewards range from discounts on gas and car maintenance, to advanced visibility on rider trip length, to online college tuition reimbursement. As of November 2022, driver surveys show that Uber is the primary choice for drivers by a three-to-one ratio.[11]

For consumers, Uber spent several years cross-marketing its services. It found that Eats+Rides customers spend 174% more annually and have a 16-point higher retention rate than the average Rides-only or Eats-only customers.[12] Inspired to do more than cross-market, in 2021, Uber launched the Uber One "loyalty as a service" program that takes a page out of the Amazon Prime playbook. For a $9.99 monthly fee, the consumer receives free deliveries on Uber Eats, discounts on Uber Rides, and various forms of priority treatment.

Pricing Edge

A coalition of laddered service providers enables a company to meet the needs of a segmented user market – realizing higher prices for customers with premium needs while remaining accessible to cost-sensitive users. In high-traffic urban centers, Uber offers up to 16 specialized classes of service and car types beyond its standard UberX.[13] From premium black car service to low-cost group rides, from pet-friendly and public-transit linked to wheelchair-assisted rides and green electric cars, Uber offers specialty drivers to meet specialty customer needs and capture a premium.[14]

Investment Edge

Companies gain an investment edge when they can reuse major fixed cost investments to build out their next customer coalition. Uber reused several investments it had made to build the Rides business.[15]

- Key Uber technologies, such as time-and-location demand prediction, matching and dispatching, trip routing, dynamic pricing, and payments, were all applicable to Eats and Freight.

- Existing Uber regional operations teams could launch new products and recruit new participants across new business lines.

- Uber descriptive product line names, tied to the same corporate brand, meant that Uber could raise awareness and consideration of new offers instantly.

Liquidity Edge

Many customer coalitions need their customers to be active in proportional ratios to create a good experience for all involved. This is known as network liquidity. In Uber's case, without the right ratio of drivers and riders, or food deliverers and orderers, either drivers or consumers will be frustrated by wait times.

Uber already has powerful tools to create liquidity through dynamic demand prediction and capacity incentive tool. The company's second customer coalition enhances liquidity by making more diverse use of the same drivers (for rides, meals, and goods). In an ideal competitive advantage scenario, the company's superior liquidity provides noticeably lower wait times than competitors.

AN EVER-EVOLVING COALITION

The evolution of Uber's Customer Coalition continues.

In 2022, Uber struck a 10-year partnership with autonomous electric car maker Motional. Autonomous vehicles will put pressure on the Uber–driver relationship. On the other hand, this partnership may deepen Uber's relationship with municipal leaders through the greening of cities via electric cars, scooters, and bikes. Uber's autonomous delivery may also help local retail storefronts better compete with Amazon's low cost and convenience.

And that's before Uber's venture investments in flying cars.

The only certainty for Uber is that the ongoing shaping of its Customer Coalition, in search of an edge, will remain key to its success. That statement likely holds true for you as well. Work through the questions below to consider how you might strategically shape your customer coalition to achieve your next edge.

KEY QUESTIONS FOR CONSIDERATION

Use Fig. 2.1.3 as an aid to answer the following questions.

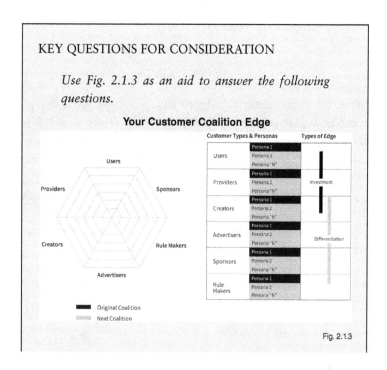

Fig. 2.1.3

1. If you already have a Customer Coalition, what are its strengths and weaknesses?

2. Which next Customer Coalition will best support your platform growth plans?

   Use Fig. 2.1.3 to display your thinking.

   If you question your marketplace liquidity, set your customer volume and mix targets.

3. What types of edge(s) could result from your planned Customer Coalition (i.e., diversification, differentiation, pricing, loyalty, investment, liquidity)?

4. If possible, think two Customer Coalitions ahead. How will you evolve again after your near-term evolution? Do you need to invest today for this longer term?

2.2

PIVOTAL PERSONA VALUE

The most complex string of time-sensitive activities that consumers will ever complete is fixing and selling their current home, buying a new home on a mortgage, renovating that new home, and moving. Little wonder that many digital innovators have tried to simplify, speed, and support the home buyer's daunting to-dos through platforms.[16]

Zillow has been the biggest platform winner, and there's a reason why. Zillow developed a feature so pivotal to the home shopper that it changed their behavior at the start of their home-buying journey. Branded the "Zestimate," this innovation launched Zillow's industry-leading platform and customer coalition. The Zestimate illustrates the strategic advantage that can come from discovering and delivering a benefit we call Pivotal Persona Value.

The Zestimate simplified an intimidating first step for every consumer – the *affordability assessment*. This step requires consumers to answer a series of complex questions: *How much is our current home worth? How much might our next home cost? Can we afford the overall transaction and manage our cash flows during the transition?*

Before the advent of the Zestimate, consumers could invest long hours in their assessment without gaining confidence that they got the answer right. Alternatively, they could ask a local real estate agent for expert help, but then they might feel beholden to use that agent without being sure they were the right partner. Even worse, the consumer might doubt the agent's advice: It could be off target or slanted in the agent's self-interest.

Zillow's Zestimate solved this major pain point. Launched in 2006, it provided a highly analytical home price estimate through a simple point-and-click. Home seekers could easily search any home (starting with their own), on or off the market, in any location, to get immediate answers. Consumers could test their new home dreams without agent pressure. As a result, Zillow received a million visits on its first day online.[17]

As consumers view a Zestimate, they also profile themselves to Zillow as well-defined real estate leads. In Phase 1 of its platform business, Zillow monetized those leads via targeted digital ads from relevant real estate agents and mortgage lenders – tapping into a $19 billion real estate ad market.

But Zillow quickly realized that its Zestimate had done more than generate an ad target. The Zestimate had helped to generate a trusted relationship with a buyer whom Zillow could serve further. In Phase 2 moves, Zillow broadened its platform's customer coalition dramatically to help home buyers (and later renters) navigate their entire set of moving-related activities, becoming a one-stop-shop broker and provider of services. Today, Zillow intermediates for consumers or directly provides them with real estate agents, mortgages, transaction services, renovation services, moving services, landlords, and tenants.[18,19]

In more-recent Phase 3 moves, Zillow is investing in a platform to directly serve real estate professionals. The platform helps them to automate their workflows and better market their services to home buyers. All told, Zillow's Phase 2 and 3 moves are tapping into a $300 billion real estate services market – 15 times the size of its Phase 1.

PIVOTAL PERSONA VALUE

The gains that Zillow made by reinventing the affordability assessment journey step illustrate the advantage a company can achieve through Pivotal Persona Value. This advantage occurs when the most influential persona in a customer coalition is provided with such compelling value at a key step in their journey that they change platform loyalties, shifting advantage to the company who provided the value. The Zestimate by Zillow illustrates four key characteristics of Pivotal Persona Value. It is:

- *Delivered to the most influential persona(s) in the customer coalition:* The buyer/seller is the most influential persona in residential real estate, followed by the real estate agent, the mortgage lender, and then dozens of niche service provider personas. By acquiring new buyer/seller relationships at scale, Zillow acquired enough influence to convince wavering real estate professionals to participate in (and make more valuable) its customer coalition.

- *Delivered in a pivotal step:* Total addressable markets are composed of a series of customer journey steps. Early-stage steps have high pivot potential because they are "first impression" experiences – targeted personas aren't committed to competitors yet. Later-stage steps can also have pivot potential, when there is a lot at stake for the customer or when the customer believes a new vendor competency is needed to take their next step. Zillow created advantage through Zestimate by winning consumers at the earliest pivotal step. Zillow defended against later-stage attackers (e.g., at the mortgage lender step) by creating a digital marketplace of lenders and making it available to consumers closer to the Zestimate step it controlled.

- *Delivered through high flow-impact features and benefits:* Each journey step contains a flow of customer activities that can be improved through platform digital innovation. Platform features enhance flows, leading to end benefits. There are two classes of flow features: *user empowerment,* often associated with Software-as-a-Service (SaaS) models, and *coalition interactions,* often associated with ecosystem connector models. These features in turn generate customer *end benefits,* which also come in two classes; some are *personal* in nature and others are *systemic.* Zillow's Zestimate innovation delivered user empowerment; its one-stop-shop innovation delivered coalition interactions. Zillow's pivotal end benefits were a powerful blend of the personal and systemic: consumers gain their next-chapter-of-life home with improved ease, speed, and cost.[20]

- *Delivered with differentiation:* Pivotal value is distinctive. When the Zillow Zestimate launched, it was. Since then, others have worked to match that original feature. As a result, Zillow has further developed its affordability assessment by adding key one-stop-shop messages like Zillow home loan availability, a three-minute Zillow home loan pre-approval, and a "Zenti-mate" of estimated home rental potential alongside home price and equity calculators.[21] Zillow's move bolstered its early-stage distinctiveness while creating bridges to its distinctive one-stop-shop solution.

It's challenging to find a high impact, differentiated benefit to provide an influential persona in your coalition at a pivotal moment in their journey. Yet it's worthwhile because it's a game changer.

DESIGNING FOR PIVOTAL PERSONA VALUE

How can you identify and design Pivotal Persona Value into your platform? To start, visually map and assess the value your platform provides per customer persona (or type), treating each persona's flows of activities as journey steps. Your articulation of journey steps and your opportunities for pivotal value will change from one customer persona to another. To keep expanding, Zillow has had to build out unique value propositions to real estate brokers/agents, mortgage lenders, home transaction and transition service providers, builders, landlords, and advertisers. These professionals each experience value in very different ways than the consumers who were Zillow's first target.

Fig. 2.2.1 provides an illustrative visual mapping of this exercise for Zillow consumers and agents. You'll carry out the same steps for every customer persona or type in your customer coalition. You should start with the most influential persona (e.g., who controls most ecosystem value and influences others) and end with the least influential.

- *Step 1: Journey Step Profile*

Name and describe each persona's journey steps, including their step objective and the flow of activities within each step. For example,

Designing for Pivotal Persona Value: Steps 1 and 2

Customer Coalition Personas | High Pivot Potential

Agent Steps

	C1	C2	C3	C4	C5	C6
Consumer Steps	■	■	■	■	■	■
Step 1: Journey Step Profile						
Step Name						
Step Objective						
Step Activities						
Step 2: Benefit Experience Profile						
Features						
Direct Empowerment		F2			F6	F8
Cross-Coalition Links	F1	F3	F4	F5	F7	F9
Benefit Impact						
Personal		B2		B5	B7	B8
Systemic	B1	B3	B4	B6		
Benefit Impact	H	H	L	L	L	H
Benefit Differentiation	L	H	L	L	L	L

Fig. 2.2.1

a step that has decision-making as its objective might include a flow of activities such as the filtering of a consideration set, options discovery, and evaluation and selection of a best option. In addition, note the steps that have high pivot potential (the black steps on the diagram). These may be early-stage steps where the persona is not committed or later journey steps where the outcome is highly important or where your persona may expect to need new platform competencies.

• *Step 2: Benefit Experience Profile*

Describe the features and end benefits that you provide to your persona. When describing features, think about how your platform directly empowers users, as well as linking your coalition members. When describing end benefits, think about personal benefits as well as systemic benefits. Fig. 2.2.2 lists typical platform features and benefits by type to stimulate your thinking.[22]

Rate the impact of the benefit by step (low, medium, high in the diagram). Additionally rate the differentiation of the benefit by step (once more low, medium, high). When judging differentiation, take into account direct competitors (they provide your features and deliver your end benefit) and substitutes (they provide different features to deliver your same end benefit).

Platform Feature and Benefits by Type

Platform Features That Improve Flows			Customer Benefits	
🎮 User Empowerment	👥 Coalition Interactions		🏆 Personal	📈 Systemic
Data Foundation	Socializing	Organizing	Essential Needs	Risk / Variance
Content Personalization	Collaborating	Knowledge Sharing	Well-Being	Cost / Complexity
Options Generation	Performing	Rating	Belonging	Revenue / Income
Decision Guidance	Service Market Making	Product Market Making	Happiness	Productivity / Agility
Intelligent Automation	Promoting	Asset Sharing	Achievement	Innovation / Creativity
Contextual Support	Currency Exchange	Event Recording	Self Actualization	Equity / Inclusion
Analytical Feedback	Employing	Investing	Reputation	Environmental Sustainability

Fig. 2.2.2

• *Step 3: Persona Value Assessment*

Strategically assess whether your platform provides pivotal value to your targeted persona. Per Fig. 2.2.3, plot benefits on a matrix of impact (L/M/H) and differentiation (L/M/H), noting whether benefits occur on steps with high pivot potential. Your goal is to have high-impact, high-differentiation benefits on flows that have high pivot potential (in our diagram a black box in the top right quadrant). You'd like to see this for personas who are highly influential within your customer coalition. If you believe you've achieved pivotal persona value after assessment, continue to Step 4; if not, design additional innovations.

• *Step 4: Persona Value Proposition*

Per Fig. 2.2.3, describe your value proposition to the persona (e.g., the reason they should choose your platform) through five key statements:

Designing for Pivotal Persona Value: Steps 3 and 4

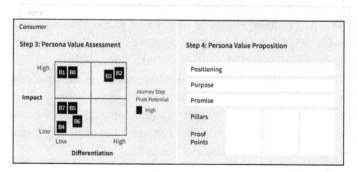

Fig. 2.2.3

- *Positioning*: who you are relative to the customer-oriented category you play in.
- *Purpose*: your motivation to provide value to your target persona.
- *Promise*: the summary or hero end benefit that you offer your target persona.
- *Pillars*: the three to five distinct ways you deliver on your promise (these should be broad strategic benefits).
- *Proof Points*: the key facts that support each of your pillar claims.

Zillow's market-facing communications[23] provide examples of each key statement in Fig. 2.2.4.

Once you've completed all of the steps, repeat them as necessary until you've designed sufficient pivotal value for all of your customer coalition personas.

Your customer centricity throughout this intensive process will pay off by making you relevant to a diverse set of customer personas. Your customer insight in a crowded market can increasingly guide your technology investments for maximum impact. Understand persona journey steps and flows, deliver persona-level features and benefit value, and watch your value propositions grow into strategic platform advantage.

Consumer Value Proposition: Zillow

Positioning:	The housing super app		
Purpose:	Give people the power to unlock life's next chapter		
Promise:	Make it radically easier for people to move		
Pillars:	Empower people with knowledge & information	Provide advanced technology, content & connections	Create a seamless & convenient real estate transaction experience
Proof Points:	[Changes over time]	[Changes over time]	[Changes over time]

Fig. 2.2.4

KEY QUESTIONS FOR CONSIDERATION

1. How can your platform deliver pivotal value to key personas in your customer coalition?

2. Who are your most important personas? Assess persona importance (ecosystem value, influence over others) to determine where to begin your insight investment.

3. Develop Pivotal Persona Value by carrying out Steps 1–4 described in this chapter for each of your key personas.

4. Reflect on the strength and weakness of your persona-level value proposition versus competitors across your customer coalition. Make a plan to capitalize on your strengths and shore up your weaknesses.

2.3

PLATFORM-WIDE DIFFERENTIATORS

"Build a better mousetrap, and the world will beat a path to your door" is a quote famously misattributed to Ralph Waldo Emerson in the late 1800s. Emerson did in fact write an ode to the power of differentiation through innovation, and he did promise that customers would create a "hard, well-beaten road" to the maker's home to buy, but his essay focused on the making of better corn, chairs, knives, and church organs – not mousetraps.[24] Ironically, whoever twisted Emerson's words into a quote about mousetraps knew something: the mousetrap became the most frequently patented device in US history, with over 4,400 versions issued.[25]

This chapter asks whether you can gain a platform advantage by designing a platform-wide differentiator, that is, something your customer sees as a better mousetrap. We'll focus on two approaches: hero platform capability and platform-level performance synergies.

HERO PLATFORM CAPABILITY

The strongest of all platform differentiators is a hero capability – a proprietary functionality that applies platform-wide, like a key ingredient, across all experience hubs that the platform offers. Google's search capability is a hero. It doesn't just power the Google Search app – it also enhances the user's experience of leading apps like Google Maps, YouTube, and Google News.[26,27] Search capability has been Google's better mousetrap that led much of the world to beat a path to its door. Now threatened to the core by generative intelligence (in the form of Chat GPT), Google is doing all it can to reinvent its key ingredient.[28]

Google Search is just one example of a hero capability as a differentiator. Uber's matching engine (linking transport tasks to nearby vehicles) and Amazon Alexa's semantic interpreter (recognizing verbal commands) also belong to the hero capability hall of fame. And hero capabilities are not limited to the tech giants. OneTrust's data discovery capability automates the classification of its business customers' data on regulatory-related parameters to empower trusted operations.[29] A BitSight algorithm converts over 100 billion cybersecurity events daily into company-specific risk ratings that inform cyber insurance policy pricing.[30] If your company can invent a broad, impactful, and protectable capability, do so by all means. It will be your better mouse trap, and your highest ROI move.

PLATFORM PERFORMANCE SYNERGIES

Many firms can't rely on hero capability breakthroughs to separate themselves from competitors. In this case, companies often seek a different path to platform differentiation. They design in platform performance synergies – that is, circumstances where the value of two or more high-performing parts of a platform work together to become more than the sum of their parts. Platform synergies come in three forms: data synergies, decision synergies, and support synergies. You can pursue any one or more of these synergies to increase your differentiation.

DATA SYNERGIES

If two data sets are intelligently linked, they can update each other to save the user costs and error risk; they can also interact with each other to create higher value data sets. Any of these data synergies have the potential to differentiate. Autodesk provides a powerful example. The company is a market leader in software that digitally helps users Design and Make just about anything, plus Operate what they have made. Autodesk software portfolio supports design, make, and use across three industries: buildings, products, and media.

Autodesk is now transforming its business into three industry-focused clouds – Forma for buildings, Fusion for products, and Flow for media.[31] Each industry cloud supports customer design, make, and operate capabilities, all running on Autodesk Platform Services. One way Autodesk differentiates its performance is by designing rich data synergies for customers. These synergies help to transform siloed business processes into seamless business processes running on linked information models (see Fig. 2.3.1).

Here are a few illustrations of Autodesk's data synergies in action:

- Commercial buildings often require custom-manufactured parts. Autodesk can associate information about the building to information about those parts. When an architect modifies a building's design using Autodesk building and manufacturing tools, building changes can ripple through to become changes in linked part designs, saving time and cost while assuring design integrity.

- When a media company animates a medieval village as a movie special effect backdrop, it may later use that animation to produce the village "for real" in a theme park, plus manufacture toy versions of the village as merchandise. Autodesk eases the transfer of data across use cases to enable multiple forms of making.

- Makers often change things from the designer's original blueprint. Autodesk's making tools support revisions of upstream design data so that what is finally produced has an accurate "digital twin." That twin can then support Operate activities, such as operations management of an apartment building or monetization of an animated character.

Autodesk Data Synergies

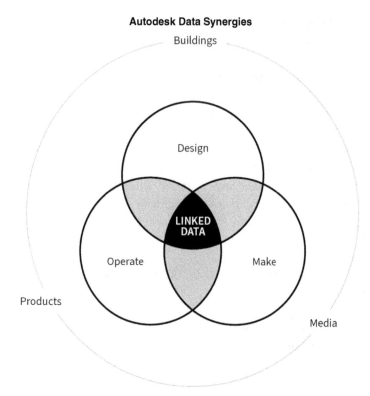

Fig. 2.3.1

Note that working on synergies doesn't keep Autodesk from also working on a hero capability. As it builds out its information model links, Autodesk is also developing generative AI tools that expand the frontiers of possibility. The tools enable designers to describe outcome parameters that they desire. Autodesk's generative AI then suggests designs that meet as many parameters as possible, sparking potential new directions. The overall result is an Autodesk platform full of efficient innovation possibilities.

You can achieve data synergies as well. Start by building a customer-centric business portfolio and then get your internal teams to work across organizational boundaries to create the data linkages that differentiate your customer benefits and experiences.

DECISION SYNERGIES

Every modern car owner or smartphone user knows what it's like to be guided by "best route" mapping software to find the fastest route from Point A to Point B. That's the best decision-making software in action. When such software takes more than one factor into account – let's say the user wants the fastest route, with the lowest carbon footprint, and the most beautiful scenery along the way – the software's performance becomes more distinctive, because it is solving a harder multi-factor problem. Platforms can provide decision synergies by tackling these complex system-level questions. Decision synergies empower users to optimize their choices across multiple, sometimes competing, objectives to achieve an overall best result.

Zebra Technologies' support of modern e-commerce warehouses provides a good example. Often bigger than sports stadiums, these warehouses are moving symphonies of goods, bins, people, conveyors, robots, and wheeled vehicles. The warehouse's shipments show up as goods on retail store shelves, medicines at patient bedsides in health-care facilities, and packages on consumer doorsteps after a delivery van comes by.

Zebra got into business over 50 years ago by helping companies track the movement of packages through barcode printing; the black and white stripes in barcodes inspired the company's name. Through organic innovation and multiple acquisitions, including software-as-service platforms, Zebra now helps customers tackle much more complex problems. It tracks the location of goods, workers, and mobile autonomous machines while considering through decision support software how they can work in harmony to achieve the warehouse management team's performance goals.

Customer operations are complex enough, and vary enough by industry, that Zebra also relies on software partners and major customer software to support best decisions that take multiple objectives into account. To extend the reach of its supply chain solutions, Zebra also provides solutions for the manufacturers who fill warehouses and for the retail stores, health-care facilities, and e-commerce companies who use what the warehouse ships (see Fig. 2.3.2).

Zebra Decision Synergies

Fig. 2.3.2

Zebra and its partners add differentiated value by generating optimal answers to system-level customer questions such as "What next order should be filled, using what next actions by available participants?" The answer needs to take into account:

- The due date and travel time of *orders*.

- The availability and location of *goods*.

- The availability, capabilities, and location of *workers*.

- The availability, capabilities, and location of *autonomous machines*.

- The possibility of restocking a former order *return* on the way to fill a new order.

Finally, Zebra's ecosystem is so rich and varied that it also provides decision support to end customers about which solution partners may be best for them. Over 10,000 partners in over 100 countries integrate Zebra hardware and software into various solutions.[32] By digitally empowering customers to find their best-fit Zebra partner, Zebra creates yet another layer of decision synergy value.

Consider whether you have an opportunity to answer system-level questions (by yourself or in collaboration) that your customers might have. Elevate your vision to see issues that your customer is only addressing in piece parts today. If you can integrate smaller answers into a bigger answer, you'll find new differentiation.

SUPPORT SYNERGIES

It's also possible to differentiate platforms through their delivery of synergistic support services. This is relevant in situations where how you help your clients use your platform may be as important as what the platform does. The interrelated markets of business accounting, financial audit, and tax preparation provide a great example. There is limited room for "innovation" when it comes to taxes and financial reporting, given their regulated nature. At the same time, a multitude of complex regulations are continuously changing, requiring continuous retraining of professional service firm employees. It's in this context that the Thomson Reuters company supplements its Onvio tax and accounting workflow platform with its Checkpoint workforce support platform to provide distinctive value.

The Canadian Thomson and British Reuters companies were both technical information publishers for many decades before they merged in 2008. From 2009 to 2012, the combined firm embarked on a new strategy that included the acquisition and integration of several professional accounting and tax software companies. After integrating and platforming those purchases, Thomson Reuters launched its cloud-hosted Onvio platform as "one place for everything"[33] shown in Fig. 2.3.3.

Thomson Reuters: Onvio Workflow + Checkpoint Support Synergies.

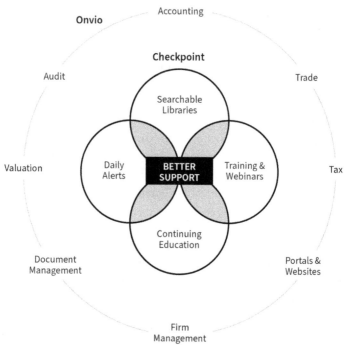

Fig. 2.3.3.

Onvio platform modules share the same database (a data synergy) and present professionals with the same look and feel for multidisciplinary problem-solving.[34] Onvio clients gain efficiency as automated entries and shared data flow into connected accounting, business analytics, and tax preparation service processes.

Yet as good as its platform is, Thomson Reuters is surrounded by stiff competition.[35,36] Every dimension of differentiation matters. Thomson Reuters relies on Checkpoint's synergistic workforce support to help distinguish its Onvio workflow offer, drawing on its legacy technical publishing competence. Checkpoint provides subscription-based support that helps tax and accounting firms optimize workforce productivity, quality of service, and cost of operations by digitally training and supporting professionals continuously. A Checkpoint support platform subscription includes the following:[37]

- Dozens of searchable libraries that generate more reliable answers than internet search.
- (Checkpoint's AI-fueled search engine enhances the usefulness of each library.)
- Over 500 continuing education modules and 450 webinars on topical issues.
- Daily alert newsletters explaining new legal rulings, regulations, and legislation.
- Virtual and in-person multi-day professional development conferences.

Checkpoint's synergistic support platform complements Onvio's synergistic data platform to doubly empower its accounting and tax firm clients.

If it's hard to differentiate your core platform's performance, consider whether you can differentiate on the user support that you provide. By structuring your support as a platform and by supporting it with its own distinctive story, you may find unexpected opportunities to distinguish yourself.

In order to grow your platform's differentiation, regularly explore each of the opportunities outlined above. Set aside a platform-level innovation budget. Maximize your returns by creating your own special mix of hero platform capabilities and platform-level synergies, whether those are data, decision, or support in nature.

KEY QUESTIONS FOR CONSIDERATION

If helpful, use the template below to capture your thinking on platform-wide differentiators.

1. What hero platform capability could help differentiate you from competitors?

2. What types of platform-level synergies might you create in order to differentiate?
   a. Data synergies for lower costs, seamless processes, and enhanced outcomes.
   b. Decision synergies for system-level best answers.
   c. Support synergies to supplement your core platform's performance.
3. How will you allocate and govern investments for ongoing platform differentiation?

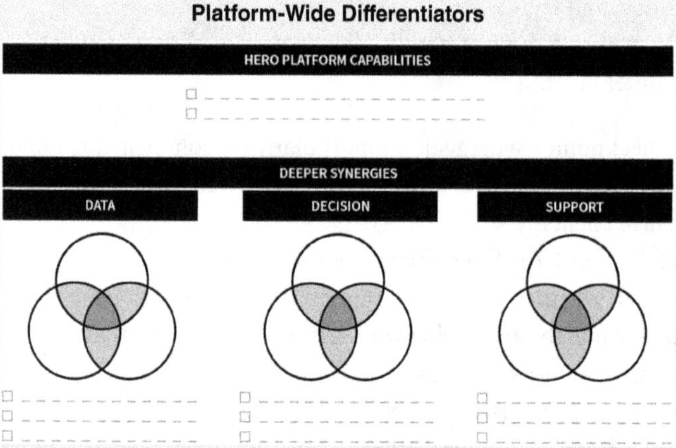

Platform-Wide Differentiators

Fig. 2.3.4

2.4

MAGNETIC OFFER ARCHITECTURE

While working at a mobile data technology firm in 2014, Kabir Barday was struck by how many of the applications that he had developed raised customer data privacy concerns. He was equally struck by how fragmented and siloed his corporate clients' approaches were to meeting customer privacy needs. Spotting a profound business opportunity, Kabir and cofounder Blake Bannon started a pioneering platform company in 2016 to address data privacy and more. Their name for the company – OneTrust – reflected the scope of their ambition.

Through that name, Kabir and Blake articulated a big idea that made OneTrust one of the fastest-growing enterprise software companies in business history.[38] They believed that privacy compliance was just a means to the end of creating stakeholder trust. The deeper they dug during prospective customer conversations, the more they discovered that building that trust was a broad and multidisciplinary task. Privacy was the start, not the end, of the trust journey. The duo went on an acquisition-and-integration sprint to create a platform that seamlessly addresses all drivers of trust.[39] Today, everyone in OneTrust's customer coalition is united and inspired by its big idea: "Make trust your competitive advantage."

MAGNETIC ARCHITECTURE FOR BUSINESS MARKETS

In parallel to its unifying big idea, OneTrust's offer architecture – that is, the offers that customers can buy and the reasons why they should buy them – attracts very different types of buyers with very different reasons to buy. And that's how it should be. Sometimes referred to as "marketecture," successful platform offer architecture attracts different customer types like a magnet. Just as every magnet has two opposite attraction poles – north and south – magnetic architecture can compel opposite types of buyers toward a sale. With platforms, the two opposite attraction types to consider are *commonality buyers* and *specificity buyers*.

- *Commonality Buyers* are drawn to *platform-wide capabilities and differentiators* that they consistently experience in every part of the platform. These buyers are typically senior executives who like the way a platform lifts the performance of large portions of their workforce. They love how a single source of data truth creates alignment. They cheer the way common and seamless interfaces encourage collaboration. They take confidence from the way that transparent and integrated decision analytics empower the right actions.

- *Specificity Buyers*, by contrast, are drawn to things that help them as individuals or small group leaders. They are drawn to specific *software modules* and specific multi-module *solutions* that precisely address their scope of needs. The Specificity Buyer may admire enterprise-wide integration, but they insist on something that helps them succeed.

Fig. 2.4.1 illustrates why OneTrust's architecture is magnetic.

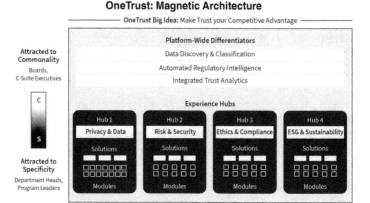

Fig. 2.4.1

At the top of the vertical axis, we see Commonality Buyers. In the case of OneTrust, these are boards of directors, business CEOs, chief operating officers, chief risk officers, and chief marketing officers. These buyers steward stakeholder trust in the company and its brand. They value that OneTrust's comprehensive Trust Intelligence Platform makes systematic trust management possible. Three platform differentiators, shown as white bars at the top of the diagram, are particularly attractive. These differentiators are as follows:

- *Data Discovery and Classification*: The platform uses AI/ML to discover and classify a company's enterprise-wide data along risk and privacy dimensions for trust management.

- *Automated Regulatory Intelligence*: The platform continuously downloads regulatory and compliance updates, so that companies are never out of date on key requirements.

- *Integrated Trust Analytics*: The platform's analytics tools help leaders interpret trust drivers – whether risks or opportunities – so that trust management can be woven into operations.

Specificity Buyers, shown at the bottom of Fig. 2.4.1's vertical axis, are a very different group from Commonality Buyers. They are functional specialists whose work only touches one part of the full system that commonality buyers desire. They might be a European personal data rights manager seeking a GDPR-compliant solution, an ESG program manager seeking a carbon accounting program, or an Ethics officer seeking a whistleblower support service. They primarily care that the OneTrust module designed for their specific role provides best-in-class functionality for that role.

To meet Specificity Buyer needs, OneTrust created a menu of 35 Lego-like modules that gives buyers the power to choose the combination that best suits them. For mid-level managers, OneTrust has 13 solutions designed to fit the most frequent multi-module patterns. These modules and solutions roll up into four clouds running on one platform, completing the ladder from Specificity to Commonality Buyers.[40]

Magnetic offer architecture can particularly help boost your growth rate when you match different levels of your architecture with diversified go-to-market motions:

- *Bottoms-up motions*: Popular, easy to access modules can be sold for little (or offered for free) through e-commerce channels that let users start using immediately and then expand over time into multiple modules and pricing systems.

- *Middle-out motions*: Promoted solutions can be sold to mid-level buyers – such as team leaders, sub-function leaders – through an internal or external sales representative.

- *Top-down motions*: One or more experience hubs (e.g., clouds, consoles, etc.) could be sold to senior executives through advisory-based sales teams who can articulate end-to-end need coverage, platform-wide differentiators, and enterprise-wide performance lift.

If you have a business platform with an unbalanced architecture or mismatched go-to-market system, consider whether improvements can open new growth paths.

MAGNETIC ARCHITECTURE FOR CONSUMER MARKETS

Magnetic architecture principles apply to consumer markets as well, with a few adjustments. Rather than having buying centers like a B2B market, consumers have a spectrum of psychographic differences. Some consumers value commonality and others specificity. Consider the Uber story we shared in Chapter 2.3. As stand-alone services, Uber Rides and Uber Eats appeal to specificity consumers. Uber One appeals to a commonality consumer. There are enough consumers in each segment that Uber expanded its offer architecture and related marketing programs to appeal to each.

It's worth noting that we're seeing the spread of "Loyalty as a Service" (LaaS) programs among platforms, inspired by the success of Amazon Prime. It is an economic appeal to commonality buyers. Uber One is a LaaS program example. The consumer is asked to *pay* a monthly fee to be loyal to the brand. In return, the consumer receives a bundle of benefits whose calculated economic value significantly outstrips the consumer's cost ... as long as the consumer is a frequent and loyal buyer from the brand.

Consumer magnetism can also be observed when specificity benefits are presented as complementary experiences, unified by a common platform differentiator, within the same app or cloud. Through personalized messaging, the platform can emphasize some specificity benefits over others, depending on consumer signals.

The MasterClass platform architecture provides a good illustration. MasterClass was launched in 2014 by David Rogier, fueled by the memory of his grandmother's struggle to access education. At the time, scale e-learning leaders such as Coursera and Udemy were established in the market, and Ted Talks had for decades been the leading forum for expert lectures.[41]

MasterClass broke through platform competition by launching a novel big idea – that "everyone should have access to genius."[42] You didn't just need an acting teacher – you needed Dustin Hoffman. A tennis pro instructor wasn't good enough – you needed Serena Williams. Want to cook modern Italian food? You need Massimo Bottura, three-star Michelin chef from Modena, Italy, as your mentor.

MasterClass has three platform-wide "differentiators" designed to lift all classes and students. These are illustrated as white rectangles at the top of Fig. 2.4.2. The first is that world-class performers know things that others don't and therefore have secrets to share. The second is that these same world-class performers "pitch" their classes to you so that you can know from their own pitches which classes interest you most. Finally, MasterClass maintains broadcast entertainment production standards when filming, so nothing gets in the way of your instructor's genius. This three-value platform value proposition appeals to a commonality buyer's mindset – perhaps a lifelong learner, definitely someone who regards learning highly and seeks a "better approach to learning," regardless of the specific topic or instructor.[43]

Within this commonality, MasterClass offers Specificity Buyers all kinds of choices. These begin with the individual experts involved (150 celebrities, who both promote and deliver classes), class topics (180+ courses, with thousands of lessons), and subject-matter categories (11, including food, wellness, arts and entertainment, sports and gaming, science and technology, home and lifestyle, and community and government).[44]

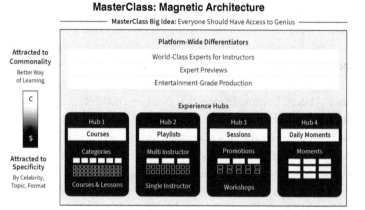

Fig. 2.4.2

In recent years, MasterClass has most creatively added specificity in learning style. This is a powerful though subtle specificity factor, because different people's minds learn in different ways. In the early years of MasterClass, critics called out that the platform only offered a single learning format – the genius speaking directly into the camera for a series of 10-minute lectures – and that this way of learning was not for everyone.

MasterClass responded by diversifying learning formats, creating a new specificity dimension. It accomplished this while maintaining their differentiators of world-class performers and high production values. MasterClass' format innovations included the following:

Playlists: students can compare and contrast multiple experts' approaches to the same general learning topic.

Sessions: Students follow a 30-day group curriculum, complete real-world projects, receive teacher assistant feedback, and join a supportive community of session-mates.

Member Wins: the outputs of high-performing session-members are promoted through MasterClass marketing channels.

Daily Moments: MasterClass geniuses provide snackable two-minute daily inspirations.

Put it all together, and the magnetic MasterClass architecture lets its members learn a specific topic, from a specific teacher, in specifically the way they want to learn. The most recent Master-Class fundraising round valued the company at $2.75 billion.[45]

OneTrust and MasterClass are shared to stimulate your own thinking. Create or improve your architecture to ensure that it is providing you with compelling avenues for growth. Review your platform's offer architecture to see whether it magnetically attracts all of the personas in your customer coalition and is supported well by your go-to-market motions. Strengthen areas of architecture weakness to diversify and accelerate your sources of growth.

In the same way that Chapter 2.2 ("Pivotal Persona Value") enabled you to develop compelling value propositions by persona, your architecture development in this chapter should enable you to develop compelling value propositions by architectural element.

KEY QUESTIONS FOR CONSIDERATION

1. What is your platform's big idea? How can you express it through your platform brand as a unifying promise and call to action to those in your customer coalition?

2. Categorize the personas in your coalition by their attraction to commonality (top-down) and specificity (bottom-up), including a third category for those in the middle (mid-level). Where do your revenues come from? Can you drive growth by adding underserved personas?

3. How can you improve your architecture to better attract underserved personas?
   a. Platform-wide differentiators for commonality buyers
   b. Multi-module solutions for mid-level buyers
   c. Individual modules for specificity buyers

4. What kind of value propositions can you write at each architecture level (platform, experience hub, solution, module, and platform-wide differentiators)?

5. Use Fig. 2.4.3 to define your architecture. Use Fig. 2.4.4 for architecture element value propositions.

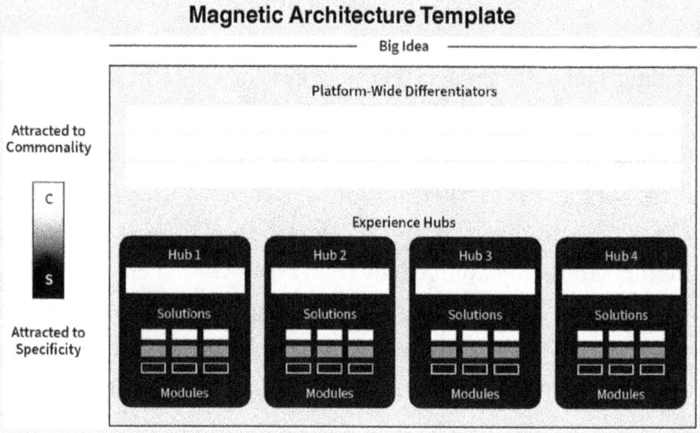

Magnetic Architecture Template

Fig. 2.4.3

Element Value Proposition Template

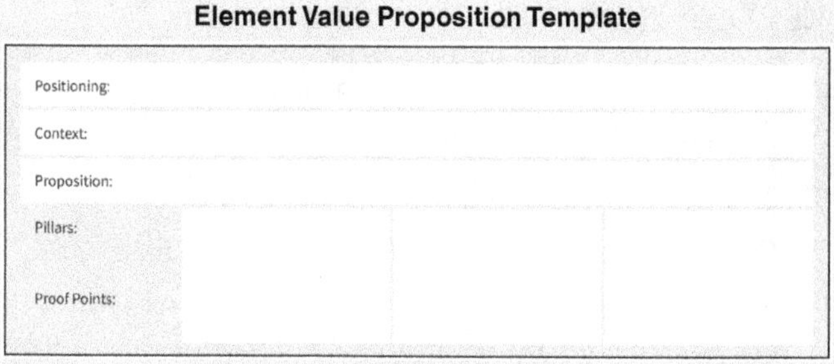

Fig. 2.4.4

Part 3

DEMAND PLAYS

Companies with platforms can grow at higher rates than companies without. Why is that? It's because platform companies have an infinite connection to customers, one that continues throughout the customer's Use journey rather than stopping at a transaction. Platform companies can use that infinite connection to build stronger customer relationships and grow stronger customer demand. Our Demand Plays show you how.

Six Demand Plays are shown as a customer journey in Fig. 3.0.1. Two Demand Plays make customer acquisition more efficient. Four more Demand Plays make customer value growth activities more effective. We depict this journey as infinite because your customer chooses, then uses; chooses, then uses again – with no end if all goes well.

- The left loop of the infinity diagram represents your company's activities during the Choose journey. These are your efforts to earn buyer choice as the buyer explores their needs and options, assesses their final choices, and transacts. Note that the outside track of this left loop is traveled by a new prospect; the inside track is traveled by an existing customer.

- The right loop of the infinite diagram represents your company's activities during the customer's Use journey – as the customer experiences value from what they have accessed.

Demand Plays

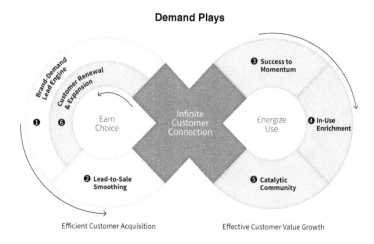

Fig. 3.0.1

The center "X" represents the infinite customer connection that a platform can create between the customer, the company, and others throughout the full journey.

Our first two Demand Plays describe how you can use your platform to make customer acquisition more efficient. In the first play, *Brand-Demand Lead Engine (Chapter 3.1)*, you'll efficiently generate a well-qualified lead. In the second play, *Lead-to-Sale Smoothing (Chapter 3.2)*, you'll efficiently convert a well-qualified lead to revenue.

The next plays describe how your company can act throughout the customer's Use journey to build energy for expansion. Play 3, *Success to Momentum (Chapter 3.3)*, describes how to spark customer momentum toward full-platform use. Your fourth play, *In-Use Enrichment (Chapter 3.4)*, explains how to enrich the customer's experience of value during use. Play 5, *Catalytic Community (Chapter 3.5)*, outlines how you can foster customer-to-customer energy by convening your community.

You'll feel the return on your Use journey investments when your customer slingshots back to the Choose journey, this time on the inside track as a return buyer. The sixth play, *Customer Renewal and Expansion*, describes how your company can use data insights it gained through Use journey customer interactions to promote optimized renewal and expansion offers. Your customer, energized by their journey interactions with your company, will be more inclined to choose positively. The result will be faster customer base growth, higher share of wallet, and larger customer lifetime value.

A NEW CUSTOMER JOURNEY

Compare the customer journey diagram we just described above to historical customer journey thought leadership below. For decades, leading business and academic frameworks have highlighted detailed steps in the customer's Choose journey but have made only passing mention of the Use journey. Consider three examples.

a. The "Purchase Funnel" is a framework birthed in 1898 and refined in the 1920s.[1] It tracks the customer's Choose Journey from "awareness" to "buy." It ignores the Use journey completely.

b. The "Buyer's Journey" was first expressed in 1965 by the marketing icon Philip Kotler.[2] It had multiple Choose journey steps but only one catch-all Use journey step – "Post-purchase Behavior" – that lacks the insightfulness of Kotler's Choose journey steps.

c. The 360° digital customer model is the most modern concept in widespread use today. It conceives a circular Choose-Use journey but shows no mechanism for value growth. It relies on generic product or service "experience" during use to achieve advocacy, rather than relying on our proposed post purchase demand disciplines.

Evolution of the Customer Journey

a) Purchase Funnel *No Concept*	b) Kotler Buyer Decision Process *Minor Concept*	c) 360° Customer Journey *Immature Concepts*
Awareness	Problem Recognition	Awareness
Interest	Information Search	Exploration
Consideration	Evaluation of Alternatives	Advocacy
Intent	Purchase Decision	The 360° Digital Customer
Buy	Postpurchase Behavior	Evaluation / Experience / Purchase

Choose step (Prepurchase)   Use step (Postpurchase)

Fig. 3.0.2

The gaps in these models are not surprising. The customer Use journey was dark to companies when these frameworks were published. But in a platform era, these classics are now incomplete.

The six Demand Plays we cover in this part of this book shape a customer journey model that we propose below. It takes platforms into account. Platforms help compress Choose journey steps while expanding Use journey steps. The result is a more efficient customer acquisition journey and a more effective customer value expansion journey – together accelerating growth.

The six customer journey stages captured in our Demand Plays (Fig. 3.0.1) are stated from the company objective perspective. These steps summarize the impact that a platform company wants to have on its customers. We can re-state these same six company steps as customer stages, with each stage expressing the customer's desired or expected experience once they are consistently served by a platform company. This re-statement moves us closer to customer-centric journey language. We call this The Platform Customer Journey model, shown in Fig. 3.0.3. We believe this is the customer journey of the future.

Several topics are worth highlighting. The customer no longer has patience for a gap between awareness and engagement (Step 1) – it should be instantaneous. In certain software or app instances, the time lag between awareness and free platform experience (through Step 2) can be measured in seconds. Paid offers take longer; for those

The Platform Customer Journey Model

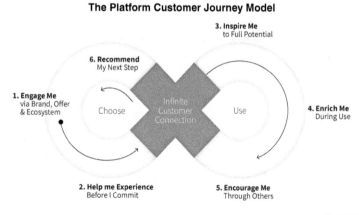

Fig. 3.0.3

the customer expects simulated use experiences that are true to post-payment experience. Once a user, the customer expects inspiration, enrichment, and community that build customer energy (Model Steps 3–5). The customer then expects that the platform company will know them well enough to make a value-added suggestion around what new product or service would next be best for them (Step 6). The customer's experience of this infinite engagement will shape their expectations of how a modern brand adds presence value throughout their journey.

3.1

BRAND–DEMAND LEAD ENGINE

You can't acquire a new customer without first generating a new lead. By this, we mean a well-qualified lead: a prospect who has become aware of and familiar with your brand and at least one offer and who is seriously considering taking the next step needed to access what you can provide. Well-qualified leads are a preliminary return on your customer acquisition investments. They have economic value because some will convert to customers. This Demand Play helps you generate more platform leads, more efficiently.

There are two underlying levers that help create a lead: prospect *attraction to your brand* and prospect *demand for your offer*, or "brand and demand" for short. These are the yin and yang of lead generation. Research shows that the most effective marketers do both, in balance and harmony, to create the most efficient lead engine.

Here's an analogy to explain why these levers work together. Imagine yourself as a solo attendee at a cocktail party, seeking to make connections. You meet two strangers and have two conversations. One stranger is easy to bond with: they share your values, have a great personality, and are doing things professionally that you admire. They invite you to join them for lunch the next day at a local café. The second stranger comes across as self-absorbed, opportunistic, and untrustworthy. But they have front-row tickets to see your favorite pop star at a sold-out music festival the next day and invite you to join them. If only the best person had the best offer, your choice would be easy!

If you own an attractive brand – the first stranger in our analogy – a prospect will want to be in relationship with your business. If you have an attractive offer – the music festival in our analogy – a prospect will want to transact. You'll be answering *the two sides of "Why?"* that all prospects ask to themselves, knowingly or not: *Why should I choose this brand?* and *Why should I choose this offer?* When you answer both in a compelling way, your prospects will soon become qualified leads.

Platforms can help you improve your lead generation by enhancing the power of your brands and by increasing the agility of your demand generation. The result is a platform-powered new lead engine. The framework shown in Fig. 3.1.1 outlines how you can use your platform to strengthen brand and demand lead generation. As the diagram shows:

- You can enhance your brand power in three ways:

  o *Elevate your purpose and make your promise more compelling* through your platform brand. Link your platform brand name to your corporate brand name if possible. That way you'll strengthen your corporate brand as you build your platform brand.

  o Shift from *product line branding* to *experience hub and ingredient branding.* You'll need fewer brands in a platform than in a product line, so you can consolidate investment and strengthen the brands you keep.

  o Make your *customer coalition* a part of your platform brand story. Your platform brand's attractiveness isn't just about your company; it comes from your coalition as well.

- You can increase the agility of your demand generation in three ways:

  o Creatively choose which persona (within your diverse customer coalition) can *best unlock new growth* through acquisition. Your best growth-generating personas will change over time.

○ Use your offer architecture's modularity to *tailor the best acquisition offer* for your targeted acquisition persona. Test and learn for best results.

○ *Adjust your acquisition value proposition* to the platform knowledge of your acquisition target. Shift your message from relevance to differentiation as your audience matures.

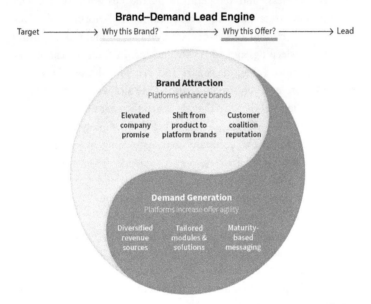

Brand–Demand Lead Engine

Target ——————→ Why this Brand? ——————→ Why this Offer? ——————→ Lead

Brand Attraction
Platforms enhance brands

| Elevated company promise | Shift from product to platform brands | Customer coalition reputation |

Demand Generation
Platforms increase offer agility

| Diversified revenue sources | Tailored modules & solutions | Maturity-based messaging |

Fig. 3.1.1

Below we share brief company stories to bring these six brand and demand opportunities to life. As you read, ask yourself how each vignette might inspire you to try something similar.

COMPANY EXAMPLES: ENHANCED BRAND ATTRACTION

Elevated Company Promise

For most of its corporate history, the mattress company known today as Sleep Number promised personalized mattress firmness, enabled by their air-filled, adjustable-firmness mattress line. Customers chose the firmness level (first 0–10 and later 0–100) that made them most comfortable. The company encouraged its customers to "Find your sleep number" for better comfort.

In 2017, Sleep Number launched a platform bed: the "Smart 360." This bed is full of sensors and software as well as air. It senses the sleeper's dynamic physical position, temperature, snoring, breathing, and heartbeat and then automatically adjusts the bed's contours, sub-area firmness, and temperature as the customer sleeps. The Smart 360 mattress meets all our criteria for a platform: It observes the customer (billions of sensor data points each night) while using the product (sleeping) and adds value during use (auto-adjustment).[3] To add yet more value, the Smart 360 provides the sleeper with a Sleep IQ score every morning, enabling the sleeper to better understand why they feel the way they do when they get up.[4]

The Smart 360 platform is elevating the company's brand purpose and promise. The company is transforming from a provider of adjustable-firmness mattresses into a science-driven sleep quality service. The Smart 360 platform promises to add "28 minutes of quality sleep each night" and that matters, because "proven sleep quality improves your quality of life."

Sleep Number acquires new leads by showing quality of sleep in action. It partners with the US National Football League to have top quarterbacks describe the difference their Sleep Number-enhanced sleep quality makes for their game-day performance. And Sleep Number is going even further, partnering with Mayo Clinic to explore correlations between sleep biometrics, cardiovascular health, and other health conditions. It's possible to imagine the day when Sleep Number's elevated brand promise includes longer customer life expectancy.[5]

Shift from Product to Platform Brands

Platforms can transform brand portfolios as dramatically as brand promises. A brand portfolio is the collection of brands that a

---

[3.] Founded in 1987, the company called itself "Select Comfort." For its first 30 years, in 2017 the same year that it launched the Smart 360 platform bed, the company changed its name to Sleep Number – a move that supported the brand promise transformation we discuss here.

company owns and nurtures in order to communicate and differentiate its market-facing offer architecture (as discussed in Chapter 2.4).

A shift to platforms gives companies an opportune moment to
transform product line brand portfolios to platform brand portfolios. When the CAD-CAM software maker Autodesk – owner of dozens of point product software brands – decided to create a platform,
it made three best-practice brand portfolio choices. Autodesk:

- Branded its experience hubs in a compelling way, then
  descriptively named modules and solutions within each hub
  for workflow-based navigation and no product brand clut-
  ter. Autodesk launched three familial cloud brands: Autodesk
  Forma for architecture and construction, Autodesk Fusion for
  product design and manufacturing, and Autodesk Flow for
  media worldbuilding and production.

- Named its platform in a way that builds the corporate brand,
  enabling platform innovations to strengthen the company's
  corporate brand rather than becoming its rival. Autodesk's
  three sibling clouds are united by one branded platform,
  Autodesk Platform Services that makes them open, extensible,
  and compatible with each other.

- Formally named or branded platform-wide differentiators.
  While all Autodesk Platform Services are valuable, some are
  particularly distinctive. Candidates for the spotlight include
  Autodesk generative intelligence that suggests design solutions, Autodesk information models that update each other,
  Autodesk large-scale collaboration management, and Autodesk
  sustainability analytics to inform planet-friendly choices.

Many Autodesk customers will still buy its branded point products (and can), but the company has laid out a new, simple, and
powerful platform brand portfolio that invites them to step into
the future when they are ready.

Customer Coalition Reputation

For better or worse, a platform company's customer coalition
becomes part of the company's brand. If a social media platform

allows hateful speech to thrive; if a ride-sharing company OKs a driver who mistreats passengers; if an e-commerce exchange admits a seller who refuses a return; the behavior of the customer coalition will be attributed to a lack of platform company standards and values. Conversely, a company whose platform supports a customer coalition known for its innovative lifestyle, its community passion, or its cultural values can do more than any advertisement to attract new prospects. One way a platform company can ready its brand for new acquisition activity is to ensure that its customer coalition hurts as little and helps as much as possible to attract others.

COMPANY EXAMPLES: AGILE DEMAND GENERATION

Diversified Revenue Sources

Platform customer coalitions provide a rich variety of acquisition growth targets. Firms like Airbnb have creatively used coalition diversity to pursue agile demand growth. In 2012, Airbnb brainstormed the idea of adding a new persona to its customer coalition – local experience creators who could bring guests closer to the local communities where they were staying (e.g., a small-group camel riding guide for Airbnb guests in Morocco).[6] The goal was both a new business line and a differentiator for its core business. Airbnb Experiences launched with 500 experience creators in 2016 and skyrocketed to 40,000 creators pre-pandemic. In a 2019 survey of 200,000 Airbnb guests, 92% said authentic local connections represented by Experiences influenced their choice of Airbnb.[7] When COVID hit in 2020, Airbnb further intensified its acquisition of experienced creators, rapidly growing its creator persona base to 400,000. Airbnb could offer creators access to long-stay lodging guests who needed a wide array of COVID-safe local activities. Airbnb could also offer creators access to stay-at-home guests who were cooped up in their living rooms and willing to pay for virtual experiences. A London magician and a Beijing pianist were equally available via zoom to someone in Chicago, through Airbnb Experiences. These new coalition member acquisitions created the foundation for long-term growth of Airbnb's experience-rich travel business.[8]

Once the pandemic eased, Airbnb pivoted back to its core customer personas to launch a new momentum campaign. "Made Possible by Hosts" featured distinctive host lodgings like LoveNests, TreeHouses, and Italian Garden Homes. This campaign built on Airbnb's experience creator differentiation by treating hosts as the creative ones. The campaign targeted lapsed travelers and dormant hosts to reenergize the core business.[9]

Tailored Modules and Solutions

The modularity of a well-designed experience hub's offers gives companies more agility than ever to propose tailored offers that will entice a prospect to respond positively. There are three dimensions that drive offer agility:

- *Scope:* Companies can tailor their platforms to the needs of every type of prospect, offering narrow modules, broader solutions, entire experience hubs, and expansive multi-hub platforms. The Adobe Creative Cloud lets prospects choose to subscribe to any one, any two, or all 11 of its platform apps.

- *Features:* Prospects can find, through filtering, offers with performance features that they care about. Airbnb makes it easy for customers to filter on 16 different categories to find their perfect getaway.

- *Pricing:* Platforms help companies to offer multiple-pricing schemes so that one of them fits a prospect's financial and experience priorities. Netflix responded to the launch of competing streaming services by introducing low-cost ad-sponsored subscriptions.

Maturity-based Messages

Your targeted customer personas may or may not be mature in their understanding of how platforms can deliver new benefits. This creates the need for a final type agility – benefit messaging agility.

If your audience is not familiar with platforms, your benefits may be unfamiliar or unexpected to them. Find a way to compete against non-platform substitutes with an accessible platform benefit. Sleep Number does this by promoting "28 more minutes of quality sleep a night" – proving their scientific sleep monitoring while delivering a highly pragmatic benefit.

If your audience becomes more platform savvy – let's say multiple platform beds launch and customers expect sensor-based beds – then messaging needs to shift to competitive platform differentiation. Here is where Sleep Number's medical thought leadership on what drives healthy sleep, size of customer database, and relationships with institutions like Mayo Clinic make a difference.

How many of the ideas and stories in this chapter spark ideas about ways you can better generate leads? How can you take advantage of the enhanced brand and agile demand opportunities that your platform provides?

KEY QUESTIONS FOR CONSIDERATION

1. How convincingly does your platform answer the prospect's two-sided questions of "Why this Brand" and "Why this Offer"? How can you re-establish balance if needed?

2. How can you enhance the attractiveness of your platform brand?
   a. Enhanced platform brand purpose and promise.
   b. Development of platform brands.
   c. Customer coalition reputation.

3. How can increase the agility of your platform demand generation?
   a. Diverse thinking and targeting of growth personas.
   b. Tailored offers by persona.
   c. Maturity-based messaging by persona.

3.2

LEAD-TO-SALE SMOOTHING

The "last mile" that a qualified lead travels before becoming a customer is a treacherous one. Typical conversion rates from a lead to a sale hover around 1%.[10] As a result, go-to-market innovators are applying the concept of digital services – originally developed to serve established, paying customers – to better serve and convert leads in the pre-purchase last mile.

This requires a platform company to offer its leads a free digital service in exchange for data visibility, observing and interacting with the lead in a more in-depth way than website browsing, and then applying powerful platform analytics and experiences to help the lead make a decision to become a customer. A good example is the way that Proper Cloth, an intelligent tailored clothing platform – creates and stores custom sizing data on all leads so that every purchase thereafter becomes simply a matter of choosing fabric and style. Thanks to the value that leads receive, they allow themselves and their histories to remain known, because they may want to return as a shopper again to receive repeat services.

These platform-powered services take aim at the most common reasons that a lead fails to become a sale. These reasons, depicted in Fig. 3.2.1, fall into two broad categories: *obstacles* and *potholes*. Obstacles are decision blockers that cause a lead's progress to slow or come to halt. Obstacles cause the shopper to delay, tire, and give up. Major obstacles include product fit and financial commitment.

Potholes are the by-product of gaps in a company's last mile operations. Potholes cause a lead to fall out of and disappear from a company's visible sales pipeline. Key potholes include lead visibility and internal alignment.

Fig. 3.2.1

This chapter will help you smooth your prospect's lead-to-sale journey through platform-enhanced initiatives.

OVERCOMING OBSTACLES

The obstacles that most commonly block lead-to-sale progress are a prospect's concerns around *purchase fit* and *financial commitment*. These concerns (shown in Fig. 3.2.2) are not new – what's new is how platforms can help alleviate the prospect's concerns.

Fig. 3.2.2

Lead Purchase Fit

Your company can help prospects overcome purchase fit concerns by allowing them to literally or virtually use the platform before purchasing it. Platforms make free trial management easier, for the company, deliver a better experience to the prospect, and provide more insights than on-premise software downloads or physical product trials. For example:

- *Enhanced free trial.* Platforms give companies better ways
  to let prospects try before they buy. For instance, Progressive
  Insurance offers a "Snapshot Test Drive" program that collects
  30 days of driver data for its observed-driver platform insurance. Snapshot enables Progressive to quote the prospect their
  personalized safe driver discount supported by collected data.[11]
  Before switching insurers, a Progressive prospect knows how
  big their personalized discount will be. The trial also gives Progressive insight into which prospects will become economically
  attractive customers (based on observed driving habits during
  the trial) so that they can prioritize their own selling efforts.

- *Augmented and virtual reality (AR/VR) simulations.* The impact
  of lead-to-sales smoothing is even more dramatic for physical
  products. AR/VR systems can provide prospects with post-
  purchase customer experiences delivered prior to purchase. For
  instance, Warby Parker's AR "Virtual Try-On" app revolutionized
  the lead-to-sales journey in eyewear. With each swipe, a virtual
  pair of glasses is superimposed on the prospect's face, filmed in
  real time using the prospect's smartphone.[12] When the prospect
  turns her head, the virtual glasses stay on her face, shifting with
  the movements of her body, as if she has already bought them and
  is wearing them. Warby Parker's try-on app connects to platform
  analytics, enabling the company to understand the impact of
  SKU-level features and presentation, plus understand the styles
  that interest a try-on participant. The app remains ever-available
  to encourage Warby Parker owners to explore additional eyewear.

Lead Financial Commitment

Your platform can do more than assure prospects of a good product fit. They can also assure prospects of good financial value. Here
are two innovative ways that you can overcome a prospect's financial commitment concerns.

- *Multiple-pricing models.* If leads can choose between pricing model options, plus flexibly change between options over

time, they grow bolder. Every pricing model unlocks a different customer experience and a different company business model. A common multi-model duo is ad funded (free to user) and subscription funded (paid by user). Spotify masterfully blends each model to achieve a 40% paid user base by 2019 (unheard of in the freemium world).[13] It provides free users with partial access to paid model benefits (personal playlists, sharing, music downloads). When paid model benefits hit limits or are withdrawn, listeners convert.[14]

- *Conditional free use.* This approach goes beyond free trial to give permanent free access to prospects as long as their usage level stays below a certain threshold (at which point platform use becomes paid). Platform companies vary their thresholds to fit their business: Dropbox's threshold is the amount of data a user stores.[15] ElasticSearch's threshold is the amount of computing resources a user consumes plus features activated.[16] Atlassian's threshold is the size of the user team.[17]

Dropbox got particularly creative by integrating a new referral rewards program into its free-use threshold program. Dropbox supplemented its conditional free-use baseline (up to 2 GB of storage) with a referral program bonus (250 MB higher threshold per friend referred) in a bid to scale quickly. The integration of the two programs took Dropbox from 100,000 to 4 million customers in just 15 months.[18]

FILLING IN POTHOLES

Two operational challenges can also hinder your lead-to-sale conversion rates. As shown in Fig. 3.2.3, these challenges are the loss of *lead visibility* and *lead management alignment* within the go-to-market team (inclusive of channel partners).

Smoothing Initiatives to Fill Potholes

From   To

Lead Visibility		Lead Management Alignment	
Visible Channels	Integrated Touchpoint Data	Team Handoffs	Team Incentives

Fig. 3.2.3

Lead Visibility

A classic visibility challenge arises when a product company creates consumer demand through advertising, but the consumer's purchase takes place in a retailer's store. There are tactical workarounds to this problem. One global cosmetics company who spent $20 million on digital co-marketing with a national department store chain wanted to observe whether its marketing efforts were generating a return. It gained visibility through an anonymized data sharing agreement with its retail partner, facilitated by a clean room data services company that matched digital ad spend to customer purchases. Anonymized analytics helped the cosmetics company improved its psychographic profiles and propensity models for a major brand, lifting in-store sales slightly despite the pandemic.

Compare this tactical solution to a more structural solution – the platform-centric approach of Sephora cosmetics.[19] A unit of the French luxury goods maker LVMH, Sephora has pioneered platform-powered experiences using a range of technologies to engage, add value to, and collect win-win data on its members as they choose and use its products. Sephora, which has over 3,000 branded points of sale and 30 e-commerce sites worldwide, captures lead shopper data seamlessly between store and home.

Sephora's latest store innovation is an AI-based mirror that analyzes the image of an in-store shopper and recommends makeup, skincare, and fragrances based on analysis of gender, age, look, and clothing. The recommendation engine also takes into account temporal factors such as local weather, season, and top trending items. Recommendations are published through a QR code that guides the shopper in-store and lets the shopper purchase at home online. Once home the cosmetics lead can access a free chat advisor and curate Sephora communities to continue finding what's just right for them, while enriching Sephora's knowledge of the customer's persona preferences and needs.

Lead Management Alignment

Many B2B firms have an internal lead-to-sale problem. They lack alignment between three teams – marketing, telesales, and in-person sales teams – who need to run a flawless relay race to turn a lead into a sale. The teams are often misaligned on incentives, data, definitions, and accountability.

- Incentives are out of sync because Marketing is incentivized to generate high volumes of leads while Sales is incentivized to reject most leads, because it will be blamed if they don't sell. Telesales teams – responsible for developing Marketing leads further before they go to Sales – are caught in the middle.

- Data and definitions are out of misaligned because each of the three teams is often responsible for their own lead scoring, naming systems, and status definitions

- Accountability is low because each team often operates in a siloed governance system.

The signs of such a disjointed system are leads that languish without agreed-upon prioritization and finger pointing around who is to blame for poor system performance.

We've watched multiple companies solve this problem, in party through technology but mostly by rolling up their sleeves. Three task force sub-teams need to work under one unified leader to address the problem as a single system. Processes and data flows needed to be mapped and rules of collaboration written. Marketing needs to raise its qualification standards using transparent methodologies, and Sales needs to sign up for speedy attention to leads through Service Level Agreements (SLAs). Everyone uses common data definitions and dashboards, running on common marketing and sales platforms that track customer touches. Everyone signs up for system-aligned performance goals and incentive structures. It's impressive to see how quickly results can turn around.

How smooth is the last mile from lead to sale at your company? Can improvement in this area become a driver of accelerated growth and advantage? Take stock of your situation, raise your expectation for what's possible, and consider how to turn this area of traditional low performance into a zone of innovation.

KEY QUESTIONS FOR CONSIDERATION

1. What is your lead-to-sales conversion rate? How has it been changing over time? How would you judge your lead-to-sales performance compared to competition?

2. What level of improvement enable lead-to-sale smoothing to become a growth driver? A competitive advantage? What improvement goals should you set?

3. How would you rank order your opportunities to overcome lead-to-sale challenges? Consider the value of improvement, the odds of succeeding, and the investment required.
   a. Lead purchase fit
   b. Lead financial commitment
   c. Lead visibility
   d. Lead management alignment

4. What initiative(s) do you recommend based on your assessment? What is the business case for each initiative?

5. What socialization and organizational buy-in will be required to achieve alignment?

6. What operating model changes will be needed to make your initiatives successful?

3.3

SUCCESS TO MOMENTUM

When platforms emerged around 2005, the function we now call Customer Success Management emerged as well. Made possible by user journey visibility, Customer Success Management represented a major step forward in the way companies could enable customers to achieve the results they intended through the products and services they had accessed. Customer Success Management – now understood and practiced in platform companies – became the latest and most advanced element in a trio of post-purchase Customer Success programs.

- *Support*: Call center programs and self-service portals when a customer needs help.

- *Onboarding*: Training and mentoring users on basic and advanced features of what's new.

- *Success Management*: Analysis of how often and well a customer or customer group use products and features they have accessed through the platform. Analytical insights help Success Management teams identify and act on customer churn risk, customer openness to renewal, and customer extension opportunities. Predictive analytics fueled by AI/ML will continue to strengthen the quality of Success Management insights. Human-centric user insights help inform adaptive product development by digital management teams.

Together, these Customer Success activities help raise customer satisfaction and net promoter scores. They generate ROI through improved renewal rates, extended revenues, and premium plan service fees. If you have a weak Customer Success function, strengthen it as a priority, because it is the foundation for what we are about to discuss.

MOMENTUM: THE TOP OF YOUR SECOND CUSTOMER FUNNEL

If Customer Success is the ultimate step in the customer's prior purchase, Customer Momentum is the beginning of all potential future purchases. While Customer Success makes good on the relationship you have already established with the customer, Customer Momentum begins the process of broadening that relationship.

Customer Momentum matters because it will become the top of your second customer funnel – not for customer acquisition (your first funnel) but for customer expansion (your second). The Customer Momentum discipline is critical to the growth of most platform companies, because newly acquired customers typically don't start out in a robust platform relationship. Customers often begin using a platform in one area where they perceive that the platform has the strongest capability to meet one of their needs. The company's new customer acquisition teams know this pattern and encourage it. They pursue a "land and expand" game plans, in which they acquire new customers in narrow relationships now and worry about broadening it later. As a result, most customers start out as partial-platform users with a large *economic value gap* between their *initial use* of the platform and their *potential full use*. Customer momentum is the first step in filling that gap.

To spark customer momentum, best practice companies do three things, shown as building blocks on the right half of Fig. 3.3.1.

- They profile customers based not on what they bought but on their potential full platform use. Full-Use Profiles segment customers by the maximum platform use that can be expected of them, given their needs and constraints.

- They create an inspiring, branded vision of the benefits that a customer's full platform use will deliver. Full-Use Vision sparks customer desire to become a full platform user.

- They generate personalized recommendations for step-by-step actions their customers can take to become full-use platform customers. Full-Use Pathing suggests the best next use cases, products, and services that lead to full use.

Our diagram additionally shows the complementarity between Customer Success and Customer Momentum. Your company will interact with your customer on both topics at roughly the same time in the customer journey, so ensuring that the customer experiences the interplay of these two disciplines positively is key. Success to Momentum is the hinge point in your platform's customer value expansion.

Let's explore each building block further.

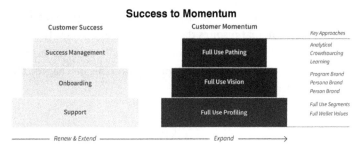

Fig. 3.3.1

FULL-USE PROFILES

Full-Use Profiles are insight-driven segments in your customer base, distinguished by how each segment will realize full use of your platform. Your customer base likely has several different full-use segments – it may have many. Each segment should be profiled on two dimensions – their full-use persona and their full wallet value.

Full-use personas are the post-purchase analog to pre-purchase buyer personas widely used in marketing. They may be the same; they may be different. If there is a difference, it's because pre-purchase segments might focus on what gets a customer to buy a first platform item, whereas post-purchase segments define full platform use given the needs and constraints of the customer's role(s), purchasing power, and attitudes.

Full wallet value calculates the future annual economic value of the customer once they become full users of the platform. This measure is a product of the economic breadth of the full-use persona's purchase basket and their size (household size and usage intensity in B2C, company size and usage intensity in B2B).

Full-use personas and full wallet values can be generated in either of two ways. The most common is through look-alike patterns, whether anecdotally observed by sellers and customer success managers or analytically observed by big data teams who assign customers to segments at scale. Platforms give analytics teams more robust data than ever for look-like insights.

The most powerful but strategically aggressive approach is to design a platform that inspires the customer to make their full wallet spend visible on your platform. This usually requires hosting competitor offers alongside your own (more on this in Chapter 1.1, "Optimal Platform Role(s)").

FULL-USE VISION

Platform companies bring full-use vision to their customer base by branding the benefits of full use. Note that this is different from branding the company itself. There are three ways to brand full use – focusing the brand on a full-use program, user persona, or specific person.

- *Full-Use Program*: Amazon brands its Prime program to infuse a vision of full use. Amazon Prime's brand promise is highly pragmatic: $139 of Prime subscription cost yields >$700 in annual Prime benefits. Amazon backs that up by structuring its vast product line offers so that nearly every part of the platform provides a Prime-related benefit. The psychological benefit Amazon promises is knowing that you got a great deal. "Spend Less, Smile More" is the message customers see with every delivery. Given their fixed investment, Prime customers are incentivized to use Amazon to their fullest. (To customer segments less inspired by its pragmatism – 18- to 34-year-old females in particular – Prime promises life-changing empowerment and control.) Prime works. Members spend $1,968 per year on Amazon,[20] roughly four times the average of non-Prime customers.

- *Full-Use Persona*: Salesforce.com brands *who* you become, if you become a full user of all that Salesforce offers. You'll be a Trailblazer. The name says it all. You'll grow as an innovative and high impact professional and person. Salesforce's Trailblazer theme plays out in each of its annual "Dreamforce" conferences where Trailblazers who made a high impact are featured. Its persona brand promise is integrated into the company's entire branding system.

- *Full-Use Person*: The investment platform ElleVest has a living icon for its full-use brand – its founder and CEO, Sallie Krawcheck. Having spent decades working in key Wall Street roles, such as CEO of Merrill Lynch Wealth Management and CFO of Citigroup, Krawcheck personifies ElleVest's full platform use message. Krawcheck started ElleVest on the belief that the investment industry's narratives had been designed *by men for men* – and therefore didn't resonate well with many women. As a result, women didn't invest as much, save as much, or achieve as much financially as they could. Krawcheck founded ElleVest to change that. Krawcheck inspires women to put their assets to work in ways that fit their earnings patterns and lifestage objectives. Her personal challenge is for women to "show up for women" – by investing, saving, and supporting each other through ElleVest.

FULL-USE PATHING

If a customer has caught your full-use vision, what should they do next? There are three ways to help customers take concrete steps, well illustrated by our same three illustrative companies.

- *Analytical* suggestions are one way, informed by pathing analysis of look-alike customers plus direct signals of individual customer interest. These shouldn't be commercial "buy now" messages but earlier-stage seeding consistent with customer experience goals and company objectives. Video use cases and content-rich reviews in areas of customer interest are great examples. The same correlation analytics that fuel Amazon's "customers who bought this also bought that" suggestions on its e-commerce sites can similarly provide pathing stimuli for its Prime customers.

- *Crowdsourcing* stories of "here's what worked for me" are a second source of pathing. One ElleVest campaign asked customers to identify the next goals they have in life – such as saving for retirement (with female longevity in mind), raising children (saving for summer camp), or starting a business (putting away two year's pay). Weekly newsletters share real-life stories about how customers are transforming their relationship with money through investing. Customer-generated content can speak to other customers with unique power.[21]

- *Learning* is the final best practice for pathing. Customers often need learning support to take the next step toward full use of a platform. Salesforce.com's Trailhead program links learning paths to expanded platform use through professional badges and certifications that additionally help learners advance their careers. Trailhead's learning brand positions it as a way to achieve the Trailblazer's vision. Learners are encouraged to define personal "trails" of sequenced courses. Trailhead's curriculum has grown in its breadth to foster personal and professional growth alongside expanded Salesforce platform use.

Consider how a strong Success to Momentum play can accelerate the growth of your existing platform customer base. Remember that Momentum becomes the top of your second customer funnel as you answer questions below and continue reading the next Demand Plays.

KEY QUESTIONS FOR CONSIDERATION

1. What benefits could Success to Momentum generate for your platform business?

2. Are enough Customer Success building blocks in place that you can focus on Momentum?

3. What full-use profiling do you need?
   a. Full-use persona classification development and assignment.
   b. Full-wallet value calculation (or full-wallet platform design).

4. What full-use vision should you infuse in your customer base? How will you achieve it?
   a. Full-use program branding.
   b. Full-use persona branding.
   c. Full-use person branding.

5. What are the best pathways from current use to full use, by persona?
   a. Look-alike analytics to provide pathing suggestions (seeding, not selling).
   b. Crowdsourcing customer "how I did it" stories.
   c. Learning systems to let customers create their own path (with optional certification).

6. What new go-to-market teaming will be needed to design and deliver your program (e.g., Customer Success, Brand, Insights, Analytics, Finance, Demand Generation, Experience)?

3.4

IN-USE ENRICHMENT

Before Apple retail stores became the shiny, open-plan, and inspiring places that we know them to be today, Steve Jobs asked Ron Johnson, a senior vice president, how he would approach store design.

In his pitch, Johnson carved out a portion of retail space for Apple owner education and support. "That's so idiotic!" Steve Jobs replied,

> *Our products are supposed to be the simplest in the world to use. Why would we want to discuss difficulties in front of other customers? And I've never met someone who knows technology who also knows how to connect with people. Our Apple "geeks" would be a disaster at the front of the house.*[22]

Undeterred, Johnson convinced Jobs that there was a strategic imperative for Apple to offer advanced user support and enrichment for the great Apple products they had bought, as users stretched their capabilities through those products to do great things. He also described a growing tech-savviness among people in their 20s who would be a great fit to work in the store.

Jobs concurred. Apple applied for the "Genius Bar" trademark the very next day.

Today, it's clear that the Genius Bar shifted customer perceptions of who Apple was. It meant more to customers and did more
to reinforce Apple's values than Johnson or Jobs could ever have
imagined. It helped the company build a collaborate-as-you-own
customer relationship that went far beyond computing. It represented a commitment by Apple to enrich users as they used, a new
way that Apple could create value for customers.

Demand for the Genius Bar swelled for use cases beyond customer support and onboarding,[23] revealing the customer's latent
desire to use Apple products to their fullest and most inspiring.
As a result, the company launched "Today at Apple," free in-store
classes to help every Apple owner learn photography, video production, coding, and digital design using Apple products.

But Apple's in-store initiatives were labor intensive. As the company looked to scale enrichment benefits to all digitally, it turned
to its customer experience delivery platforms. COVID only intensified Apple's platform approach. Apple now has in-use enrichment
modules embedded throughout its products and apps, including:

- *Today at Apple at Home*: a self-paced online equivalent of
  courses available in-store.

- *Siri*: the voice-controlled personal assistant available in-use on
  all Apple devices.

- *Apple Guides*: curated and augmented city experiences embedded in Apple Maps.[24]

- *Apple Classroom*: an instructor's content manager for a classroom full of Apple products.

As Apple enriched its customers during use and the company
became enriched in turn, its stores achieved the highest sales per
square foot in the world.[25] Apple's brand entrenched its position in
Prophet's Brand Relevance Index as the most relevant brand in the
world, across all industries. Customers say they can't imagine living
without it.[26]

IN-USE ENRICHMENT MODEL

In-use enrichment takes advantage of platform connectivity to supplement, enhance, and deepen the value of the user's experience – as they use – beyond the core functionality of the product or service. This is most effectively achieved when a company seamlessly suggests features, support, short-form learning, and learning extension opportunities that would not be as available if not connected to the platform in real time. In-use enrichment can be one of the most noticeable experience improvements that a customer receives when a company first adopts a platform.

There are six ways your platform can help you enrich the customer's experience during use. These are the honeycomb cells shown in Fig. 3.4.1, arrayed to indicate their interrelationships and holistic user impact. They include intelligence features, embedded support, embedded learning, personal analytics, embedded community, and embedded commerce.

The center cell represents the benefits your company stands to gain as its ROI on in-use enrichment investments. These include market preference, customer loyalty, greater ability to price to

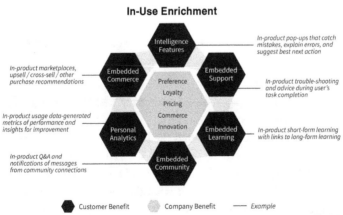

In-Use Enrichment

In-product pop-ups that catch mistakes, explain errors, and suggest best next action

In-product marketplaces, upsell / cross-sell / other purchase recommendations

In-product trouble-shooting and advice during user's task completion

In-product usage data-generated metrics of performance and insights for improvement

In-product short-form learning with links to long-form learning

In-product Q&A and notifications of messages from community connections

Intelligence Features — Embedded Commerce — Embedded Support — Preference Loyalty Pricing Commerce Innovation — Personal Analytics — Embedded Learning — Embedded Community

⬡ Customer Benefit   ⬡ Company Benefit   —— Example

Fig. 3.4.1

value, permissible in-use commerce, and user insights for adaptive innovation and messaging.

Enrichment Elements

Here is a brief description of each in-use enrichment possibility:

- *Intelligence Features:* intelligence-powered interactions that upgrade user performance – from spellcheck to a prompt that says, "it's been 3 months since you emailed this client."

- *Embedded Support:* user tips and links to efficient forms of customer support typically found through a call center or self-help portal – without leaving the experience.

- *Embedded Learning:* short-form learning nuggets for in-use absorption (3–7 minutes long), with long-form learning link-outs, ideally sponsored by a company learning program.

- *Embedded Community:* crowdsourced community customer support, learning, and encouragement (without creating user distraction).

- *Personal Analytics:* metrics that empower individual users and teams to monitor and improve their effectiveness, with appropriate worker privacy safeguards.

- *Embedded Commerce:* "permissible commerce" opportunities during use that enable users to enhance or add to what they already own in order to achieve their goals.

Note: the term "permissible" commerce describes how a company must strike a customer-centric approach to embedded commerce. Permissible commerce has the following characteristics:

- It self-monitors a key messaging ratio: How many messages provide added value for what the customer has already purchased, and how many suggest ways the customer could achieve more by spending more? The ratio should be very high in favor of existing value added!

- It maintains an advisory tone and suggests to the customer only offers that make sense based on what their keystrokes or screen motions indicate they are trying to achieve.

- It suggests small, micro steps (extensions, plug ins, tiered support levels) rather than major offers that distract during use. It lets customers transact and keep using without leaving the platform environment. Micro e-commerce carts can be helpful.

- It easily takes "no" for an answer – no hounding the customer with repeated attempts.

Most critically, embedded commerce retains the spirit of in-use enrichment.

Collaborators Required

Given the array of experiences delivered, it will take a multidisciplinary village to pull off in-use enrichment.

- A clear leader is needed to orchestrate experience strategy and execution. You'll want someone with rule-based digital experience and content competence who can lead a cross-functional team with a high level of customer centricity.

- Contributions will be required from many teams, spanning Product Management, User Experience/Interface Design, Customer Success/Support, Learning, Community Management, Marketing/Demand Generation, Third-Party Marketplace, Analytics, and AI/ML operations. The team will often share a common pop-up user enrichment "billboard" during use and will need to orchestrate through content strategy what content appears, triggered by user signals.

- Motivated alignment is key. In-use enrichment doesn't deliver short-term lift to any single group's bottom line, plus it pulls fractional time from multiple teams. Without attention and prioritization from senior leadership, its execution could suffer from misalignment.

PROFESSIONAL IN-USE ENRICHMENT

Salesforce.com is one of the world's premier B2B practitioners of in-use enrichment. A Salesforce user – typically part of the go-to-market team – can experience a rainbow of enrichment in a single-user session. To illustrate, we'll create the scenario of Tom, a Renewals Manager in a B2B energy supply company, who just received the results of a customer satisfaction survey. He is reviewing them within the Salesforce.com platform as he prepares to personally carry out annual renewals for several strategic accounts.

- Einstein (a major Salesforce *intelligence feature* running machine learning in the background) informs the manager that a subset of B2B customers may be interested in upgrading their product at renewal. Their satisfaction scores have significantly exceeded norms for three consecutive quarters.

- The manager hasn't implemented renewals through Salesforce before, so Einstein shows him where he can find *embedded support* that provides step-by-step guidance through a renewal process for each customer that Einstein has identified.

- After following the step-by-step guide, the manager sees the link to Trailhead (Salesforce's hub for *embedded learning* and its *online community*) and clicks through to see which renewal-related courses his peers are finding useful. As he watches a series of 10-minute mini-courses over lunch, he also chats with colleagues in the Trailhead community.

- The manager's colleagues chat about how they love Salesforce's integration with Tableau visualization tools. Since he is a visual learner and communicator, he is immediately attracted. Salesforce lets him easily add his team's renewal results to a Tableau dashboard via the *embedded upgrade* button without any extra authorization. The platform administrator had authorized all managers on his level so that it was instant.

- Before signing off for the day, he checks the "My Status" tab on his dashboard to see how his team performed against their weekly targets. Tom's team and his personal *productivity* had been the best yet!

KEY QUESTIONS FOR CONSIDERATION

1. What current experiences of in-use enrichment (beyond core product and service functionality) do you deliver to users today? Document your activities on the template (Fig. 3.4.2) below.

2. What is your vision for future in-use enrichment? Plot future activities on the same template. Remember to specify your current state year and planning horizon year for clarity.

In-Use Enrichment Strategy

	Current Year: _____		Transitional Year: _____		Future State Year: _____
Elements	**Current State**	→	**Transitional State**	→	**Future State**
Intelligence Features					
Embedded Support					
Embedded Learning					
Embedded Community					
Personal Analytics					
Embedded Commerce					

Fig. 3.4.2

3. What is your business case for in-use enrichment? Refer to Fig. 3.4.1 for inspiration; select from the five benefits listed or add others based on your circumstances.

4. How effective is your organization in mobilizing and coordinating the "village" that it takes to deliver In-Use Enrichment? How will your go-to-market team deliver with seamless excellence, given the multidisciplinary capabilities and motivation that are needed?

3.5

CATALYTIC COMMUNITY

Emily Weiss, a 28-year-old former Vogue styling assistant, faced a personal moment of truth in 2014. She had amassed 184,000 blog followers after four years of posting and responding to comments on her blog *IntoTheGloss.com* plus her Facebook and Instagram feeds. Through social dialog, Weiss realized that her cosmetics followers weren't satisfied with the products that they were buying. The biggest brands in the cosmetics industry were focusing their attention on inventing and selling makeup that made skin appear flawless. Weiss kept hearing that her followers really wanted better skin, not better makeup.

Emily ultimately asked her followers if they would co-create a new line of products – and brand – with her. Not by completing a customer survey or joining a paid panel but by becoming a living, breathing part of how she built a business.

The answer was yes. In October 2014, Weiss took the plunge and launched a community-centric beauty brand called Glossier that aimed to focus on product innovation that really mattered to members. "I saw the need for a beauty brand that speaks to its consumers directly, offering them a chance to engage beyond the traditional touch points of purchase, use and mass marketing," said Weiss. "Glossier's ability to listen to and communicate directly with its customers sets it apart and allows the brand to leverage customer feedback towards continual product innovation."[27]

Over the next several years, Weiss built a community-powered platform business. Weiss fostered so much community interaction that the company could – through its community platform – observe, interact with, and add value to users on their Use journey. What's more, in this platform business, the customer coalition did a lot of the work. Members created and shared content, established connections with each other and the brand, and took part in developing successful products. The result was a living community that had a reason to be interested in, purchase, and advocate for the brand's products and overall success.

Weiss primed the Glossier community by doubling down on quality content volume and by modeling a spirit of collaboration, honesty, and generosity. It didn't take long before the community Weiss had primed became self-perpetuating, with rising initiative, reflecting Weiss' philosophy that "Every single persona is an influencer."[28]

All the positive energy built through Glossier's platform community spilled out onto the sidewalks of Manhattan when the company announced its early products. Customers formed lines that rivalled the front of the Apple Store at a new iPhone launch. But Glossier's lines were even more impressive because they took place at pop-up stores well above the street level, with no established address or windows to attract foot traffic.

By 2018, the revenue per square foot of Glossier's New York flagship store (~$5,000/sq ft) overtook that of the Apple Store ($4,500/sq ft) and Tiffany & Co ($2,900/sq ft), the retail revenue magnates at the time. Driven by a steady run of blockbuster products and an expanding community, Glossier's revenue more than doubled every year to over $100 million per year in 2018, and its enterprise value rose to over $1 billion.[29]

CATALYTIC COMMUNITIES

Emily Weiss achieved platform business success through a *catalytic community*. A catalytic community is a collective of members and observers – some customers, some not – who feel so inspired and well served by a brand's purpose and its community programs that they perpetuate their own involvement, attract others to join, and work for the brand's success.

Positive community experiences fuel brand advocacy in a way that positive product experiences alone can't. Community experiences retold to friends and acquaintances add human authenticity. The stories are rooted in more than a product's performance. They are rooted in a brand's and its customers' shared purpose and values.

It was possible to create a community in the analog past. The first annual Comic Con (comic book convention) was gathered in 1964. Harley Davidson motorcycle owners began formally riding together in 1983. But community platforms – both group sites on social media channels and dedicated third-party community management platforms – have enabled companies to make catalytic community a scalable strategy for customer loyalty and expansion.

Three catalysts – connection, content, and commerce – help make communities catalytic (see Fig. 3.5.1). Great communities combine all three.

- *Connection* is the recognition of common interests and the experience of social interaction between two or more users. Connection can be encouraged through searchable member profiles, shared interest groups, and large group gatherings, to name a few.

- *Content* is any valued informational or experiential asset. It can take myriad forms; a user might publish a video of their experience, power users might crowdsource a solution to another user's problem, or a member might share work they've done.

- *Commerce* is the exchange of valuable goods and services among users or between users and a company. Again, the forms are many – members respond to recruiter ads on community job boards, consumers take part in the product development process, and community marketplaces enable members to buy and sell from each other.

These catalysts are brought to life through five types of programs. Program types vary from company to company.

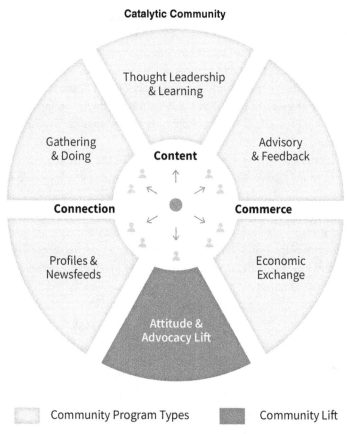

Catalytic Community

Fig. 3.5.1

- *Profiles and Newsfeeds programs* provide the information backbone of the community, updating members on coming events and enabling members to find others. In the Salesforce Trailblazer community, member profiles include Trailhead learning program badges, reinforcing its learning ethos.

- *Gathering and Doing programs* bring together team members for group events and achievements, ranging from annual extravaganzas – like the Nike community's Super Bowl half-time run – to monthly local chapter meetings.

- *Thought Leadership and Learning programs* enable community members to grow in the areas of personal and

professional growth that matter to them – such as healthier
skin in the case of Glossier.

- *Advisory and Feedback programs* give companies an in-depth
  assessment of how customers are experiencing its in-market
  activities. They also provide knowledgeable, early-stage product development input, as is the case with Nike's dedicated
  Sneakerhead community.

- *Economic Exchange programs* provide community members
  the opportunity to market personal outputs, build a reputation,
  or review job postings. Adobe's Behance community of over 30
  million creative artists who can display (and, if they choose, try
  to sell) their work is a great example.[30]

THE COMMUNITY LIFT

Communities don't just happen because a company sets one up.
They succeed if they become authentic human networks that tap
into a purpose that a brand shares with its customers, creating a
chemistry and community mission. They need well-designed programs that achieve catalytic outcomes. And they need a priming
investment from the company until they become self-perpetuating
systems.

If your community does emerge and succeed, it can deliver tangible and valuable community lift outcomes. Community lifts are
not directly financial. But if you track lift metrics, you can correlate
them to financial metrics in order to assess the business case. Community left metrics include:

- *Member experiences of the brand's benefit*: Do members feel
  the brand has better delivered on its core purpose and promise? Do they feel better connected, supported, empowered to
  receive the brand's benefits?

- *Member attitudes toward the brand and company*: How much
  affinity, loyalty, and expansion momentum do members and
  observers feel over time? Has their view of key brand attributes
  changed for the better?

- *Member advocacy and program engagement levels*: Do members post socially and take part in reference and influence programs for their personal and professional networks? Do they participate in learning and output exchange programs?

A final benefit of the community is customer understanding. Appropriately collected and managed touchpoint data can help build customer profiles that improve future messaging and offers.

B2B: THE ATLASSIAN COMMUNITY

Communities aren't just for consumer products companies. They are powerful forces in B2B as well. Atlassian's purpose and promise are to unleash the power of business teams. It helps software developers and knowledge workers to improve their collaboration and group output through industry-leading products like Jira, Confluence, and Trello.

Launched in 2017, Atlassian's community has the same purpose-driven ethos as the company – to unleash the power of its biggest team (its community) for everyone's advancement. Run on a unified community platform, the community had 1.2 million developers (users) registered as members and received 20 million annual visitors in 2020.[31]

The community is a content treasure mine. In 2020, through gatherings and community-led thought leadership forums, users posted 57,000 new how-to-use questions, with a focus on building and integrating applications using Atlassian products. Over 16,000 users replied to these questions, maintaining the community's cultural ethos of responding to a member's question within 48 hours. These questions and answers were then housed on the Atlassian forum and subsequently viewed 70 million times.[32] Atlassian then facilitates forums for distinct personas who share similar needs and questions: users, administrators, partners, and more.

The community is not just about day-to-day work, however. Meetups around the world bring Atlassian users together for social get-togethers, creating a global–local cohesion well beyond the typical reach of a company Atlassian's size. What's more, Atlassian provides teams with activities they can do together, such as hack-athons and group learning.

Energized by the value of the community, members agree to serve as references, participate proactively as social channel influ-encers, and volunteer for ambassador roles within the community. Community leaders are personally recognized and celebrated by the company's most senior leaders. The community has become a vital asset for Atlassian's growth and for its members' professional advancement.

Consider whether a community platform could become a growth driver for your company. Start with the fundamentals – your basis for community chemistry and the value you would gain from community lift. If those check out, design and develop your community platform to catalyze new business success.

KEY QUESTIONS FOR CONSIDERATION

1. What brand purpose and groups of personas could create your community chemistry?

2. What member and business community lift will you strive to achieve?

3. What ultimate business outcomes will you want that community lift to produce?

4. What program additions will allow you to launch or build out your community?

5. Is the end result a balance of connection, content, and commerce?

6. How many of the five program families described in this
   play will you activate?
   a.   Profiles and Newsfeeds
   b.   Gathering and Doing
   c.   Thought Leadership and Learning
   d.   Advisory and Feedback
   e.   Economic Exchanges

7. How can you prime your community to become
   self-perpetuating?

8. What leadership, team, operating model, and investments
   are needed for you to succeed?

3.6

CUSTOMER RENEWAL AND EXPANSION

Every customer relationship holds a story of investment and return. Your company makes an investment to acquire a new customer and then receives a partial payback with a first-time customer transaction. Often, positive customer lifecycle economics are only achievable through customer renewal and value expansion. Without renewal and expansion, lifecycle economics turn negative, and your company can't grow. With improved renewal and expansion, additional revenues can bring you higher than average margins.

Platforms can transform your company's economics by transforming your customer economics. Fig. 3.6.1 reminds us that the success formula for profitable lifecycle platform growth described in our other Demand Plays is:

- Lowering acquisition investment by *compressing your acquisition cycle*. This comes from strengthening your Brand–Demand Lead Engine (Chapter 3.1) and smoothing your Lead-to-Sale last mile (Chapter 3.2).

- Utilizing your platform's *infinite customer connection* to *energize your customer's Use journey experience*. This requires a second lifecycle investment to deliver Customer Success and Momentum, In-Use Enrichment, and Catalytic Community (Chapters 3.2–3.5, respectively).

143

- Reaping the rewards of your investment through best-practice Customer Renewal and Expansion – the focus of the rest of this chapter.

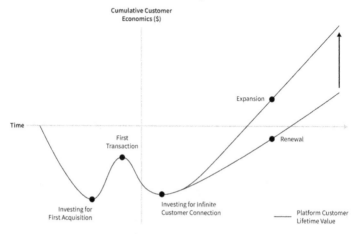

Platform Customer Lifecycle Economics

Fig. 3.6.1

PLATFORM INSIGHTS – BETTER THAN EVER BEFORE

Platforms provide companies with more insight than ever about how to renew and expand customer value. That's because platform insights go beyond the *point of sale* to the *point of use*, yielding much more powerful and actionable insights. To gain the economic benefit of platforms, renewal and expansion teams need to collaborate with company data architects and the teams who generate data from Customer Success and Momentum, In-Use Enrichment, and Catalytic Community activities. These add unprecedented insight to traditional data sources like known customer websites and digital touchpoint interactions.

It's also important to note that in some cases, platforms can yield *category-wide insights* rather than *single brand or channel insights* – even more valuable for opportunity spotting. Consider the difference for yogurt sellers.

- Point of sale: today a grocer captures a consumer's yogurt purchases at checkout and then analyzes data on a loyalty card account for patterns that trigger personalized coupons. Third-party data services may show market-wide yogurt segment-level purchase volume.

- Point of use: a new model refrigerator has a barcode reader that "sees" how fast the yogurt is moving off of the consumer's refrigerator shelf, pot by pot, relative to other product use velocity. One flavor might disappear quickly while another waits until after expiration, indicating it was thrown out. New yogurt additions reflect the customer's full-wallet spend, from all stores and all channels.

How much better off would a retailer be if its loyalty card included a premium tier of benefits for permission to see the consumer's refrigerator data? How could insights fuel home delivery services, new packaging, digital coupon timing, and overall category growth messaging?

Category-level insights can also increase if your company commits to what we call a "full-wallet" platform design – one that attracts category-level spending. Charles Schwab pioneered a full-wallet investment brokerage platform three decades ago: Schwab OneSource. It offered competitor mutual funds (and later ETFs) alongside its own to incentivize investors to manage all of their investment assets on just one site: Schwab's. By providing unflinching transparency – including just-the-facts scorecards that showed investors when competitors were outperforming Schwab – Schwab gave investors the confidence to bring their full investment wallet.

Schwab gained strategic advantage because it could see the customer's full-wallet as it supported the customer. It could market its own products to investors when it could offer a better deal than competitors. Schwab's full-wallet platform played an important role in its innovation-fueled rise from a 1973 upstart to a company with $1.85 trillion in assets under management today.[33]

ACHIEVING RENEWAL AND EXPANSION

There are three steps that support successful renewal and expansion: Best Opportunity, Best Strategy, and Best Execution (see Fig. 3.6.2). We recommend you first focus on best practices for customer value expansion (vs renewals), as that requires additional process steps. Then explore how a subset of your expansion processes can support and improve renewals. This will improve your integrated data management, team management, and hybrid renew-and-expand motions.

Customer Renewal and Expansion

Fig. 3.6.2

BEST OPPORTUNITY

In the Best Opportunity step, you'll determine what growth opportunities deserve your highest priority attention. There are two sub-steps: best customer type and best accounts.

Customer Type

Start by reviewing your customer coalition. Select which customer type(s) or which customer persona(s) within a type merit-prioritized investment for value expansion. This is not a choose-one-only or winner-take-all thought process; you can build a portfolio of expansion programs to diversify risk and maximize learning. You might focus value expansion efforts on:

- End users who pay and use.

- End users who don't pay, but whose increased usage activity grows payments from sponsors, creators, providers, or advertisers.

- Sponsors, creators, providers, advertisers, or rule makers, holding constant user activity levels.

Selection of these customer type(s) and personas within type should occur during annual or semi-annual growth program planning. Your company should have a process that lets best ideas compete for resources. Customer-focused value growth teams may find themselves competing with product-focused teams for scarce growth funds. Customer type analytics should help you back up your expansion opportunities.

Account Prioritization

Your expansion program might target every single customer account that belongs to the type or persona that you selected. But resource constraints, such as program cost or sales force bandwidth, may require you to prioritize at the customer account level. There are different shortcut criteria that you might apply – key accounts, recently won accounts, high NPS score accounts. To prioritize based on value potential, we recommend a calculation that your analytics team could run focused on *Expected Expansion Value* of each account. This same calculation, described below, might also be applied when you are selecting your customer type.

Expected Expansion Value

Expected Expansion Value is the cross-multiplied product of two inputs: Expansion Value and Expansion Likelihood. By taking both factors into account, modest expansion value opportunities with higher odds of success can compete for resources with larger expansion value opportunities that have lower odds.

- *Expansion Value* calculates the absolute economic value of the gap between the customer's *current use value* and *full-use value*. Full-use value is part of your account's full-use profile, discussed in Chapter 3.3, "Success to Momentum."

- *Expansion Likelihood* represents the probability that value expansion will occur.

Use journey data collected by the platform can be particularly helpful in calculating Expansion Likelihood. Today, many companies rely heavily on "small data" inputs about the customer when deciding odds of success. An NPS survey score, an onboarding experience from the Customer Success teams, and a conversation with a sales rep are all "small data" examples. Platforms add the predictive value of big data analytics to a company's toolkit to determine whether and where to best pursue expansion growth. Likelihood calculations, often called "propensities," can be built on more robust data streams with greater cumulative predictive power and improved over time, increasingly with the help of AI/ML. Propensities enable companies to become more predictive, and therefore more proactive, in pursuing expansion.

Renewal and Extension Use Cases

The approach we describe above for value expansion can equally be applied to renewals and same-product volume extensions.

- Expected Extension Value is calculated just like expansions:

  Extension Value × Extension Likelihood.

- Expected Renewal Value is similar in logic but distinct in calculation; it can be negative:

  Renewal Value × [Positive or Negative] Renewal Likelihood

Renewal Value is the customer's current use value – what a company stands to keep or lose. Positive propensity identifies likely renewal; negative propensity signals renewal churn risk.

It is valuable for renewal, extension, and expansion teams to use common risk and opportunity analytics like the one we described above. It can create a collaboration bridge between what are often two different go-to-market teams. Both teams can watch customer scores change using consistent metrics. When it's time to pass an account from a churn prevention team to a value expansion team – or to run a renew-and-expand hybrid play – teams can hand off and integrate seamlessly.

At the end of your Best Opportunity step, you'll know what renewal and expansion opportunities you are prioritizing, and why.

BEST STRATEGY

In the Best Strategy step, you'll decide on your best move to drive customer value expansion. There are two parts to your best strategy: a best offer and a best experience blueprint.

Best Offer(s)

Now that you've prioritized your target accounts, you'll want to identify the *best offer* that each customer should receive. Consider three factors when choosing your offers.

- What platform offers *could* your company propose to each customer? To answer this question, you'll start with the full-use profile for each customer described in Chapter 3.3, "Success to Momentum," and then subtract the offers that the customer currently uses.

- What platform offers *should* your company propose, based on *expansion pathing pattern* insights? You'll study what offers look-alike customers bought first and then bought next to expand their value. Look for patterns among customers with the same full-use profile, who started with the same initial purchase(s) as the account in question. Refine your pattern search further if needed by comparing paths of look-alike customers who share similar demographic, psychographic, and firmographic characteristic as the account in question.

- What platform offers *should* your company propose, based on customer *offer-level propensity* signals? This is the most granular use of platform-powered propensities, this time focused on the offer level. Has the business user watched a certain use case video, taken a certain learning course, or attended a certain community thought leadership forum? Has the consumer followed a certain actor's film and TV work, followed the advice of certain fashion influencers, or driven past the same storefront every day?

You'll need to learn from and choose between different Best Offer answers that different methods propose. In addition, for large B2B accounts, you'll receive Best Offer recommendations from sales teams based on their account plan and latest intelligence. After weighing your inputs, you'll select the Best Offers needed to expand account value.

Experience Blueprint

Just as a Best Offer is a key to your strategy, so too is a *Best Experience Blueprint*. A blueprint captures all of the elements and conditional "if ... then" rules of a customer value growth campaign. If in the past an offer and an experience blueprint together succeeded in expanding customer value, it's possible that partial credit for success should go to the experience blueprint rather than the offer. That blueprint should be kept and tried again with another offer.

For a concrete blueprint example, consider the activities of a B2B health services provider who wanted to market a new offer: an employee wellness service for corporate employees during COVID. The best offer addressed the mental health challenges and needs of remote workers. The best experience blueprint featured:

- A personalized account rep video as a door opener.

- Multichannel distribution of a data-backed e-book on remote work health trends.

- Comparison of the offer to other employee wellness services in each customer region.

- A company-specific webinar with company-dedicated themes and a sign-up landing page.

- A company-specific executive workshop with a company-dedicated, sign-up landing page.

You can create libraries of experience blueprints and maintain dashboards of their outcomes so that your teams gain pattern recognition of the best blueprint for a given situation. It's similar to a chess master who learns which moves should be triggered by a certain layout of pieces on the board.

BEST EXECUTION

In the Best Execution step, you'll carry out your value expansion campaign using as much account-customized content as needed to drive profitable results.

Customized Content

Each experience blueprint makes use of automated content templates to pull in customized customer content, creating unique assets. One might personalize ads, email, text messages, and web pages while mixing and matching research, white papers, videos, and demos. The key is to make content as modular as possible so that it can be generated in an agile fashion within the limits of the blueprint. For the remote worker mental health offer, customized content showed employers how the featured plan compared to competitive local service providers.

The time required to collect and align data for custom asset content, then create and manage that content, can make this process the most time-consuming among the five we have discussed. The cost of the labor involved can become a bottleneck to scaling customer value growth programs.

Generative AI (e.g., ChatGPT and others) may help unlock this process by making custom content generation more affordable. In the future, generative intelligence may also suggest best offers and even best blueprints. Platform companies who plan to scale customer-base growth efforts should carefully follow the capability expansion of these technologies. (For more, see "Agile Content," Chapter 5.3.)

Agile Adjustment

To build an effective customer value expansion program, a company needs strong analytics and a willingness to adjust. Think of all factors that affect success or failure: the choice of customer type and persona, the prioritization of specific accounts, the offer and experience blueprint, and the kinds of content that are customized. Odds are high that you can successfully expand customer value if you do the hard work to discover which factors drive success.

You can structure your campaigns to learn faster. For instance, some planners might choose one impact strategy (offer × experience blueprint) for many customers. Other planners might deploy several different impact strategies, each one covering a few customers. There are yet other times when one impact strategy for one account makes sense, given the size of the opportunity. These one-to-many, one-to-few, and one-to-one impact strategies can be structured as tests to understand when strategy variations make a real difference. The better structured your experiments, the quicker you'll learn how to grow your customer's lifetime value.

AND THE JOURNEY CONTINUES

When you succeed once at customer renewal and expansion, don't stop. An account with positive energy is a strategic asset to be valued and built out further. If your expansion customer responds to become a new lead (a first-time buyer of the next thing you are promoting), use a variation of Lead-to-Sale Smoothing (Chapter 3.2) to convert it. Check to see if the lead-to-sale initiatives you put in place will be as effective at converting existing customers as they will be for new customers. Returning customers may not have as many predetermined barriers and potholes to their next purchase with you … or they may have new ones. Repeat your energy-generating Use journey Demand Plays. Continue to renew and expand as you and your platform customers make progress toward your full potential.

KEY QUESTIONS FOR CONSIDERATION

1. How much of your company's current revenue growth rate can be explained by customer-base growth (vs new customer acquisition)? How will your company's overall growth rate change in the future? How much of that growth will you achieve via customer-base growth?

2. What is the state of your renewal marketing and sales? If you struggle, do you have to pay exclusive attention to renewals first, or can you, at minimum, focus resources in parallel on value expansion?

3. How operationally excellent are you at processes that deliver customer value expansion?
   a. Best Opportunity (Customer Type Selection, Customer Prioritization)
   b. Best Impact Strategy (Best Offer, Best Experience Blueprint)
   c. Best Execution (Customized Content, Agile Adjustment)

4. If you are not yet excellent, where would you start to deliver the highest positive impact with least investment and risk?

5. What transformation of processes, data, and roles are needed for you to achieve customer renewal and expansion success?

Part 4

INNOVATION PLAYS

After designing your platform for strategic advantage and then growing it through journey plays, it will be time to spice things up. How can you maintain platform growth and differentiation by bringing ongoing innovations to market? Your ambition should be to establish your company as an outperforming innovator – both within your industry and across industries – through customer-centric creativity.

We've identified six Innovation Plays that reflect platform innovation hot spots. They put your customers on Better Paths – in business and personal life – with Broader Powers than they've ever had. These innovations are shown in Fig. 4.0.1, developed and deployed in an infinite loop, enabled by your platform's infinite connection to your customers on their Choose and Use journeys. Your teams can be innovative in a continuous and adaptive manner as technology advances and as customer feedback tells you where they are experiencing value.

Our first three Innovation Plays encourage you to envision and empower *better paths* in life and work for your customers – the bedrock value that platform innovations deliver.

"Reimagined Flows" (Chapter 4.1) challenges you to deliver new types and levels of customer benefit by making possible new workflows (business) and life flows (consumer) for your customer coalition members. When innovative flows that could delight your customers require functionality or data that your company doesn't have, "Extended Ecosystems" (Chapter 4.2) outlines how you can

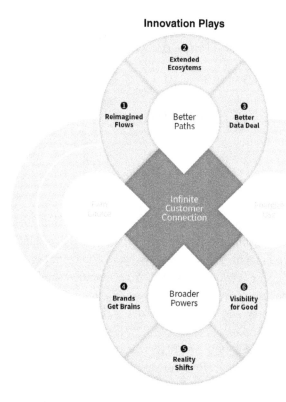

Fig. 4.0.1

harness an ecosystem of partners to fill your gaps. If the data you'll need to deliver innovation resides with your customer, "Better Data Deal" (Chapter 4.3) explains the types of value-for-data exchanges that can unlock that data responsibly.

Our next three Innovation Plays describe how cutting-edge platform functionality can give your customers *broader powers* than they've ever had before.

"Brands Get Brains" (Chapter 4.4) challenges you to make your brands more than just smart – to develop the living brands your customers want to experience and use. "Reality Shifts" (Chapter 4.5) asks what new benefits you can bring by helping customers change realities at key moments of their journey through three-dimensional (3D) worlds, augmented reality, and virtual reality. "Visibility for Good" (Chapter 4.6) shares powerful data-driven ways that platforms can help your customers make a distinctive difference in the world by supporting your organization.

4.1

REIMAGINED FLOWS

On November 1, 2020, a Peking Roast Duck Festival was the talk of China.[1] To everyone's surprise, the festival's sponsor wasn't a group of Beijing restaurants – it was the home appliance maker Haier. The $32 billion company[2] was famous for having the highest global market share of home appliances, including refrigerators, ovens, and washing machines[3] – but they wanted to be known for what their appliances could do *for* customers to improve their lives.

For the last decade, companies in the home appliance space had been innovating to win customers through new technological features – such as Internet of Things (IoT)-connected appliances that meant a consumer could switch their oven on/off from their mobile phone. This brought new control and convenience to the busy consumer's life. While Haier's innovators wanted to extend technology benefits further, their most ambitious goal was to add a rich new layer of experiential benefits.

The festival gave Haier the opportunity to redefine itself based on its new ambition. Haier unveiled a new digital services platform that could uplevel the Haier consumer's home activity flows. Haier creatively marketed its concept under a new sub-brand, Sanyiniao, and gave the name "Scenarios" to its family of smart home flows. Through each "scenario," Haier promised that customers could "flow" through a home activity with much less mental and physical effort and with more joy. What's more, the latest technological innovations on Haier's platformed appliances worked seamlessly with its scenarios to make the combined effect yet more distinctive.

Please note that what Haier redefined through its innovations are the same customer "flows" that we discussed briefly in "Pivotal Persona Value" (Chapter 2.2). Flow describes a set of sequential activities taken by a customer to achieve a desired objective.

At the festival, Haier revealed its Sanyiniao Peking Roast Duck flow, offering consumers a new path to culinary joy. Instead of spending hours shopping for ingredients and days preparing a duck and then following over forty cooking steps, Haier's new cooking flow empowered customers to cook a restaurant-quality Peking duck at home in just three steps.

- Step 1: Using the Haier Smart Home app, say, "I want to make Peking roast duck."

- Step 2: Put the pre-prepared frozen duck into the oven.

- Step 3: Click one button on the platform-connected oven to cook the duck.

Activating this flow sets Sanyiniao's customer coalition of local farms, distributors, and grocery providers into action to deliver a pre-prepared frozen duck to the consumer's door within a few hours. No need to manually set temperature and timer, wait for the oven to preheat, or open the door to check on the cooking progress.[4] Haier's artificial intelligence – branded Chef@Home – does all the work. The oven's sensor technology identifies the type, size, and temperature of the food; activates the ideal cooking settings; and continuously adjusts the oven to the appropriate cooking stage (defrosting, steaming, cooking, crisping) until the item is cooked to perfection.

Digital experiences bring joy beyond cooking. The oven's platform shares live video (that can be shared with others), timing updates, and side dish recipes on its app and touchscreen door interface. The consumer can learn about the breeding time, growth conditions, and quarantine status of the duck in the oven. If the consumer wants to get hands-on in the kitchen, they can ask for Cook With Me, Haier's voice-activated cooking assistant.[5]

In just its first month, Haier Sanyiniao delivered 20,000 Peking Roast Duck scenarios – as many roast ducks as a top Beijing restaurant sells in a year.[6] And the duck scenario was just one of many. Today, consumers can choose from over a thousand scenarios from Haier Sanyiniao's smart home business unit – everything from ordering a whole house renovation through to selecting the best classes for you to do on your smart exercise bike. Many of these scenarios have been contributed by consumers, either online or through personal interactions at Haier's network of Sanyiniao retail kiosks.

As with any platform initiative, Haier's innovation has benefited an entire customer coalition, not just one customer. In this case, Haier has created new economic value for a wide network of food preparation, delivery service, and home experience providers. The Peking Roast Duck scenario alone increased the total revenue of each provider involved by an average of 5%.[7]

Customers love Sanyiniao scenarios, which have vastly improved their culinary experiences. Haier loves them, too. Haier customers who bought a platform-enabled appliance and at least one Sanyiniao scenario have higher than average income (typical for early adopters and great for Haier's brand). They engage 212% more than customers who purchased a traditional product, and they reroute spend through Haier that would otherwise go to restaurants or grocery stores – an economic flow from which Haier and its partners benefit.[8]

REIMAGINING FLOWS

Haier's Peking Duck illustrates the common benefit that all platform innovations provide: *better customer flows, enabled by platform features, leading to new end benefits.* Each step in a customer's Use journey contains granular activities, together comprising the customer's current state flows. When these activities are digitally enabled through platform software, they can be reimagined as new activity flows. There may be hundreds or thousands of flow steps that your company could reimagine to improve customer outcomes.

- In *consumer* markets, we call these activities "life flows." A life flow could be the steps someone takes to choose what to wear in the morning, grab a coffee before they arrive at work, or reunite with friends remotely. Providing a satisfying home dinner is a life flow, too.
- In *business* markets, these same sequential activities are called "workflows"; a workflow could be the steps that a warehouse team takes to prioritize and fill an order, the decision a bank takes to approve or deny a loan, or the assessment a company undertakes to promote a high performer.

To reimagine flows for your customers, it's most helpful to split what can be a daunting innovation exercise into two parts, as shown in Fig. 4.1.1.

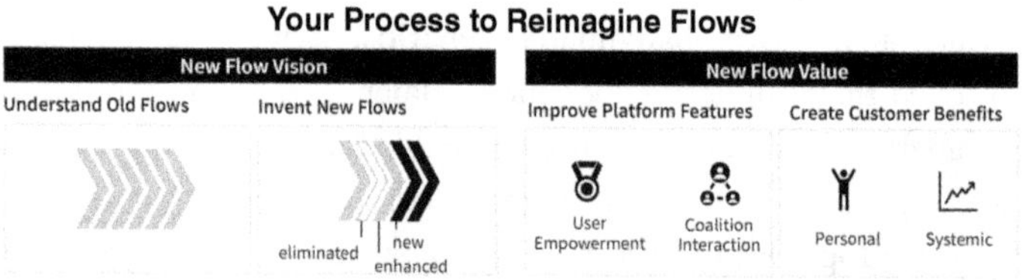

Fig. 4.1.1

The first part, creating a *new flow vision*, invites you to establish a firm understanding of what your customers do today to accomplish their objectives (old flows) and then invent what a new possibility would look like (new flows). The second part, delivering *new flow value*, asks you to select platform features that can deliver your new flow vision, plus identify the customer end benefits that those features will generate.

NEW FLOW VISION

What could the future of your customer's flows look like? With a customer coalition and a new benefit hypothesis in mind, radically reinvent them. Eliminate old steps no longer needed; enhance current steps that can serve a better role; introduce new steps that were not possible prior to your platform. Be aware that your team may be more comfortable with point-in-time benefits versus flow benefits – invest in understanding that difference if you are new to platforms.

Teams can draw on three sources of insight to help with this process:

- *Ethnographic research* provides deeper understanding of customers in the context of their daily lives and frames their behaviors in relation to your customer coalition personas and data. Gain an ethnographic journey understanding at the activity and data flow level, from a multi-persona viewpoint, with equal focus on what is and what might be.

- *Pattern recognition* draws on cross-industry and expert trend analysis. What are your customers drawn to in other industries? What new ways of living or work enabled by other platforms could apply to your platform? What new trends or capabilities are just arriving?

- *Current usage data analytics* converts actual customer usage data into insights about favorite features and areas of frustration. These can stimulate new hypotheses about new areas of innovation to explore further through research (for more, see "Adaptive Innovation," Chapter 5.4).

Best-in-class companies look to a blend of these three sources of insight to reinvent their new flows. For example, Haier had *ethnographic research* on 180 million homes from its 36 years of operations, had more recently gathered *usage data* from tens of millions of IoT connected devices (through its platform-connected appliances), and had *identified patterns* that pointed to what their future customer wanted to experience. Haier concluded that some customers wanted to save time and effort in the kitchen, others wanted preparation help, and both wanted restaurant-quality meals at home. This new flow vision guided the transformation of a 40-step Peking Duck flow (old), to just a 3-step flow (new) through a Sanyiniao scenario.

NEW FLOW VALUE

The *new flow value* process translates your *new flow vision* into something that makes a difference in your customers lives. It deploys platform features for tangible customer benefits – often features and benefit levels that your market hasn't seen before.

To stimulate your innovation thinking, we have catalogued patterns of common platform features and customer benefits produced across industries. While our list is not exhaustive, it should give you a quality start. There are two classes of platform features: *user empowerment*, often associated with Software-as-a-Service (SaaS) models, and *coalition interactions*, often associated with ecosystem connector models. There are two classes of customer benefits produced by these features; some are *personal* in nature and others are *systemic*, that is, more structural. The best platforms deploy a blend of both classes of features to deliver a blend of both classes of customer benefits. Fig. 4.1.2 lists these flow-enhancing platform features and customer benefits.

New Flow Value: Platform Features and Customer Benefits

Platform Features That Improve Flows			Customer Benefits	
🎛 User Empowerment	👥 Coalition Interactions		🍸 Personal	📈 Systemic
Data Foundation	Socializing	Organizing	Essential Needs	Risk / Variance
Content Personalization	Collaborating	Knowledge Sharing	Well-Being	Cost / Complexity
Options Generation	Performing	Rating	Belonging	Revenue / Income
Decision Guidance	Service Market Making	Product Market Making	Happiness	Productivity / Agility
Intelligent Automation	Promoting	Asset Sharing	Achievement	Innovation / Creativity
Contextual Support	Currency Exchange	Event Recording	Self Actualization	Equity / Inclusion
Analytical Feedback	Employing	Investing	Reputation	Environmental Sustainability

Fig. 4.1.2

Features that empower users include the following:

- *Data Foundation:* sensing, cleaning, transforming, and applying new high-value data.

- *Content Personalization*: modules/filters that help users self-configure capabilities/content.

- *Options Generation*: intelligence that generates options based on user inputs or criteria.

- *Decision Guidance:* best move recommendation based on algorithmic learning.

- *Intelligent Automation:* autonomous execution of best move so the user doesn't have to.

- *Contextual Support:* prompts, advice, tools, and learning that enrich the customer as they use.

- *Analytical Feedback:* analysis of user activity and output to enable future improvement.

Features that enable customer coalition interactions include the following:

- *Socializing:* personal and group connections that create and strengthen human bonds.

- *Organizing:* hierarchical links that support planning, alignment, execution, and reporting.

- *Collaborating:* task-related content creation, editing, and governance among team members.

- *Knowledge Sharing:* user access to and provision of subject matter expert knowledge.

- *Performing:* creative performances made available to and enjoyed by audiences.

- *Rating:* users who have experienced something provide scores for those who haven't.

- *Service Market Making:* facilitation of service transactions between providers and buyers.

- *Product Market Making:* facilitation of product transactions between producers and buyers.

- *Promoting:* advertisement of goods, services, and work opportunities to targeted prospects.

- *Asset Sharing:* owner-to-renter and peer-to-peer sharing of assets.

- *Currency Exchange:* exchange of established or new currency units for goods or services.

- *Event Recording:* ledger of information linked to an event or a transaction.

- *Employing:* mutual employer and talent discovery, assessment, and contracting of work.

- *Investing:* buyer and seller negotiation and ownership transfer of economic assets.

Haier built several of these features into its reimagined consumer cooking flows and then spotlighted them through its go-to-market activities. Some features enable user empowerment: Sensors and video cameras create a real-time *data foundation* about the food as it cooks. Chef@Home artificial intelligence provides best *decision guidance* and *intelligent automation*. The Cook with Me assistant provides *contextual support*. Other features enable customer coalition interaction: Haier's prepared meal assembly and delivery is a catalyst for *food service market making*. Haier customers *socialize* by posting in-oven pictures of their upcoming dinner. They *collaborate* by contributing their own scenarios back to Haier.

Platform features change over time because of new technological innovation. In contrast, *customer benefits* are evergreen: They are rooted in human and organizational needs. End benefits fall into two classes: personal and systemic (see Fig. 4.1.2). We won't define them here as they are well understood by innovators and marketers alike.

- *Personal end benefits* that improve a customer's essential needs, well-being, belonging, happiness, achievement, self-actualization, or reputation.

- *Systemic end benefits* that improve the balance of a customer's risk exposure, cost or complexity, revenue and income, productivity and agility, innovation and ability to create, equality and inclusion, and environmental sustainability.

While customer benefits address timeless human and business needs, they are produced in new ways and applied to new use cases through platform innovation. They can deliver unprecedented levels and intensity of benefits.

Haier Sanyiniao's scenarios promised functional and experiential benefits such as ease, time saving, and delicious home-prepared meals. Haier's go-to-market campaigns targeted higher-order personal end benefits. While prior campaigns may have focused on the *well-being* of a customer that can be achieved by using their appliances, Haier's new campaigns portrayed *self-actualization*. One web campaign showed a stay-at-home father and a single woman each expressing fulfillment and self-esteem by making their home uniquely theirs with Sanyiniao. These benefits were complemented by *reputation* (positive social image) and happiness (a strong sense of joy).

Move beyond point-in-time benefits to consider how your platform can deliver new flows to your customer coalition, through innovative platform features, for distinctive customer benefits.

KEY QUESTIONS FOR CONSIDERATION

1. How many personas in your customer coalition should receive focus for your innovation?

2. How would you map each persona's current journey with each step viewed as an activity flow (i.e., an activity sequence)?

3. Using ethnographic research, patterns, and usage data as inputs, what is your vision for a new customer flow from your next round of innovation (by persona)?

4. Using Fig. 4.1.2 as reference, what new platform features could deliver your flow vision? What customer benefits would those platform features deliver (by persona)?

5. How should you update your brand portfolio, offer architecture, and go-to-market messaging to communicate your reimagined flows to customers?

4.2

EXTENDED ECOSYSTEMS

In 2011, Jeff Bezos stood at a whiteboard and sketched out the device that would become the Amazon Echo,[9] a smart speaker that would soon compete for a place in the world's homes. He wanted it to cost $20, run on Amazon's cloud computing platform (AWS), use Amazon's virtual assistant Alexa, and be voice-controlled to allow users to order products on Amazon.com while going about their day. For the platform to succeed, Bezos asserted, Amazon would have to become more than a successful e-commerce company; it would need to become "an invention machine."[10]

Amazon began with internal platform innovation investment. It acquired artificial intelligence capabilities to give its speaker voice control, increased its speech recognition vocabulary by a factor of 10,000,[11] and developed Alexa, a software platform that would become the brain, heart, and voice of the speaker. Amazon equipped Alexa with several use-case skills, such as delivering the news and weather, setting timers, creating shopping lists, and playing music.[12]

Next, Amazon built out the Alexa *customer coalition* – a platform company's ecosystem that enables direct connections between coalition members. In a successful domestic land grab, Amazon built a bigger customer coalition by far than other voice-controlled appliances in four ways, illustrated in Fig. 4.2.1. It:

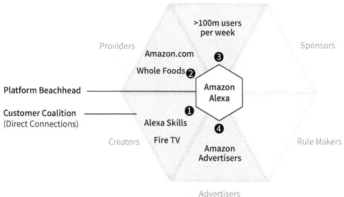

Alexa's Customer Coalition Build-Out

Fig. 4.2.1

1. Grew Alexa's use-case "skills" from 135 to 130,000 by mobilizing third-party developers (*Creators*); published 17 language variants across 80 countries in 2022.[13] Added an Alexa-controllable living room platform, Amazon Fire TV (*Creators*).[14]

2. Acquired Whole Foods for local fresh grocery delivery that complemented Amazon's e-commerce supply chain (*Provider*).[15]

3. Incorporated Alexa audio-based experiences into Amazon Ads (*Advertisers*).

4. Grew Alexa user base to 72 million users (*Users*).[16]

What Amazon built was amazing, even by the tech titan's high standards. It was strong enough to form a beachhead that enabled Amazon to take the next step – building an Extended Coalition. We define a beachhead by when the company has sufficient market share, brand status, and capability distinction to attract the partners it wants with positive or neutral economic effect. Amazon did just that. To enhance its value proposition further, Amazon built an Extended Coalition – an ecosystem built on indirect connections. This is illustrated by the outer ring in Fig. 4.2.2.

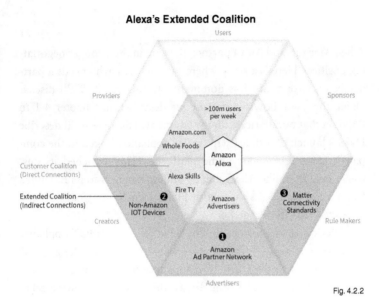

Fig. 4.2.2

1. Alexa was included as an advertising channel and ad product line in the launch of the Amazon Ad Partner Network in 2021. This network enables third-party ad agencies to integrate Amazon Ad programs into the advertising services they provide their clients[17] (*Advertisers*).

2. Alexa partnered with Bose, Sonos, Sony TV, and others for home entertainment; Phillips Lighting, iRobot's Roomba vacuums, Aeris, Google Nest, and others for home control; and Bosch, Samsung, and others for home appliance control (*Creators*).

3. Amazon partnered with its competitors, Apple and Google, to set industry standards. They unified their IOT protocols into a single, royalty-free global standard called "Matter." This protocol has been adopted by over 400 companies, so that users can buy and use devices from any competitor on a single IOT network in a seamless and secure way[18] (*Rule Makers*).

Amazon's winning Customer Coalitions and impressive Extended Coalition combine to give it the richest ecosystem in the voice-controlled personal assistant market. In the process, Amazon became the holistic invention machine that Bezos had envisioned.

PARTNERSHIP AMONG EQUALS

When Amazon and Alexa partner, they are in the stronger negotiating position. Here is a story where the company who needs a partner has a strong, but less dominant, starting point. We'll discuss Haier, the "new flows" company we described in Chapter 4.1 to build on that familiarity with the company. This time we'll describe Haier's launch of a smart wine cellar appliance, linked to the company's same IOT smart home platform. Haier enriched its customer coalition, like Alexa did, by adding partners to its Extended Coalition. Fig. 4.2.3 shows both Haier's Customer Coalition and Extended Coalition together.

Haier's first step was to link its wine cellar to its IOT appliance customer coalition. In this case. it was a matter of "plugging in" the wine cellar to the Haier IOT appliance platform and the Haier Sanyinaio Scenarios platform. Today, this gives Haier's wine cellar access to 80 million consumers (*Users*),[19] to the Sanyinaio scenario food service network (*Providers*), and to Haier's 50,000 strong commercial network of home décor companies, designers, and home appliance dealers (*Sponsors*).

Haier's Wine Cellar: Customer and Extended Coalitions

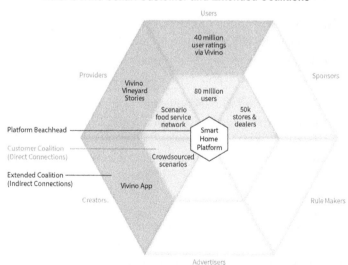

Fig. 4.2.3

Equally critical were Haier's smart ovens and food refrigerators (sibling experience hubs). These were both key because they had valuable food information to share that could be paired with wine, making Haier's appliances work "better together" due to data synergies. Haier's oven knows what's cooking thanks to its in-oven camera and scenarios menu choices. Haier's refrigerator knows what food's inside through an embedded barcode reader. It can organize refrigerator contents information by expiration date, food category, and meal potential. The development of wine and food pairing suggestion could be appliance to appliance – if there were a database that could link the two – something Haier lacked.

To make those pairings and much more, Haier created a partnership with Vivino, the world's largest wine marketplace with over 40 million active users, a database of over 11 million different wines, and a sophisticated food- and wine-pairing database. This partnership instantly brought Haier a full ecosystem of indirect connections that it could use to enrich its customer coalition value proposition. Through its partnership, Haier gained access to:

- A wine super app developed by Vivino (*Creator*). Developed for its own customer coalition (Creators), world-class wine and food pairings, individual and community wine ratings, winery backstories, and grape blend and production year information by harvest. The two firms collaboratively developed a Vivino module to snap into Haier's smart home app.

- Community ratings from Vivino's community (*Users*) that could be added to Haier's.

- Vineyard backstory and wine information from Vivino's winery community (*Providers*).

The partnership has room to grow (particularly cross Advertiser opportunities) given the strength and size of each company's community.

BUILDING YOUR RICHER ECOSYSTEM

To enrich your own ecosystem, work through the four steps outlined below. We'll refer to Haier's wine cellar and Smart Home IOT platform ecosystem development, shown in Fig. 4.2.4, to illustrate these steps.

1. Understand clearly how your Extended Coalition will enable you to offer even better flows to customers. Envision ideal new customer flows without regard to your internal limitations. Where do you have gaps? How could the right partner(s) fill those gaps? *Haier sought to provide a world-class food- and wine-pairing flow for its wine cellar (and oven and refrigerator) customers. Only with an expert wine partner could Haier fill gaps to achieve its new flow vision.*

2. Consider building out internal partnerships if they are not already part of your platform offer. *Haier didn't need to create new internal partnerships; its IOT wine cellar fit seamlessly onto its IOT appliance platform and into its Sanyinaio providers network, making those all part of its core customer coalition.*

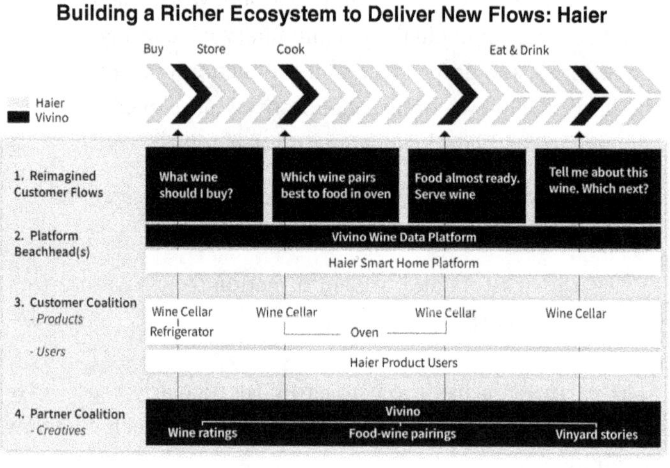

Building a Richer Ecosystem to Deliver New Flows: Haier

Fig. 4.2.4

3. Enrich your ecosystem through an Extended Coalition and its indirect connections. Consider potential partners by ideating along your "six-types-of-coalition-customers" categories. Ask whether partnerships could bring you indirect versions of *Users, Providers, Creators, Advertisers,* or *Sponsors.* Ask whether your partnerships could improve your outcomes with *Rule Makers. Haier's partnership with Vivino brought more than a wine-pairing database. It brought multiple wine use-case apps (Creators), backstory-telling vineyards (Providers), and consumer user ratings (Users).*

4. Understand whether you have a platform beachhead strong enough to attract your desired Extended Coalition (ideal partners are attractive to your customer coalition but not strategically threatening). If your platform beachhead isn't strong enough, choose between further internal investment (e.g., stronger product or brand, larger customer coalition) or accept a less attractive partnership, at least in the short term. If your coalition partner candidate is strategically threatening, prior to accepting, consider the impact it will have on your platform's value (might you need to split value unevenly, or might customers leave you for the partner). *Haier's customer coalition of IOT appliance consumers and Sanyinaio service providers was sufficient to attract Vivino, a strong wine industry player. Vivino did not threaten Haier strategically.*

Executing these four steps successfully will require your company to adopt the role of ecosystem "orchestrator." This is a significant mindset and culture shift for any company that is accustomed to doing business within its four walls. It will also require you to be mindful not just of your strategic intent and business model but also of the intents and models of your partners. Quality partner agreements will cover everything from economic sharing to legal boundaries to data rights. You'll finally need to stay innovative as a partnership in an ongoing adaptive manner.

KEY QUESTIONS FOR CONSIDERATION

1. Have you envisioned ideal customer flows without regard for your internal limitations (believing you can fill gaps through partners) or do you limit your innovation thinking based on internal business constraints?

2. Follow the four steps described above in "Building Your Richer Ecosystem," to uncover your opportunities. What can you conclude? What action steps will you need to take?

3. What organization, mindset, and culture issues might you need to address to successfully enrich your ecosystem through an Extended Coalition?

4.3

BETTER DATA DEAL

Every platform is built on a data-for-value exchange. Customers provide data, allowing platform companies to observe and interact with them during use. In return, companies provide customers with something they value.

Like any deal, the customer may view a platform's data deal as compelling, acceptable, or unfair. Furthermore, in many instances customers may have options to share limited visibility, more visibility, and maximum visibility. The latter may enable a platform company to both serve the customer better for faster growth and to more fully monetize their customer relationship. Finally, customers will view a platform's data-for-value exchange in a competitive context. How does it compare to the data deal offered by another platform?

The Better Data Deal play seeks to expand customer data-driven visibility for growth, or differentiate from competitors on customer data-driven value propositions, or both. Given data pervasiveness and society's growing sophistication around it, we believe that this play will increase in frequency and importance as data-for-value platform innovations continue to advance as a factor in customer choice.

STARTING POINT: SECURITY AND COMPLIANCE

Sound data management practices are table stakes. Customers demand that platform companies practice secure, compliant, and ethical use of the data they hold. Governments and regulators have responded to citizen concerns with a raft of new laws. Consider the following:

- A company's data security reputation is considered by nearly half of all consumers when choosing whether to use it.[20] Little wonder, given that the top 10 security breaches of all time put 9 billion customer records in jeopardy.[21]

- In total, 137 out of 194 countries in the world now have legislation to protect an individual's data and privacy.[22] The European Union (EU)'s General Data Protection Regulation (GDPR) requires companies to get consumers' consent before sharing their data and gives them the right to access, delete, or control it.

Meeting security and compliance requirements is critical. It can keep a company from a reputational disaster. But it's not enough to differentiate them from other companies. To that, they'll need to go even further.

FOUR TYPES OF DATA

There are four types of data covered by value-for-data exchanges:

- *Zero-Party Data:* information that a customer intentionally shares with a company (e.g., contact forms, interests, preferences, and contest entries).

- *First-Party Data:* information the company collects and owns through daily customer interactions on its platforms and other digital touchpoints (e.g., product and service usage, website activity, and social media commentary).

- *Second-Party Data:* first-party data owned by another organization that your company knows and trusts; these data are made available to your firm via partnership, for a purpose.

- *Third-Party Data:* first-party or third-party data bought, sold, or exchanged by independent marketplace organizations that your company may or may not trust. Data are typically gathered by tracking cookies from multiple sources (e.g., browsing and advertising). Laws increasingly limit or prevent third-party data transactions.

THE "BETTER DATA DEAL" LADDER

Companies can take steps to win over customers and differentiate their offer from other companies through a better data deal, as Fig. 4.3.1 illustrates. Think of the y axis as a four-step ladder that companies can climb, if needed, to offer increasing value to customers. Best practice is to use every step of the ladder during the climb, without skipping any. This allows the company to build the customer's trust and goodwill, in turn allowing the company to ask the customer to expose additional data that may be required for the company to make stronger, more innovative, competitive moves.

At the first step of the ladder, the company delivers trusted data experiences (Step 1). It next adds value through personalization (Step 2), then increases incentive through value-added services (Step 3), and finally offers a form of economic sharing to unlock data visibility (Step 4).

Better Data Deal Ladder

Economic Sharing	Can I offer the customer economic value in return for a portion of the value their data creates in my economic model?	
Value-Added Services	Are there services I can offer the customer that meet or exceed the perceived value of data they share?	If customer preferences include 3rd party data...
Personalized Experiences	Can I deliver personalization as an experienced benefit? On how many valuable dimensions can I personalize?	...then within legislative and customer experience limits, do I have an acceptable model for 3rd party data?
Trusted Experiences	Have I provided customers with trusted data experiences by soliciting and maintaining customer data preferences?	
	Zero Party 1st Party 2st Party 3rd Party	

Fig. 4.3.1

You can use the ladder to achieve a more innovative path to deliver one or more strategic objectives, such as:

- Win or retain customers who may be reluctant to use your platform due to prior data issues.

- Launch a new value proposition that requires more, or new types, or data from customers.

- Boost your company's insight into customer flows and needs relative to competitors.

Given that each step up the ladder will cost your company more, you should try to only climb as high as necessary to achieve your business goals. We'll start with Trusted Experiences.

Trusted Experiences

The first step to improving data-for-value exchange is designing trusted customer experiences – moments in the customer journey where a company transparently engages with customers on the management of their data. Data trust is a huge part of overall trust. In total, 58% of customers will buy new products from companies they trust, and 67% will remain loyal and advocate for brands that they trust.[23]

OneTrust became the fastest-growing enterprise software company in US history by helping corporate clients turn customer-focused trusted experiences into a competitive advantage.[24] Above and beyond providing *security assessment and compliance management* tools, OneTrust helps clients make trust a competitive advantage in multiple ways. One of those is data-related trust; OneTrust provides trust experience services such as:

- *Website Preference Management.* Client users can change how they want, or don't want, the company to use their data. This gives agency back to users, providing a way to engage with users on the topic of data, and provides granular choices in place of a catch-all unsubscribe.[25]

- *Omnichannel Preference Management.* Clients can ensure user data preferences are honored across all relevant use cases, by all business units and functional teams within their company. A seamless omnichannel experience for users and differentiated client brand framing can lead to better opt-in rates.

If trusted experience management rewards your company with the data it needs to innovate and grow competitively, stop here on the ladder. If it doesn't, then continue to the next step, *personalized experiences*. Keep in mind that each step up the ladder has an associated cost/effort trade-off. You want to reach the sweet spot, not the top.

Personalized Experiences

Companies often promise customers that if they provide the company with their data, they'll receive *personalized experiences*. Some companies might view this mechanically – *How can we personalize?* – and not get far, because they miss the need to create a data-for-value exchange. Other companies ask, "How can personalization increase customer relevance?" and learn that driving that question to its conclusion is highly valuable for both the company and the customer. In fact, the percentage of customers who say a brand would lose their loyalty if it lacks personalized experiences has steadily increased (from 45% in 2021 to 62% in 2022).[26]

L'Oréal pinpointed personalized experiences as the right data-for-value exchange for them when it launched an email-based data capture program that went out to 70% of its European brands. The company wanted to create a large, updated, and enriched customer relationship management (CRM) database that they could use to hyper-personalize content over the longer term. L'Oréal invited email recipients to create a "beauty profile" that stored new data into L'Oréal's cross-brand CRM. The company gained zero-party consumer data (such as skin type, hair type, brand preferences, and product preferences) and in exchange offered recipients insider access to hyper-personalized product promotions that were paired to each customer's self-identified needs. The result was astounding: 60–70% of 5.5 million email recipients created beauty profiles.

If personalized experiences are the sweet spot for your user data-value exchange, then you can pause here. If you require more, then move on to the next level of the ladder.

Value-added Services

Offering a superior data-related service in exchange for data visibility is next up the ladder. The insurance provider Lemonade chose to differentiate itself from other insurance providers by delivering insurance claim payouts at an unmatched speed. Lemonade asked the customer for permission to access and integrate a series of trusted second-party data regarding the customer's activities prior to a car accident. It then integrated that data into its payout policies through its AI-enabled platform.

Lemonade's claim process required a significant degree of customer trust and reassurance that the data used would create a personalized response. After receiving a customer's cell phone video showing damage to their vehicle, Lemonade asked permission to access the car's onboard data platform (second-party data) to review pre-accident driving behavior (e.g., speeding, tailing distance, or hard breaks). Lemonade also asked permission to access distraction data (e.g., mobile phone use while driving). This unprecedented customer visibility led to unprecedented speed of claim payments. Lemonade's platform could approve insurance claims in seconds or minutes (rather than days or months, the industry norm). Lemonade asserts that it offers the fastest insurance claim payouts ever. Its first AI-powered payout took just three seconds.[27]

For many companies competing in the mainstream platform era, delivering value in exchange for data at this level will enable profound innovations and value to be delivered back to the user. However, if your company operates in one of the earliest industries to innovate through platforms (such as social media, search engines, or website development), you may need to offer more in exchange.

Economic Sharing

The fourth and final rung of the ladder is for a platform company to share economic value with customers who share their data, a rational step to take if accessing more, or new, data improves the company's economics.

Progressive Insurance improved their ability to match their automotive rates to risk – a key competitive advantage for the company – by launching a program that relied on a big data-to-value exchange. Typically, car insurance rates are based on factors related to a driver's history or the histories of similar drivers. Progressive's Snapshot program instead uses data gathered from a users' car diagnostics port to monitor their driving habits and returns a share of the annual insurance rate back to safe drivers. This win–win exchange saved Snapshot drivers $156 per year by driving better. And Progressive has paid back over $1.2 billion in discounts through the program[28] – a highly differentiated approach that the company has cited as a key to their competitive position.[29]

BEYOND THE DEAL

Best-in-class companies don't design an innovative data deal and then move on to the next. They also look for better paths to achieve their desired strategic objective beyond the terms of the deal itself. These include, but are not limited to:

- *Best way to ask.* Your customer's likelihood of saying "yes" to your data deal could be significantly improved by when and how you ask. In the automotive industry, a new car owner's opt-in rate to an auto-services-for-data deal can be improved dramatically purely based on when (e.g., before, during, after car sale) and how (e.g., as part of a "let's now personalize the settings on your car" conversation) the better data deal is conveyed to the customer.

- *Best internal incentives.* It can be difficult for companies to identify which "one" business unit benefits from a particular better data deal. It may be one, it may be many, or it may be data required to design the future of your business. Senior leaders should assign responsibility for data creation to a clear team with scorecard objectives that maximize quality and quantity of data collected within a cost constraint. The team would propose strategies to offer a better data deal, if more data are needed and evaluated as a corporate investment for everyone's benefit.

KEY QUESTIONS FOR CONSIDERATIONS

1. Do you have a sound starting point of data security and compliance? If not, start there.

2. What improved level of customer data sharing do you seek? What business goal(s) could you achieve if you had better access to these data?

3. What are your best strategies for offering the customer a better data deal (trusted experiences, relevant personalization, value-added services, economic sharing)?

4. What else "beyond the deal" do you need to innovate to succeed?

4.4

BRANDS GET BRAINS

When the British genius Alan Turing published his seminal paper "Computing Machinery and Intelligence" in 1950,[30] no one knew that he had planted the seeds of a branding revolution. Turing encouraged his fellow computer scientists to stop asking the philosophical question "Can machines think?" and instead focus on a more pragmatic challenge that Turing called the "Imitation Game." *Can a digital machine imitate the way that a human being behaves to the point that a human judge can't tell the difference?*[31,32]

For decades thereafter, popular belief in what artificial intelligence could do outpaced actual technological progress. That's no longer the case. Now, IOT sensors and user interfaces create enough data, cloud-hosted computing platforms provide enough processing power, and AI software provides enough accessibility that the Imitation Game is on. Every company has the option to imbue its corporate brand, its product brands, or a dedicated intelligence brand with the customer-facing appearance and experience of a sentient being. One that senses, empathizes, decides, acts, and learns. A living brand.

This is a major shift in technology; it's an even bigger shift in branded experience.

- Brands have traditionally used mass media symbols to *represent their promise*. They pull from a robust representational toolkit: logos, colors, taglines, tone of voice, sonic signatures, mascots, and spokespeople. Think of McDonald's golden arches, its Happy Meals, and its popular jingle, "I'm Lovin' It."

- Digital media have helped brands *engage customers in their promise* by deploying personalized brand content, facilitating branded community experiences, and telling experiential signature stories around brand purpose and values.[33,34] Dove's Real Beauty self-esteem campaigns featured a wide range of women experiencing Dove's encouragement to see their own beauty.

- Platform-enabled living brands *perform their promise* in real time by interacting as the brand would interact if it were truly alive, based on brand attributes, values, and personality. We don't mean that a machine should masquerade as a human – everything should remain transparent to the customer – but that brands are increasingly capable of intuitive human behavior.

This play will challenge you to consider whether owning an intelligent (or living) brand can bring in-market advantage to your customer and company. If the answer is yes, this play further challenges you to develop an intelligence architecture and experience strategy for your brands.

A LIVING BRAND HAS MORE THAN A BRAIN

The advent of AI has led many brand thinkers to celebrate brand intelligence, but a living brand can be much more than just a thinking brand. Living brands can make experiential the functions of a whole person when performing a platform company's brand promise:

- Sensing (input gathering including vision and listening, and interpreted objectives).

- Empathy (values tension recognition, empathic anticipation, and expression adjustment).

- Decision making (options generation, best choice decisioning, and alignment).

- Acting (digital execution, physical action, and content generation).

- Learning (evolution).

While each of these could be experienced by customers, not all of them should be. As Fig. 4.4.1 illustrates, it is possible to assess your brand's actual performance against a desired experiential performance profile on each of these dimensions. You can set where you want to be as a differentiated brand (from seen and felt to invisible) and score where you are today to identify the investments that will drive your living brand ROI.

A Living Brand can:

Sense: Gather data that are foundational to understanding and responding to a customer.

- Collect and curate data needed to become aware of potential responses.

- Collect and curate the contextual data that empower quality interpretation of data found.

- Accurately infer intent of customer's verbal, written, or physical inputs.

Living Brand Assessment

Brand's ability to:	Performance

		Weak	Strong
Sense	- Collect and curate customer data - Collect and associate contextual data - Infer intent, interpret data meaning		
Empathize	- Anticipate emotional response - Evaluate points of tension - Adjust and personalize expression		
Decide	- Generate options - Assess options - Determine best options		
Act	- Generate new content - Execute tasks with governance - Execute tasks autonomously		
Evolve	- Re-weight decision criteria - Update defaults based on patterns - Improve best options		

Key: – – Performance   → Opportunities

Fig. 4.4.1

Empathize: Recognize and modulate responses based on a customer's emotions to help them feel understood.

- Anticipate a customer's potential emotional response to data, based on customer information.

- Evaluate potential values tension from data, based on known brand and customer values.

- Adjust a brand's verbal/visual expression for the customer's emotional needs in the situation.

Decide: Process implications of data to give accurate advice that also adds value to a customer.

- Generate a range of options based on a well-understood customer objective.

- Assess options against customer-centric criteria that ladder to their objective.

- Determine the best option or best option candidates with transparent rationale.

Act: Automate tasks in a way that reflects the customer's desire for control along the way.

- Generate new content via synthesis and extrapolation of core and associated content resources.

- Execute digital and physical tasks with stepwise visibility for permission or override.

- Execute digital and physical tasks autonomously within customer-prescribed execution limits.

Evolve: Learn lessons from past outcomes to improve next results.

- Re-weight decision criteria based on patterns in customer preferences.

- Create default option(s) based on the customer's most frequent choice(s).

- Improve best option recommendations based on past outcomes.

COMMUNICATING LIVING SYSTEMS

A platform brand may represent an interconnected set of modules, well beyond a single product. In this context it may be important to also show how multiple modules work in harmony with each other to form a living system. If this is true in your case, you'll want to add to the performance characteristics shown in Fig. 4.4.1 to include cross-product communication and teaming capabilities.

Trellix, a new cybersecurity platform company, provides an example. It chose to communicate at launch how its entire product line, coordinated through a common platform, could team intelligently to provide business customers with "living security." Trellix defined living security as the ability of its ecosystem of products to "learn and adapt at the speed of dynamic threats," including shared learning. Trellix made its promise real by articulating how its advanced threat labs, its intelligent platform, and similarly intelligent connected products worked as one to deliver better resilience for business success.

In a world where cyber criminals are continuously changing their tactics, Trellix' living security promise had high relevance. Backed by a launch campaign, Trellix's new brand emerged strongly after just six months in market. The lesson is that powerfully architected intelligent systems, aimed at solving mission-critical customer problems, can break through in-market for advantage.

DEVELOPING YOUR LIVING BRAND

Fig. 4.4.2 illustrates three steps you can take to develop your own living brand. First, you should develop a *Living Brand Strategy*, then construct a *Living Brand Architecture*, and finally design a *Living Brand Experience*.

Living Brand Development Framework

Decisions		Key Questions	Illustrative Descriptions
Living Brand Strategy	Living Brand Flows	What customer flows are enhanced by intelligence-powered platform features?*	Mapping of pre- and post- intelligence customer flows to identify priority intelligence-power features
	Living Brand Benefits	What end benefits do Intelligence -powered platform features deliver?*	Identification of the end benefits produced by intelligence-powered platform features
	Humanized Brand Role(s)	What human analogies best capture the role(s) that the living brand is playing?	Roles like Scout, Expert, Coach, Helper, Driver, Learner, Ideator, Crowdsource, Magician, Administrator, Guardian
Living Brand Architecture	Living Brand(s) Portfolio	What brands will be assigned Living Brand attributes?	Brands may be dedicated/stand alone, corporate/business unit, product line/product, or key ingredient/flow
	Living Brand Physiology	Describe how each Living Brand functions, and how multiple brands work together?	How does each brand do one or more of the following: sense, empathize, think, align, act, learn.
	Naming System Integration	How do the Living Brand(s) mesh with the platform / product line naming system?	Guidelines for how Living Brands integrate witho other brands, names, and descriptors in the product line
Living Brand Experience	Psychology & Expression	What is the psyche of the living brand? How does it express itself verbally/visually?	Guidelines for brand psyche, voice, and form(s), including situational adaption and customer personalization
	Journey Touchpoint Mapping	When in their journey should customers experience our Living Brand?	Journey based touchpoints: When, Where, Why, How Customer experience: thoughts, emotions & perceptions
	Feature & Benefit Messaging	What distinctive messages describe the Living Brand's activities/features/benefits?	Translate value proposition (promise, pillars, proof points, etc.) into tangible & relevant full journey audience messages

*= refer to Chapter 5.1, Reimagined Flows, for additional detail

Fig. 4.4.2

Develop a Living Brand Strategy

A living brand strategy outlines what distinctive benefits your brand will deliver to your customers through intelligence and other living attributes. It articulates the distinctive *new flows* your platform company enables, powered by intelligence. It then identifies the *end benefits* that those new flows deliver plus provides a *humanized role* that your brand will fulfil in your customers' lives. Each of these should be unmatched by competition.

Trellix' intelligent ecosystem learns and adapts in ways that improve three major cybersecurity workflows. Each workflow improvement leads to better business resilience and confidence. Trellix learns and adapts:

- *Before attack* for <u>optimal readiness,</u> acting as a lookout scout and preparedness expert.

- *During attack* for <u>best-in-class response,</u> acting as an analyst and response commander.

- *After attack* for <u>continuous improvement</u>, acting as crowd-sourcer and forensic detective.

For you to do this too, break apart each of your customer flows into their component steps and identify the steps that are powered by intelligence, unique versus your competition, *and* deliver valuable end benefits to the customer. These will likely form the most disruptive foundation for your living brand strategy. When you look at these disruptive steps together, what human analogy best captures what they do?

Construct a Living Brand Architecture

Living brands exist in relationship to other brands. To construct your brand architecture, you need to define those relationships next. Determine *which brands in your portfolio* will become your company's living brand(s) Describe how each living brand will *physiologically function* – optimizing each dimension from Fig. 4.4.1. Finally, make any needed adjustments to your current *brand and naming architecture*.

When deciding *which brands will become your living brand(s),* you have several choices:

- *Dedicated Living Brand*: This approach makes one brand the focal point of intelligence claims and benefits. Salesforce.com launched Einstein as its AI-powered seller productivity helper. Amazon launched Alexa as its voice AI assistant. Both companies chose a human name for their brand, giving it a personality and spotlighting performance. If you go this route, watch out for two risks: overusing your living brand (sometimes called "intelligence-washing") and making your corporate and product brands seem unintelligent by comparison.

Go to market teams with dedicated living brands may need to adopt taxonomy for an AI brand family that reflects sub-capabilities (e.g., Computer Vision, Natural Language Processing, Machine Learning Relationships and Classifications, and Generative Intelligence). This contrasts with treating AI as a monolith. Companies who brand an AI family may need to adopt descriptive sub-brands for sub-capabilities. The very adventurous might develop an AI brand portfolio, hoping its distinctiveness will outweigh communication complexity.

- *Living Corporate Brand*: This approach credits the corporate brand for intelligence. Tesla attributes intelligence to its corporate brand. Trellix does the same. Having a living corporate brand allows you to spend efficiently; a single investment can build a platform brand and strengthen the corporate brand – all at once. If you choose this route, just be sure your corporate brand's intelligence claims are credible.

- *Living Product Brands:* Microsoft chose to embed intelligence into each of its hero products (Office 365, Power BI, Bing, GitHub, etc.) rather invest in an all-encompassing intelligence brand (previously called Cortana). More recently, Microsoft has introduced a personal assistant brand called Copilot that will run in each of its Microsoft 365 products. This is a great way to modernize product brands that have already earned a place in customers' hearts. For a company that makes this choice, the challenge is to ensure that product brands display living attributes in coherent ways across products.

Once you've decided which brands will get a brain to become a living brand, you'll need to determine each living brand's physiological functions. How does each one sense, empathize, assess, decide, generate, act, and learn? If you have multiple living brands, is there a division of labor and specialization (i.e., one brand senses and another brand acts) or does each brand do everything, just in different circumstances? These living roles will be reflected in your brand, naming, and modifier nomenclature systems to reflect living brand capabilities and architecture decisions you have made.

Design a Living Brand Experience

Your final part of the living brand development framework is to map what, when, and how your living brand shows up throughout the customer journey. This requires you to define the *brand's psychology and manners of direct expression* (verbal and visual), determine at what customer journey *touchpoints its expressions will be experienced*, and update the *brand's messaging*.

Each organization's living brand can come to life in different ways to meet their unique business objectives. For verbal expression, a consumer goods company could use AI in its customer service chatbot to detect customer sentiment and shift the tone of its responses accordingly, meeting frustration with empathy or satisfaction with celebration. For visual expression, companies across industries can use a living approach to design to enhance the customer's experience. For Trellix, several design choices came together to do exactly this:

- Trellix uses small line segments that move together, like waves of grain in the wind, to communicate intelligent data flows from one part of the Trellix system to another.

- Trellix uses color to communicate where its system is learning and adapting. Blue implies learning, green implies adapting, and white signals the system has adapted.

- Trellix shows its product line working intelligently in harmony from a bird's-eye (or drone's) perspective.

RISKS OF INTELLIGENCE

The use of AI to power living brands has risks as well as benefits. Management and marketing teams need to take these risks into account as they add new platform value through AI.

- The introduction of generative intelligence (Chat GPT being a conversational use case) creates concerns about the trustworthiness of AI-generated content. How can companies and customers know if their generative intelligence application synthesizes or extrapolates from a "true fact" database when it generates output? To solve this challenge platform companies are increasingly offering "trusted" databases for their AI – large data sets built and updated under strict protocols – to increase the safety of generative AI output. And there is a second, yet deeper challenge. Because generative AI outputs original content through novel applications of patterns in existing data, it can generate "creative" (untrue) output even if it is drawing on true inputs. These challenges may be solvable, but they must not be ignored.

- If AI-fueled automation reduces employment in various areas of the economy, the phrase "AI-powered" may become a negative association. The more your company innovatively uses AI to produce benefits that the customer couldn't get before, versus simply producing traditional benefits with less labor, the more robust of a value proposition you'll have.

- As AI is disseminated and strengthened, experts are raising significant new concerns around the risks of unintended consequences and malevolent applications. AI could become harmful to those it is intended to serve. Those who participate in platform intelligence should redouble their commitment to responsible use that serves customer needs.

All of these factors raise the need for a risk management approach to communication about underlying AI technology, and a redoubled focus on articulating the practical benefits it produces, plus the safeguards that are in place.

KEY QUESTIONS FOR CONSIDERATION

1. How can an intelligent brand(s) modernize your company and differentiate your platform?

2. What benefits can it drive for your customer coalition?

3. If you have a living brand(s), how can you improve its performance? Use metrics in the Living Brand Dimensions framework (Fig. 4.4.1) to assess actuals, set targets, and develop initiatives.

4. What steps do you need to take to develop your living brand(s)? Follow the steps in the Living Brand Development Framework (Fig. 4.4.2) to find your answers.

4.5

REALITY SHIFTS

The democratization of the metaverse began at 1:47 a.m. in a Danish basement. Nicholas Francis, a Copenhagen-based video game programmer, was frustrated as he tried to make a piece of "shader" software work (to create light and shadow effects) in his video game engine. Francis posted a request for help on his chat board that caught the eye of a German programmer named Joachim Ante, who was also awake, and intrigued, despite having expertise with a different type of gaming engine. What began as a chat about making a more versatile shader tool quickly turned into an incredibly ambitious conversation. Why not build a better, open, maker-centric tool set for all three-dimensional (3D)-experience creators, one that would let programmers build new worlds seamlessly across all gaming engines?

"Unity" became the name for the business that emerged.

That was 2002. Up to that point, gaming engines had been all about programmer *entrapment*; once you chose your engine, you were locked into the limited tools designed to run on it. Unity's goal was programmer *empowerment*.

THE MAKER SIDE OF EXTENDED REALITY

Nicholas and Joachim enabled a whole industry to move forward at faster pace, with greater agility, thanks to a developer platform that enabled bottom-up maker innovation and collaboration.

Unity's intuitive maker environment let teams of video game programmers, designers, and script writers collaborate in one place. Unity built a catalytic community of gaming programmers who could share, buy, and sell reusable code blocks to speed up and lower the cost of projects.

Unity then broadened its capabilities *beyond gaming* to encompass *every type of extended reality* experience: immersive, augmented, mixed, and virtual (definitions coming later). Today, nearly half of the world's extended reality experiences are created on the Unity platform.

Some of the world's 3D gaming and social platform giants are now competing to surpass Unity as the programmer's platform of choice. Epic Games is the strongest and best known challenger. Facebook created its own metaverse platform for its massive customer base, changing its company name to Meta to shine light on its strategic shift.

Here's the good news for any company who wants to use 3D experiences to differentiate their customer's journey: The "maker" half of the equation is no longer an obstacle. Tools exist, talent can be found, and cloud-hosted platforms provide sufficient processing power. While reality-creation technology is still in its early years and not yet suitable for every imagined use case, it will only continue to become more realistic and robust over time.

As a result, it's time to seriously consider empowering your customer to shift their reality at key points in their journey. Where might that add customer value? Where might it bring you in-market advantage? That's the focus of this chapter, and play.

THE CUSTOMER SIDE OF EXTENDED REALITY

Where's customer value? That's now the bigger challenge. Your customers probably won't be impressed by the novelty of a new reality experience. On the one hand, the experience may seem *too foreign* to your non-gamer customers (who will skew older). "Why swap out reality for a poor substitute?" is what Baby Boomers and many Gen X leaders might ask. On the other hand, the experience may feel *too familiar* to be interesting to generations who grew up on gaming. "What's the big deal?" your Millennials, Gen Zs, and next gens might ask.

This means that new reality experiences alone won't drive new levels of customer engagement or other desired customer behaviors. The power of extended reality experiences will be propelled by the benefits they provide the customer at the journey moment when they deliver that benefit. If a new reality is truly a new enabler of a new or improved benefit experience, it stands a chance of capturing the customer's head and heart.

FOUR WAYS TO SHIFT REALITY

There are four types of reality-shift experiences that fall under the umbrella term "extended reality." Each requires a platform to run and some form of user hardware to view or project. Each can be used at any moment in the customer journey. We list them in order of current market use frequency:

- *Immersive Reality (IR)*: Video and digital animation are produced for an immersive effect and watched on a screen (e.g., streaming YouTube video or a watching a video ad campaign). This is not a novel experience but is still extremely effective.

- *Augmented Reality (AR)*: Digital elements are virtually superimposed onto the real world. There is no actual contact between digital and physical elements (e.g., superimposing the heat signature of a patient's vein on the skin to improve first-time injection rates).

- *Mixed Reality (MR)*: Digital elements are virtually superimposed onto the physical world, but physical and digital elements interact (e.g., Digital Pokémon Go characters have spatial and contextual awareness of their surroundings, so that they can hide behind trees or avoid bumping into people).[35]

- *Virtual Reality (VR)*: A digital world that has digital elements in it. Most useful for fully immersive experiences where it's safe for the real world to be entirely blocked out (e.g., viewing the digital twin of a building through VR glasses at work or learning new skills while seated at home).

CREATING VALUE THROUGH REALITY SHIFTS

To identify opportunities to shift customer reality, it's helpful to consider how extended reality use cases can add value for both your platform's customer coalition and for your company. Fig. 4.5.1 illustrates the most common benefits that extended reality can produce, by stage of the platform customer journey. Every time extended reality is used in the customer journey, it should answer the customer's question of "why?" plus deliver against clear company objectives. Consider these opportunities by journey stage.

1. *Brand–Demand Lead Engine*: To attract new customers and increase current customer brand engagement at the start of a journey, companies can use extended reality experiences to make a great first impression that is accessible, engaging, and points to next steps.

   Over the last decade, more than half of Paris has been turned into a virtual reality model. Originally designed for architects and builders, it has become a multipurpose tool to introduce and engage citizens in potential new urban projects – the first steps toward buy-in and support. The interactive model engages citizens who hadn't been "in the know" before and therefore not engaged in change. It empowers citizens to crowdsource their voice in the future of their community. This "digital twin" is photo-realistic, covering 2 million structures on 1,000 square kilometers. It is made of modular interfaces to fit all accessibility and use case requirements.[36]

2. *Lead-to-Sale Smoothing*: To increase sale conversion, companies can help prospective customers shift reality to a future state where they have already made their purchase – letting them better evaluate and gain confidence in their choice. To do this, extended reality experiences should be available wherever the customer wants and be hyper-personalized to their own situation, as well as provide effective post-decision simulation.

   As part of its choose-to-use journey initiative, retailer IKEA empowers shoppers to scan spaces with their smartphones, erase their real-life furniture and art from the screen, and insert new

Creating Value by Shifting Reality

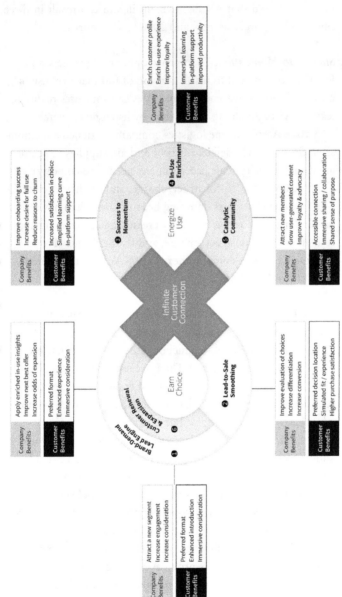

Fig. 4.5.1

items from the IKEA digital catalog.[37] Home furnishing companies have found that AR deployment in situ can result in three times higher purchase rates and 20% lower returns.

3. *Success to Momentum*: To improve onboarding of new platform customers, and to instill a vision of full-platform use in partial-platform customers, companies can shift user reality to learn by virtually doing rather than by listening or watching.

   Swoop Aero, a drone logistics company, designed a medium-sized drone to help deliver medical and aid supplies to remote areas of Africa. To scale, the company needed to empower hundreds of locals to construct, charge, and fly their drones. The learning curve was daunting because many had never seen an airplane up close before. They created an AR training app to help anyone construct, charge, and fly the drones. Proudly supporting remote communities, Swoop Aero just delivered their one millionth item.

4. *In-Use Enrichment.* This customer journey step breaks into two very different scenarios. In one scenario, a platform's reason for being is people-to-people interaction (e.g., social media, teleconferencing, collaboration, etc.). There are myriad ways that interaction may be enriched through extended reality; there are others by which it might be diminished. Given limited space, we'll acknowledge this rich discussion topic but won't venture into it.

   In a second scenario, companies can deliver real-time user support, enrichment, and ongoing training through extended reality, leading to improved user (or managerial sponsor) satisfaction and loyalty. This experience must deliver tangible benefits such as on-the-job learning, reduced errors, improved worker capabilities, and/or improved productivity.

   The accurate placement of intravenous injections and catheters to children and adults provides a strong example. Hospitals can now provide AR support to detect a patient's heat signatures and superimpose a map of veins (many invisible to the eye) onto the patient's skin. AR use boosts first-time injection success by 350% and reduces procedure time by 78%.[38]

5. *Catalytic Community.* Through communities, companies seek to achieve higher levels of engagement, expanded use, loyalty, and advocacy. Extended reality can support key drivers of community such as member connection, content, and commerce. Deployments should ensure required and desired privacy, enable sharing and collaboration, and foster a shared sense of purpose.

To host the 2020 World Expo in Dubai amid global COVID lockdowns, the organizers created both real and extended reality tickets. Users who attended on-site and remotely were able to interact using a mixed reality that consisted of real venues in Dubai, three-dimensional (3D) booths from online vendors, and virtual reality. AI-powered avatars and AR anchors enabled both on-site and remote users to share these experiences in real time – and empowered visitors from anywhere to connect with the WorldExpo displays.

6. *Customer Renewal and Expansion.* Companies seek to improve take up rates on their "next best offer" to expand customer lifetime value, while consumers want to assess whether they should deepen their brand relationship and broaden their brand purchases. Extended reality can gather hyper-personalized insights and seed higher engagement in the company's next offer, improving take up.

Disney makes extensive use of extended reality innovations to enhance guest park and hotel experiences. That enables the company to gather personalized park and hotel guest insights from guest activities and then combine those with insights from streaming media consumption and merchandise purchases. The results are vivid Disney customer profiles that help the company improve its next offer and bring more member happiness.

Having traversed the platform customer journey, we come back to our original question. Where might you create new customer and company value by giving your customers the opportunity to shift their reality?

KEY QUESTIONS FOR CONSIDERATION

Use Fig. 4.5.2 as an aid to outlining your shifted reality plan. Consider how many areas of your business worth a dedicated thought cycle. Think of each area as a "card" on the diagram.

For each card, select a persona in your customer coalition as your customer journey focal point.

Shifted Reality Plan Template

Business Unit A
Customer Coalition Persona _____

	Step 1 Where in the journey might you create new customer & company value?		Step 2 What expanded reality experience would have the biggest impact?				Step 3 How could data be of benefit?
Customer Journey Stage	Customer Benefit	Company Benefit	Immersive Reality	Augmented Reality	Mixed Reality	Virtual Reality	Data Capture & Use
Brand-Demand Lead Engine							
Lead-to-Sale Smoothing			Existing	Purchase visualization			
Success to Momentum						Virtual twin	
In-Use Enrichment							
Catalytic Community							
Customer Renewal & Expansion			Existing	Virtual learning lab			

From ▬▬ To

Fig. 4.5.2

Answer the following questions, one card at a time. Once done, look for synergies across cards.

1. *Where in the customer's full-platform journey might you create new customer and company value through reality shifts?* Choose the appropriate row(s) on each business area card and write down the paired customer and company benefits that shifted reality could help you achieve.

2. *How will you shift reality to deliver your desired benefits?* Write in the box your customer's headline experience. Choose the extended reality *technology* that delivers the experience.

3. *How might new data captured serve the customer and company?*

4.6

VISIBILITY FOR GOOD

An annual global research study, first started in 2000, has tracked the evolution of customer trust in four institutions that affect public life: government, nonprofits, media, and business. Which institution do consumers trust the most? Business now comes out on top, having risen steadily for two decades.[39] Here are a few highlights[40]:

- *Higher business trust is rooted in a blend of competence and ethics.* In the survey, business scored 53 points higher than the government on competence and 30 points higher on ethics.

- *Consumers want business to do even more on societal issues.* Nine out of 10 consumers want businesses to either continue taking action or take more action against climate change, economic inequality, and health-care access.

- *Consumers back up their desire through purchase and advocacy behavior.* Sixty-three percentage of consumers (73% of Gen Z) are likely to buy from and advocate for brands that align with their values.[41]

COMPETING ON GOOD

The result is that purpose-based communication and activation – the expression of a company's desire to do good – has become a new dimension of business competition. Companies now seek to differentiate their purposeful perspective and activities to earn the loyalty of talent, customers, and investors. But differentiation is hard to achieve. There are three reasons that keep firms failing to stand out.

First, when companies express their societal benefit, they often rely on badges that their competitors can also collect and claim, such as Fair Trade®, Certified 100% Organic, or Certified Carbon Neutral. All badges are valuable starting points. However, over time, they become a cost to stay in business, not an investment to win it. The badges usually hide unique data-driven "backstories" that companies could be telling.

Second, companies often go it alone when customers want to be part of the solution. Fifty-eight percentage of consumers prefer to help a brand address societal issues, rather than watching the brand do all the work itself.[42] Among consumers who want brands to make the world a better place, a third also want the brand to help make them a better person. In contrast, many companies implement their purpose outside the realm of their customer's experience. A customer might only occasionally hear about a brand's corporate social responsibility (CSR) initiatives or read its environmental, social and governance (ESG) report online.

Finally, companies often fail to personalize the customer's experience of the company doing good. One aspect of a company's purpose may be especially relevant to some customers, while a different aspect may be more relevant to others. Purpose has all the same potential for segmentation and personalization that a product or service has.

The upshot is that across many industries, even leading companies might commoditize their actions around doing good. Their purpose might be distinctive; the way customers experience it is not.

PLATFORMS AND VISIBILITY FOR GOOD

Platforms can help on all three dimensions that hold companies back. They do this by facilitating reverse visibility. We say "reverse" because platforms *typically give companies visibility into customers* as they use what they've acquired. This time, roles are reversed: Platforms *give customers* (or donors or taxpayers) *visibility into companies* (or nonprofits or governments) as they do good (Fig. 4.6.1).

All the principles of "standard" platform marketing apply in creating this reverse visibility. Instead of a company putting sensors on its products. The company most creatively put "sensors" on the good it does to make it visible. The company must enable digital dialog between the good it is doing and those who are watching. The company must personalize and learn what is most relevant to each observer and then amplify that.

If you succeed, your reverse visibility platform will become a streaming source of stories rich in human meaning and data-driven

Reversing the Role of Platform Visibility

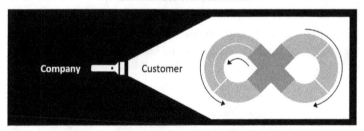

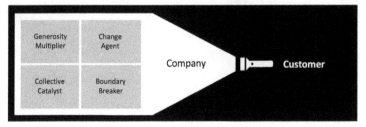

Fig. 4.6.1

impact. It will differentiate your company and product through purpose. In the best scenario, your company's reverse visibility platform will become integrated into the beating heart of your company's core business operations.

DESIGNING VISIBILITY FOR GOOD

The framework below (Fig. 4.6.2) illustrates four leading examples of how platforms can provide visibility for good. This framework has four quadrants based on *the income level of the key platform participant* (y axis: *low-income beneficiary* to *high-income purchaser*) and the *type of company "good" that the platform enables* (x axis: *focused* to *structural*).

A *"Collective Catalyst" uses platforms to empower low-income populations to advance individually and collectively.*

Poverty Stoplight, a nonprofit organization founded in Paraguay and serving needs worldwide, is a platform designed for community advancement. Its Stoplight Survey acts as a giant IOT sensor of stepwise progress made by low-income groups with the help of economic support programs. The survey defines 50 ways that poverty shows up in daily life (e.g., my shoes, toilet, stove, transportation, mindset, and relationships) and provides pictures for users to click on to visually match each user's situation to levels of poverty: extreme poverty (red light), poverty (yellow light), and leaving poverty (green light).

Visibility for Good: Platform Use Cases

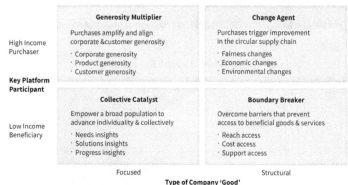

	Generosity Multiplier	**Change Agent**
High Income Purchaser	Purchases amplify and align corporate &customer generosity	Purchases trigger improvement in the circular supply chain
	· Corporate generosity · Product generosity · Customer generosity	· Fairness changes · Economic changes · Environmental changes
Key Platform Participant		
	Collective Catalyst	**Boundary Breaker**
Low Income Beneficiary	Empower a broad population to advance individuality & collectively	Overcome barriers that prevent access to beneficial goods & services
	· Needs insights · Solutions insights · Progress insights	· Reach access · Cost access · Support access
	Focused	Structural

Type of Company 'Good'
Visible to Customer

Fig. 4.6.2

A group's first-time survey provides the benchmark of red, yellow, and green starting points. As an economic support program takes effect, subsequent surveys track patterns of color change that reveal whether, where, and how a program is working. Like any platform, the database provides kaleidoscopic value to different members of a customer coalition. Program managers use insights to advance programs. Program sponsors use color change to celebrate and report impact. Program beneficiaries share with each other how they changed their colors, crowdsourcing anti-poverty innovations. Finally, because the survey asks individual participants to click the next three areas where they seek color change, it guides programs to focus on where a target population has personal and collective energy to progress.

The Poverty Stoplight's collective catalyst platform has been adopted by nonprofits, villages, national governments, and low-wage private sector employers to literally help light the way for change.

A "Boundary Breaker" uses platforms to overcome barriers for low-income populations to access beneficial products and services that are otherwise out of reach, too costly, or that otherwise require unaffordable labor-based support.

MicroEnsure was a small nonprofit with sky-high ambition: to bring life-changing global insurance coverage to poor families who had always lacked access. The obstacle was distribution; it was too costly to find, qualify, and administer insurance to small insurance customers. Yet poor families suffered the most when a family wage earner died or when an unexpected cost occurred.

In 2012, MicroEnsure's founder, Richard Leftley, had a flash of insight. Why not distribute insurance through the platforms of mobile phone companies? He envisioned a win-win scenario. Telecommunications companies suffered economically from customer churn because customers in low-income markets did not purchase long-term contracts, only pre-paid cards. Customers could hop from one cell phone company to another when they "topped up." Leftley's "aha" moment came next: What if microinsurance coverage was provided as a perk to loyal mobile phone customers, like frequent flyer miles or loyalty card discounts in other industries?

And Leftley's idea worked: Today, MicroEnsure provides insurance coverage to 60 million people in Africa, Asia, and Latin

America, and the company has received multiple global honors for financial services innovation. Two-way telco platform visibility was the key. Participating families agreed to make their top-up purchase loyalty transparent by participating; that visibility equally enabled rapid benefit payouts if needed.

A "Change Agent" uses platforms to create structural change per purchase by improving fairness, economics, and environment across the supply chain.

Provenance.org, a blockchain platform, is helping companies and consumers reclaim visibility to influence choice and fairness throughout FMCG supply chains. "Every time we buy a product, we're voting on the way we want the world to be," says Provenance founder Jessi Baker at Europe's leading technology conference, Next Web.[43] The Provenance platform works with companies to verify the origin of materials and products throughout a supply chain, embed the blockchain tokens required to continuously monitor and track verification, and then directly communicate this verification to consumers through e-commerce plugins and marketplaces.

Just one example of this in use is Princes' efforts to prevent illegal intermediaries from exploiting farm workers and violating minimum wage requirements in the Italian agricultural industry. Princes processes around 250 million tomato products each year in Italy for its brand Napolina. Through Provenance's blockchain-powered platform, Princes deployed in-field inspections, on-truck traceable GPS, on-tomato-can QR codes, and more. This gave buyers of Princes products verification of their choice for human rights for farmers and drivers of the tomatoes they buy. It also enables Princes to ensure that tomatoes they purchased would create local structural change.[44]

Provenance's blockchain platform has been adopted by companies looking to make any type of structural impact through supply chain visibility, spanning climate, waste, nature, work, and community. Bringing this visibility from the farm to the consumer, in Jessi's words, helps combat "exploitation of people and the environment [which] thrive in opaque supply chains."

A "Generosity Multiplier" uses platforms to amplify and align corporate, product, and customer generosity programs.

Patagonia, the outdoor clothing and gear retailer, has an inspiring history as an innovator of multifaceted, highly engaging generosity programs. Founded in the 1970s by a teenage mountain climber, Yvon Chouinard, Patagonia has provided visibility for good through platforms to amplify its efforts to reverse climate change:

- In 2002, Patagonia launched 1% for the Planet, a certification and advisory platform for companies looking to amplify their generosity by giving 1% of their gross sales each year to vetted environmental groups. The result? The platform has certified over $435 million in funds since 2002 – four times the $100 million that Patagonia has contributed since 1985.

- In 2018, Patagonia launched Patagonia Action Works, a platform designed to give its loyal base of over 10 million retail customers visibility into local events, petitions, and volunteering opportunities hosted by Patagonia's ecosystem of over 1,000 environmental groups. In the first six months alone, the groups received 1.6 billion new impressions, 120,000 direct acts of generosity, and over 7,000 hours of high-skill, high-pay volunteering – the equivalent of $1.9 million in value.[45]

And Chouinard embodies this spirit himself, by aligning his personal acts of generosity with his company's values. In 2022, Chouinard donated his family's entire shareholding in Patagonia to climate change. "Every dollar that is not reinvested back into Patagonia will be distributed as dividends to protect the planet," he said, "We made Earth our only shareholder."[46]

THE RISING BASELINE

There's a final reason to differentiate through visibility for good platforms now. It can help you get ahead of an ever-rising visibility baseline created through legislative or regulatory requirements. Consider the Fashion Act, a proposed bill in the New York Senate as of

October 2021. It requires New York apparel and footwear retailers with global revenues over $100 million to identify and disclose[47]:

- *End-to-end supply chains:* the top 50% of suppliers that pose the highest environmental and/or social risk, from seed to storefront.

- *Impact goals and effects:* a roadmap for reducing corporate and supply chain impact on the environment and society, and they also must disclose any adverse events or effects that occur.

- *Reporting and public access:* due diligence actions taken to account for risks and all information available on the retailer's website for public viewing.

By investing now in visibility for good platforms, you'll be well positioned to move to the next level of visibility for good while your competition scrambles to play compliance catch-up.

KEY QUESTIONS FOR CONSIDERATION

1. How thoughtfully, clearly, and authentically has your company articulated its purpose?

2. How sensitive is your customer base, talent base, and/or investor base to a distinctive expression and activation of purpose?

3. How could a platform provide your customer coalition with greater visibility for good?
   a. Unique content-rich storytelling
   b. Two-way customer engagement
   c. Personalization for relevance

4. What platform uses provide you the visibility for good that your company needs?
   a. Collective Catalyst
   b. Boundary Breaker
   c. Change Agent
   d. Generosity Amplifier

Part 5

INTERACTION PLAYS

The way a prospect or customer thinks and feels about your platform-related offers will determine their preferences and choices. Their perceptions will be shaped not only by how well your products perform but also by the experiential quality of their interactions with your experience hubs and your brand.

In the past, when go-to-market executives spoke about the importance of a consistent, on-brand customer experience, they meant some combination of visual systems (the way the brand looks), verbal systems (the way the brand speaks), and interactions with a company's employees (the way a brand's values show through its people). Those remain critical.

But it's distinctive digital interaction that lies at the heart of today's customer experience. Through experience hubs, the platform interacts in a way that anticipates the customer's flow needs. It understands who the customer is and what the context is and personalizes content accordingly. It is a good dialogue partner, listening and responding naturally when the customer "speaks" first and starting a new conversation based on inferred customer signals. And it's always looking for ways to do better through innovation. Growth of generative intelligence capabilities, immersive realities, and multi-sensory experiences will continue to transform digital interaction going forward.

Distinctive digital interactions, delivered throughout the full customer journey, can create a *differentiated* customer impression.

They can help your company win through platforms by becoming the customer's preferred experience. The result will be better prospect acquisition and customer value growth.

Four interaction plays can help you upgrade your digital customer interactions. They are shown in Fig. 5.0.1, underpinning both the Demand Plays (the horizontal infinity loop) and the Innovation Plays (the vertical infinity loop) described earlier in our book. Powered by the platform's infinite customer connection, these four plays are summarized below and detailed in the next four chapters.

- *Full-Journey Engagement (Chapter 5.1)* helps you distinctively interact with your customer through the full Choose-and-Use journey, applying consistent drivers of engagement excellence.

Interaction Plays

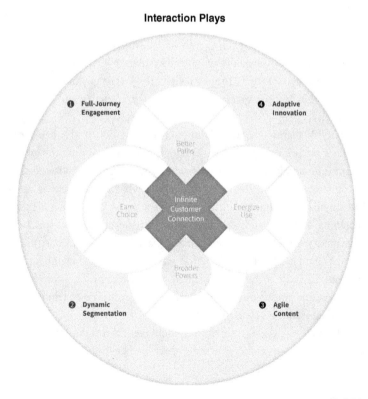

Fig. 5.0.1

- *Dynamic Segmentation* (*Chapter 5.2*) describes how multiple simple and composable segmentation schemes can be combined like building blocks at different journey steps to call for personalized content that's right for the moment.

- *Agile Content* (*Chapter 5.3*) outlines how to establish a strategy and action plan for personalized content journey-wide through modular content strategy, digital operations management, and governance.

- *Adaptive Innovation* (*Chapter 5.4*) explains how to make innovation a part of your customer interaction, enabling you to accelerate innovative products or practices that matter to market first while crafting a customer experience of meaningful collaboration.

Together, these Interaction Plays can turn your platform into a dynamic dialog between company and customer, each continuously communicating with and learning from each other. The result is a far more enhanced customer experience that will pay dividends in loyalty and growth.

5.1

FULL-JOURNEY ENGAGEMENT

It's hard to think of a more digitally engaging brand than Nike. In a 15-year marathon to become a premiere platform company, Nike transformed different parts of its customer journey through a series of strategic digital investments.[1,2,3,4,5,6] This has taken Nike from a company that excelled at top-of-the-funnel marketing to one that can engage the customer at every step of the journey with compelling, relevant digital interactions – something we call Full-Journey Engagement.

Key Nike customer experiences are mapped against our platform journey model in Fig. 5.1.1.

In its early years, Nike's "Just Do It" slogan could be read as an individual challenge to a solitary jogger, a call to buy a pair of Air Jordans, or a cultural challenge to let girls play sports. Now, thanks to Nike's platforms, "Just Do It" is also an invitation to join a community of those determined to stay fit and those ready to be of support.

Nike brings curious prospects to its website, where they can engage with three things: Nike's brand attitude, Nike's latest shoes, and Nike's invitation to "become a member." This last call to action, featuring three different communities, is now an integral part of the brand. Downloading one of three community apps immediately makes the prospect a member. It's a digitally scaled example of how

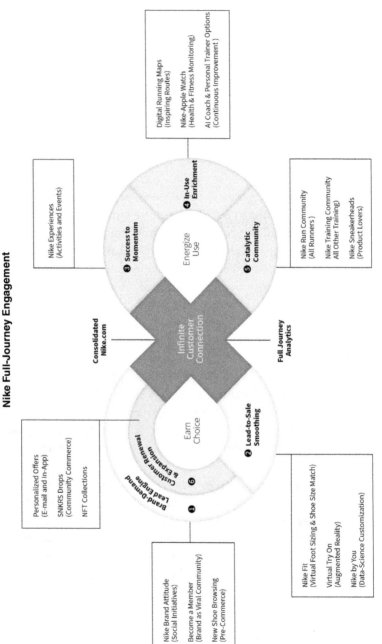

Nike Full-Journey Engagement

Fig. 5.1.1

the final "use journey" experience – the catalytic community (see Chapter 3.5) – can become a first viral point of engagement in the "choose journey" of the next prospect.

Nike smooths the prospect's lead-to-sale stage through a blend of platform innovations that add engagement "wow" to the shopper's shoe and apparel buying experience, both online and in-store. For example, with Nike Fit, shoppers can scan their foot with a smartphone and be told what size of each shoe model fits them best. Virtual Try On lets shoppers view Nike products as holograms on human models. Nike by You enlists the shopper to become a co-creator – by adding personalized touches to core Nike shoe elements based on personal taste, cultural association, or favorite sports team.

When a shopper becomes a Nike shoe owner, Nike's digital engagement continues to grow. Nike Experiences creates momentum by enlarging the shoe owner's vision of how they can expand their fitness journey via personalized activity and event recommendations.

When the owner slips on their shoes or shorts to become an active user, Nike engagement platforms kick into overdrive. Nike collaborates with leading makers of fitness monitoring apps to capture and store the user's exercise, vital statistics, and fitness progress to the Nike platform. The Nike Run app provides digital maps that guide runners through inspiring outdoor routes and facilitates group runs. The Nike Train app includes training content, coaches, and communities across a wide variety of fitness activities.

Nike's third engagement platform, SNKRS (pronounced "sneakers") is for self-proclaimed Nike Sneakerheads. These are diehard product lovers who view shoes as art. To keep this "catalytic community" engaged, Nike drops limited-edition shoes and sneaker NFTs to give this community the opportunity to snap them up and turn them into collector items. Nike interacts with Sneakerheads not as a seller of goods but as a fellow fan, concierge, and event host.

Nike closes the customer journey loop by using data generated from its engagement platform apps to curate product innovations and customize customer demand expansion offers based on each customer's evolving interaction and behavior. Customers receive personalized offers via email and in-app messages, demonstrating that Nike is recognizing them as a unique individual through messages and prompts that reflect their unique needs and behaviors.

Nike's full-journey engagement isn't just a nice-to-have feature; it's a hard-edged discipline that yields significant business results.[7] According to Nike CEO John Donahoe, these programs help retain a higher proportion of engaged members and create an increased buying frequency with lower customer acquisition costs, increased return on ad spend, and an immensely positive impact on demand creation. The bottom line: Nike found that customers who engage with the brand on two or more of its platforms have a lifetime value that's *four times higher than the baseline customer.*

ENGAGEMENT EXCELLENCE DRIVERS

Achieving full-journey engagement results like Nike's is both process-intensive and technically complex work. Fig. 5.1.2 lists key engagement excellence drivers must work in harmony for your company to outperform competition through full-journey engagement. Excellence should feel to the customer like intuitive digital dialogue. By that we mean a two-way engagement with the customer through your experience hub where you are able to say and do the right thing at the right time, in the right way, through the right experiences to deepen your customer relationship.

We grouped these excellence drivers into three clusters: Pre-Market Strategy, In-Market Capabilities, and Enablers.

- Pre-Market Strategy excellence drivers map your goals and plan for digital engagement along the entire customer journey (or your stage of it as part of a full-journey team).

- In-Market Capabilities bring your engagement plan to life by making the most of your existing infrastructure through process, decision constructs, and content management.

- Enablers underpin engagement through advanced technology and data infrastructure.

Full-Journey Engagement: Excellence Drivers

Engagement Capabilities & Definitions... ...Across Full Journey Stages

Pre-Market Strategy	Brand-Demand Lead Engine	Lead-to-Sale Smoothing	Success to Momentum	In-Use Enrichment	Catalytic Community	Customer Renewal & Expansion
1 Touchpoint & Process Standards	Document company and ecosystem participant interactions by touchpoint, data flow & data source					
2 Program Strategy & Blueprints	Design data-driven, omnichannel engagement program that achieves stage-level KPIs					

In-Market Capabilities

3 Segments, Targeting, & Recognition	Create actionable segments for account & buyer types to target (outbound) and recognize (inbound)					
4 Best Move Decision Rules	Classify audience / channel activities and automate best-move responses using optimized decision rules					
5 Content Strategy & Customization	Guide, create, and manage content customized for best-move intent, audience persona, and channel					
6 Channel Mix & Management	Data-driven media plan that responds dynamically to behavior and optimizes spend based on objectives					
7 Owned Touchpoint Experiences	Effectiveness and personalization of digital site interactions and user behavior sharing on & across sites					
8 Status Advancement & Nurture Loops	Lead scoring and status qualification, with nurture programs for non-advancers					
9 Customer Choice Support	Interactions that empower the customer to make their best choice					

Enablers

10 Tech Architecture & Integration	Technology tools needed to achieve stage-level KPIs with integrations for full journey synergies					
11 Data Management & Analytics	Data strategy, governance, access, and compliance needed to achievement of all-stage KPIs					
12 Organization & Skills	Structural effectiveness of digital dialog operating model and talent maturity against roles					

Fig. 5.1.2

PRE-MARKET STRATEGY

Touchpoint and Process Standards

When your teams create a new campaign, do they have a standards-based foundation to start with, or are they reinventing the wheel each time? Best-practice platform companies empower their teams by mapping a standards-based starting point. They plot ecosystem-wide touchpoints with process and data flows across all six platform journey stages. The mapping spans digital and physical touches between the user, the company, and other customer coalition members. Teams can be trained on standards and then create variations for their unique campaigns. This approach saves time, trains teams by doing, and guarantees baseline engagement quality.

These standards maps might differ from your traditional customer journey maps in three ways. First, some Use journey stages might be new, thanks to new platform connections. Second, multi-customer interactions enabled by the platform might also be new – you might currently only track customer to company. Third, you might need to map standards from the viewpoints of different customer personas on different journeys – that is, from their unique angles – to understand their experience well.

Program Strategy and Blueprints

Given high-quality standards as a starting-point foundation, your company's next capability area is the strategic design of a go to market program that achieves specific objectives within and across journey stages, using omnichannel engagement with target personas. This activity creates a blueprint for that stage's digital interactions. Best-practice blueprints anticipate certain leaps and zig-zags across sub-stages and channels versus linear journeys. Blueprints can be saved through knowledge management for team reuse and refinement.

IN-MARKET CAPABILITIES

Segments, Targeting, and Recognition

In order to power personalized digital dialog, it is important to have multiple Lego-like segmentation schemes that can be composed in varying combinations at different parts of the journey. Equally important to segment insightfulness is practical segment identification. How well can your company target prospects using its segments? How reliably can you recognize and classify new prospects and customers into segments? This topic is so fundamental that our next play, "Dynamic Segmentation" (Chapter 5.2), takes a closer look.

Best Move Decision Rules

Full-journey digital interaction uses dynamic segmentation and scoring signals to shift from "first deliver this, then deliver this" rules to "if this happens, then do that" rules. Modern tools use machine learning to recognize and categorize customer signals and then recommend next-best actions in real time, whether it's a follow-up ad, an in-product pop-up message, a call from customer service, or a link to helpful video.

Content Strategy and Customization

New segmentation flexibility is creating explosive growth demand for content variation. Because it's quicker for an "if this … then that" rule to ask for new content than it is for a creative team to deliver it, the time and cost of content creation is becoming the new bottleneck to full-journey digital engagement. As a result, content teams are making content modular, creating module variants, and pre-approving these content ingredients so that they can be recombined for customer personalization. They are beginning to use generative AI and machine learning to help automate and refine content creation. Like segmentation, this topic is so critical to journey-wide operations that we take a closer look, in "Agile Content" (Chapter 5.3).

Channel Mix and Media Buying

Best-practice digital interactions make use of robust media mix strategies. Omnichannel plans include paid, earned, and owned channel mix optimization. Traditionally, advertisers and marketers have used prior look-alike campaigns, plus sequential test and learn waves within a program, to evaluate how media mix should shift. Now AI/ML analytics are helping companies optimize channel mix within one go-to-market wave, adjusting budgets in real time on programmatic ad platforms based on audience responses or behavioral patterns.

In addition, platforms are providing new types of owned channels: Augmented or virtual reality experiences, single sign-on home pages, in-product pop-ups, link-outs to learning sites, digital community sites, and digital marketplaces are just a few examples.

Owned Touchpoint Experiences

Websites, mobile sites, and customer portals are the three owned touchpoints that companies typically utilize to enable digital dialogue. Platform-fed sites are the newest owned touchpoints to get right. They may take the form of mobile apps, computer interfaces, AR/VR environments, or interactive IOT product displays (a GPS car dashboard, for instance). It was important for Nike to present a consistent, unified digital experience for its customers across all journey stages. To achieve this, it consolidated more than 70 disparate digital properties owned by the brand under a single Nike.com banner. This resulted in a singular, optimized experience for full-journey engagement.[8]

Status Advancement and Nurture Loops

At various stages of the full-journey, your company will want to advance the status of your prospect or customer – into a deeper programmatic relationship, into a more valuable commercial relationship, or both. There are two challenges that arise from status advance moments. The first challenge arises when a status advance means a handoff from one journey team to another. The second challenge arises when either the customer or the company says "not ready" for the advance.

In the first case, excellence calls for coordinated decision-making between the "sending" team and the "receiving" team. What scoring system (lead scoring, churn risk scoring, etc.) is being used to deem the prospect or customer is ready to advance? What defines a seamless customer experience during the handoff? Is there shared or conflicting motivation and accountability for status advancement to occur?

In the second case – the "not ready to advance" case – a nurture loop is needed. A nurture loop is a mini-program that keeps the relationship between company and customer intact with forward momentum until the moment is right for next-level advancement. A lack of well-designed nurture loops hurts customer experience and lowers journey advancement rates.

Customer Choice Support

We are used to thinking of customer choice support at the purchase decision stage only, particularly e-commerce. But there are many other decision support moments throughout a customer journey (does the customer sign up for a loyalty program, take a learning course, or join a community forum?) that might also require decision support and customer fit tools. Best-practice companies support "just right for me" decision-making in each decision moment.

ENABLERS

Technology Architecture and Integration

Full-journey digital interactions require the right set of technology tools to execute in a consistent, data-driven way. As Fig. 5.1.3 shows, key tools fall into four categories: channel experience tools, customer information databases, analytics and programmatic tools, and content management tools.

- Engagement tools manage communication channels. They include marketing automation tools for content management and messaging across digital marketing channels plus new uses of the platform experience hub as a channel.

- Customer information databases[9] store data generated from engagement platforms and provide a place for analysis, visualization, and storage of that data. These include DMPs,

CRMs, CDPs, or any databases that store customer profiling and interaction data to help power next-best moves and personalization.

- Analytical middleware assesses signals brought back from engagement channels and then uses programmed responses, enriched through AI/ML, to determine next-best moves, both within the engagement channel that brought the customer signal and across other channels.

- Content management tools turn content strategy into digital execution. Key support elements include Content Management Systems (CMS) that allow multiple contributors to create, edit, and publish content on digital touchpoints. These in turn are supported by Digital Asset Management (DAMs).

The rise of platforms is triggering several new tech stack challenges.

- Companies need to deploy new engagement tools within the use journey. In-use journey tools are enabling new data creation and capture. They span customer success, learning, in-use product, community, and customer advocacy.

- AI-driven analytics tools need to produce account relationship propensities (negative churn propensity, positive expansion propensity) based on in-platform telemetry and user journey activity. These support customer lifetime value marketing for consumers and account-based marketing for business customers.

- AI (in particular machine learning and generative AI) are taking increasingly important roles within analytics and programmatic tools, as well as content management tools.

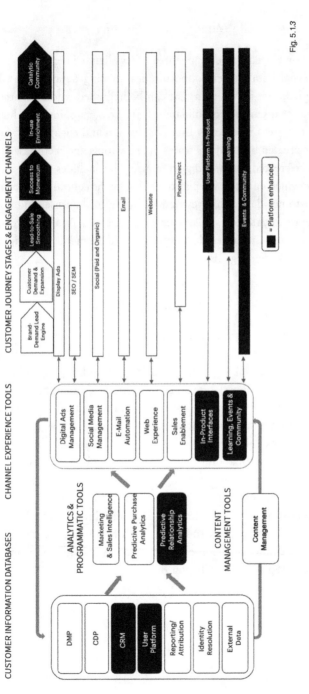

Full-Journey Tech Stack

Fig. 5.1.3

Data Management and Analytics

Data flows need to be mapped to every digital interaction. This will reveal improvement opportunities: missing data that can be appended, best moves data that can be upgraded, and data architectures that can be consolidated. Data flow mapping also highlights the areas where new user observation and engagement data can be created by analytics teams via new tools and methods.

Once created, data need governance. This includes processes to decide which data storage platforms will be the central repositories for customer data, what restrictions apply to data use, and who has rights to data access. Data also need analysis. Analytical teams should define strategies that link data and metadata to insights, KPIs, and business goals.

Organization and Skills

The full-journey engagement needed for platform alignment advantage requires brand, demand generation, sales, and customer success teams to collaboratively use their skills, techniques, and tools in new combinations. Companies are increasingly treating their go-to-market teams as one collaborative system (vs traditional silos). This forces a rethink in responsibilities so critical that we address it further in "Collaborative Go to Market" (Chapter 6.2).

To support collaborative go to market, platform companies are introducing an integrated operational support function called "RevOps," shorthand for Revenue Operations. If digital service innovation is also integrated, the idea broadens to become Growth Operations or GrowthOps. This new unit is so critical to future best-practice operations that we cover it in greater depth in "Growth Operations" (Chapter 6.3).

KEY QUESTIONS FOR CONSIDERATION

1. How effective is your organization across each of the capabilities needed for full-journey digital interactions? Which ones require the most improvement and investment?

2. Where and how can you advance toward excellence this year in Pre-Market Strategy and In-Market Capabilities? How can you extend advances over the next two to three years?

3. What technology, data, and investments will you need to support your excellence goals?

4. How suited is your operating model and organization to advance?

5. Which leaders and teams are on point for improvement? How will you measure their success?

5.2

DYNAMIC SEGMENTATION

Imagine your company uses six distinct segmentation schemes to capture differences in your customer base (e.g., one scheme for age, one scheme for geography, and one scheme for income, plus three more schemes). Assume that each of your six segmentation schemes has eight segments (eight age groups, eight geographies, eight income levels, etc.). How many unique segments could you build by creating unique combinations of your 6 × 8 schemes and values?

Let's go one step further. How would your number of unique combinations grow if you could cluster segment values within each scheme (e.g., cluster the two lowest ages, the three highest income levels, or six of the geographies) and treat each clustered value as a segment too?

If your head hurts, you may understand how Gotdfred Kirk Christiansen, former president of the Lego toy company, must have felt in 1958. Christiansen had come to the patent office over lunch to patent his family's Lego design. To his surprise, the Danish patent officer asked how many uniquely combined structures he could build by stacking just six of his family's proprietary Lego bricks in every way possible.[10] Each of the six bricks had eight studs (small cylindrical bumps) for combining, just like our segmentation math problem. Lego's official estimate to the patent officer's question was 102 million combinations.[11,12]

Today, go-to-market professionals need to build segmentation systems that treat customers as a "Segment of One." The reason is intuitive: if the customer receives just the right offer with just the right message at just the right time, response rates should increase.

Modern personalization approaches are built on a Lego-like segmentation model that breaks from the past. Old fashioned segmentation schemes were built for analog media. They packed many different variables into one single segmentation scheme, which usually meant categorizing audiences primarily by a clustered blend of factors like demographics (age, income, location) and purchase priorities (e.g. key benefit orientation). In our digital world, this rigid approach can be replaced. Now, multiple simpler segmentation schemes can be designed separately, then combined in nearly infinite ways to match the unique reality that is one customer.

This breakthrough is valuable all by itself. But there's another critical advance that a Lego-like segmentation provides, especially valuable for platforms. Combinations can be made and remade throughout the customer's full journey to create dynamic personalization, through time. For example, in early journey stages, segmentation might rely more on a combination of demographic and browsing behavior data. Further down the funnel, product interest dimensions become visible and critical. After purchase, usage and expansion dimensions rise to the top. Reflecting changes through journey time is critical to maximizing response rates, because true personalization is a product of both individual and journey context.

DYNAMIC SEGMENTATION IN ACTION

An online prescription fulfillment company illustrates the use of dynamic segmentation throughout the full choose-and-use journey. This prescription service created three segmentation families, each with topically similar types of segmentation schemes. One segmentation family focused on *personal* segmentation, another on *patient therapeutic and medication* segmentation, and a third on patient *vendor choices and economics.* Each family of segmentation schemes was constructed in a modular way so that different schemes could be mixed and matched – both in and across families – as the drivers of patient behaviors shifted.

Fig. 5.2.1 visualizes this segmentation. It represents personal segmentation schemes through white cubes, therapeutic and medication segmentation through gray cubes, and vendor economics segmentation through black cubes. At each customer journey stage, *a blended color block of cubes represents the combined segmentation schemes used at that moment in the journey.*

The figure shows that during initial journey stages (left of the infinity loop), patients were segmented on demographic and psychographic dimensions, therapeutic goals, and medication use. As they moved closer to purchase, the segmentation scheme adds commercial behavior data. Once the patient receives their medication, segmentation switches to new dimensions such as therapeutic needs, usage data, and community engagement to support personalized patient messaging.

Dynamic Segmentation Example: Prescription Fulfillment

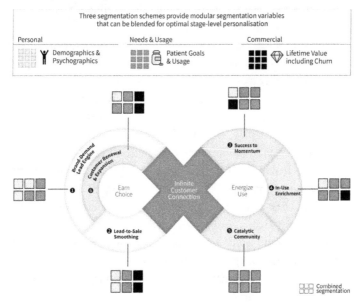

Fig. 5.2.1

The company applied dynamic segmentation to millions of members, deploying all three segmentation families across the entire journey. This modular segmentation system improved patient acquisition effectiveness, extended patient loyalty, and increased share of the patient's medicine cabinet. Use of the system generated new data relationships that, through analytics, generated new predictive, propensity-based scoring and refined segment value ranges.

DESIGNING YOUR DYNAMIC SEGMENTATION SYSTEM

The rest of this chapter provides starter tools for you to develop a dynamic segmentation system for your own platform. Fig. 5.2.2 provides a segmentation building-block framework. On the left hand axis are three generalized segmentation families: *Identity Segmentation*, *Need and Use Segmentation*, and *Commercial Behavior Segmentation*. In the text following the framework diagram, we provide examples of segmentation schemes used within these families. You can select dimensions you'll need plus add your own.

Remember your segmentation dimensions will shift as the customer travels across their full journey. We have put platform journey stages on the *x* axis. After developing your *y* axis, you'll want to identify where your schemes are applied at the cell level.

Also remember you'll need a segmentation system for every member of the platform's customer coalition. We have represented each coalition member as a "card" in the framework, on the *z* axis.

If you run this play, it will help you maximize relevance for your customer and maximize their response rates at every step of the journey. It will also help your go-to-market teams think about engaging the customer across the whole journey, rather than focusing only on their assigned stages. Finally, it will enable your go-to-market teams to work better together.

Here are examples of segmentation schemes by Segmentation Families. Given our platform focus, we provided Use journey and lifetime value segmentation examples. Your thinking should encompass every journey step.

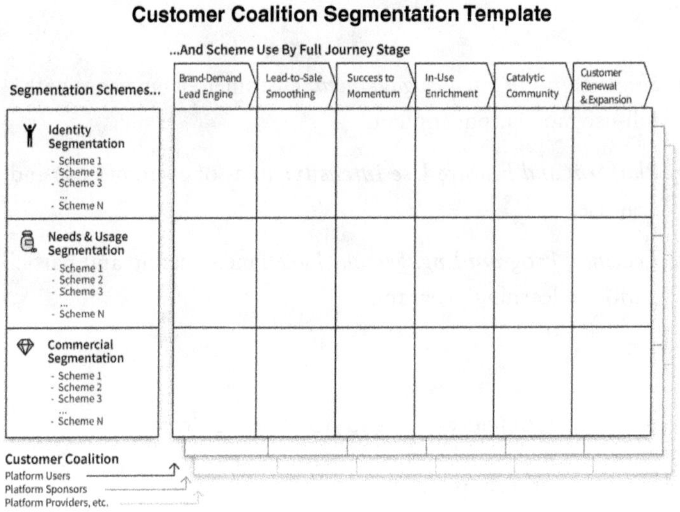

Customer Coalition Segmentation Template

...And Scheme Use By Full Journey Stage

Segmentation Schemes...	Brand-Demand Lead Engine	Lead-to-Sale Smoothing	Success to Momentum	In-Use Enrichment	Catalytic Community	Customer Renewal & Expansion
Identity Segmentation - Scheme 1 - Scheme 2 - Scheme 3 ... - Scheme N						
Needs & Usage Segmentation - Scheme 1 - Scheme 2 - Scheme 3 ... - Scheme N						
Commercial Segmentation - Scheme 1 - Scheme 2 - Scheme 3 ... - Scheme N						

Customer Coalition
Platform Users
Platform Sponsors
Platform Providers, etc.

Fig. 5.2.2

Identity Segmentation

- *Account/Household Type:* B2B business size and industry/B2C household type.

- *Role/Buyer Type:* B2B professional responsibilities/B2C household roles.

- *Psychographic Profile:* attitudinal characteristics of individual B2B and B2C buyers.

Needs and Usage Segmentation

Needs related:

- *Full-Use Scope:* the scope of a customer's ideal platform use, given their identity.

- *Current/Potential Use Cases:* the use cases that drive current and then ideal, platform scope.

- *Next Use Case(s) Path:* the next use case(s) that should be promoted to the customer.

Usage related:

- *Single Sign-On Page Engagement:* customer engagement with full-use momentum content.

- *Platform and Feature Use Intensity:* areas of customer use and non-use.

- *Learning Program Engagement Level:* membership and participation in learning program.

Commercial Behavior Segmentation

Economic relationship related:

- *Historical/Current Value:* annual value of actual platform use, prior year trends.

- *Full-Use Value:* economic value of ideal platform use expressed as annual and lifetime value.

- *Churn and expansion propensities:* predictive metric of likelihood to churn or expand.

Expansion purchase related:

- *Brand-Product Line Attitudes:* target's attitudes toward brand by product line segment.

- *Website/Mobile Site Behavior:* target's browsing focus area(s), duration, and engagement.

- *Lead Scoring:* criteria-based scoring (by marketing and sales) to inform lead status.

How could dynamic segmentation advance your platform's growth? Meet with customer-facing teams in your organization. Identify where dynamic segmentation could have the biggest impact.

KEY QUESTIONS FOR CONSIDERATION

For each customer persona that you select, do the following:

1. Describe the business objectives you will achieve by developing a dynamic journey-wide segmentation system (or by improving one you have).

2. Given your objectives, who should be involved in your initiative?

3. Document your current segmentation system using Fig. 5.2.1 as a template.

4. Consider how to improve the full-journey design of your segmentation system:

   a. What overlapping and conflicting segmentation schemes need rationalization?

   b. What Use journey and Renewal/Expansion dimensions might be missing?

5. Consider how to create a Lego-like series of building-block segmentation schemes:

   a. Which segmentation schemes should you disaggregate further?

   b. Which segmentation schemes should you aggregate?

6. How should your teams work differently after your new system is developed?

   a. Who will have new segment system access? How will they use their new access?

   b. Who will govern segment definitions, data integrity, and compliance monitoring?

5.3

AGILE CONTENT

As digital marketing and experiences have become the primary way that companies interact with customers, content creation has become the new bottleneck to achieving interactive customer impact. Creative content teams were historically staffed to prepare "one-to-many" messages for large audiences at the top of the pre-purchase funnel. To meet the needs of a platform business, content teams now need to support individualized customer dialog throughout the prospect's initial Choose journey, the new customer's Use journey, and the ever-expanding customer's Choose and Use cycles thereafter.

Content output is struggling to keep up. With the availability of full-journey engagement technology (see Chapter 5.1) and with the granularity of dynamic segmentation (see Chapter 5.2), the pressure is on for content teams to do more.

The answer is agile content, This means content whose requirements are informed by modular segmentation schemes, and whose response is efficiently produced in a similarly modular way. Modular content can then be assembled in different combinations to meet the personalization needs found in a customer engagement plan. Fig. 5.3.1 visually depicts how agile content (the lower row in black) needs to serve, through dynamic segmentation (the middle bridge) the messages and experiences needed to deliver personalized digital dialog (the upper row in gray).

The overall aim of agile content is to help go-to-market teams build strong personalized customer relationships within affordable cost

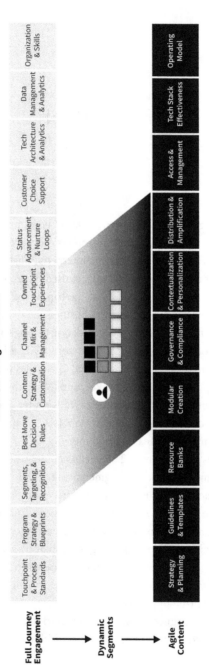

The Role of Agile Content

Full Journey Engagement

| Touchpoint & Process Standards | Program Strategy & Blueprints | Segments, Targeting, & Recognition | Best Move Decision Rules | Content Strategy & Customization | Channel Mix & Management | Owned Touchpoint Experiences | Status Advancement & Nurture Loops | Customer Choice Support | Tech Architecture & Analytics | Data Management & Analytics | Organization & Skills |

Dynamic Segments

Agile Content

| Strategy & Planning | Guidelines & Templates | Resource Banks | Modular Creation | Governance & Compliance | Contextualization & Personalization | Distribution & Amplification | Access & Management | Tech Stack Effectiveness | Operating Model |

Fig. 5.3.1

constraints. This is easier said than done. Content departments need to rethink their mission, processes, technology stacks, and skill sets. They need to ask new questions, such as "How do we reimagine content packages for a platform-enabled full digital journey?" and "How do we use generative intelligence to reshape content modules into unique combinations that serve customer needs?"

To do this, companies must become competent in 10 key areas of agile content excellence, outlined in Fig. 5.3.2. Improving any one driver is helpful; improving them together can be transformative.

Agile Content Excellence Drivers

Agile Content Capabilities & Definitions...   ...Across Full Journey Stages

Pre-Market Creation	Brand-Demand Lead Engine	Lead-to-Sale Smoothing	Success to Momentum	In-Use Enrichment	Catalytic Community	Customer Renewal & Expansion
1 Strategy & Planning	Evolve content strategy and planning for in-use journey, segmentation, and modularity to achieve goals					
2 Guidelines & Templates	Translate central strategy into business unit, regional and agency distributed guidelines and templates					
3 Resource Banks	Content teams populate Resource Banks with segment-aligned content for multiple stages and channels					
4 Modular Creation	Creative content teams, working to program briefs, create modular content linked to segment strategies					
5 Governance & Compliance	Compliance, business, and brand reviewers approve modular content for multiple permutations					
In-Market Application						
6 Contextualization & Personalization	Content deployed in test & learn manner for contextualization, personalization and optimization					
7 Distribution & Amplification	Content is distributed and amplified across an optimized mix of 1st and 3rd party channels					
Enablers						
8 Access & Management	Content is available across channels, stages and businesses, with insightful tagging at sustainable costs					
9 Tech Stack Effectiveness	Decoupled/open tools that fit full journey and stage-level objectives, with seamless integrations					
10 Operating Model	Structural effectiveness of content operating model and talent maturity against roles					

Fig. 5.3.2

The first five excellence drivers address Pre-Market Creation of content. The next two address In-Marketing Application of content. The final three drivers are infrastructure-level Enablers.

PRE-MARKET CREATION

Strategy and Planning

Increased content productivity begins with holistic planning. By understanding content needs for go-to-market program blueprints, including journey stages and dynamic segments, content teams can create strategies to use and reuse content in multiple contexts. For example, research for a product marketing whitepaper in the chosen stages can be further mined to create support content repurposed for the use journey.

Guidelines and Templates

Content strategists can embed segmentation dimensions into guidelines and templates for implementing a modular approach. Their goal is to empower geographic and business unit teams, as well as third-party agencies, to create content for modular segmentation in ways that align with personalized digital dialogue needs. Templates can define modular breakpoints that can feed into segmentation schemes, along with test-and-learn optimization.

Resource Banks

If content strategy and planning has identified opportunities for related use and reuse, then multiple teams need to access and draw from centralized content banks across business market and geographic boundaries. These banks, or digital asset management systems, can scale content production and reuse by providing features to categorize, store, and edit content, all while providing multiple teams a common space to collaborate and approve creative assets.

Modular Creation

One area where technology will make the biggest difference is in the affordable creation at scale of variable content linked to segmentation dimensions. The creative team breaks down content into smaller modules and then modifies that modular content in alignment with segmentation strategies. Module-level variants can then be combined with each other to create new overall content variations.

To illustrate, cold sore relief medicine maker Abreva created 119 video ad variations out of four base videos using YouTube's

Director Mix tool. Each ad variation was tailored to a particular interest or viewer characteristic and then was shown to them based on the type of video they were watching.[13] As a result, Abreva saw a 41% improvement in ad recall, and a 342% increase in search interest with its target audience.

Companies will increase efficiency further by using generative intelligence plus AI/ML, to first generate module variants and then combine different modules based on customer knowledge and prospect behavior or prior results with others. We are in the early days of AI creating endless variations from existing resource banks. Generative AI can produce net new content and variations with a few smart prompts. Generative AI tools, such as OpenAI's ChatGPT, enable the instant generation of copy to fill emails and ads. The automaker Lexus took this generative capability one step further by getting AI to generate the entire script for a video ad.[14] While it won't win any awards today, it's a glimpse into the future of how AI will power the creation of content at scale.

Governance and Compliance

Another benefit of modular content is how it speeds up approval. Almost 40% of companies still approve every piece of content through a compliance department or senior executive. This is especially true for highly regulated industries such as health care and finance. Modular approval enables recombined variations without undergoing a new review. A digital approval tool can streamline this process further by contacting all reviewers simultaneously and tracking their responses to overcome bottlenecks. Citizens Bank reduced its approval time from 14–16 days to 4–6 days, plus reduced legal workload by 70%, after installing such a tool.[15]

IN-MARKET APPLICATION

Contextualization and Personalization

You can apply your content resource bank to specific in-market scenarios in ways that matter most to your customer's context and persona. Many variables can be used to contextualize content such as time of day, geographic location, weather patterns, etc. Other variables reflect personal preferences – product line arrangement, messaging sequence, templates used, personas shown, use cases shown, article color – and the list goes on. Contextualization and personalization tools, such as Optimizely or Adobe Target, let content teams test and optimize all forms of variation through no-code, point-and-click interfaces in a relentless search for improved yields. These tools were first designed for pre-purchase digital engagement, but they will be equally powerful going forward in a platform setting when used to optimize post-purchase user engagement.

For example, a large international quick-service restaurant chain started to contextualize its drive-through and kiosk displays dynamically, based on the time of day or local weather conditions. This could mean recommendations for cold breakfast items – iced coffee, yogurt parfaits, and frozen smoothies – on a hot day in California or hot items – hot chocolate, soup, and hot sandwiches – for lunch on a cold day in Minnesota. The item recommendations showed up at the top of the drive-thru screen or kiosk with large, attractive food imagery and text, increasing the chances that customers would order these choices impulsively and in larger quantities. The restaurant was able to implement this type of content personalization without having to track anonymous user behavior, simply by utilizing data already available to them.[16]

Distribution and Amplification

Company-owned channels are often not the most powerful distribution systems for content. Teams can make their content work harder through distribution and amplification strategies. Content syndication tools can enable companies to efficiently multiply their content reach through third-party channels to achieve their impact goals. Objectives range from new acquisition and current customer growth to post-purchase participation in customer momentum, learning, or community programs.

ENABLERS

Access and Management

Cloud-based digital asset management (DAM) software helps power content productivity. These DAM platforms have more storage space than local file servers and can better accommodate content variations. They integrate with multiple content delivery systems (website Content Management Systems, social media, and email marketing technologies) making it easier to accurately track content use. The most innovative DAMs offer machine learning-powered content tagging and categorization, solving one of the biggest challenges of content duplication and repetition. Cloud-hosted DAMs increase the chance that content will be found and used by all those who need it, lowering content creation costs and approval delays.

Technology Stack Effectiveness

The content management tech stack has improved over time, evolving from rigidly coupled publishing (front-end) and management (back-end) systems into more open front-end and back-end systems, each capable of integrating with other systems to share data and link operations. Key technology stack components include content planning systems, collaborative content creation systems, content approval systems, content access and management systems, content delivery systems, content optimization, and corresponding analytics. The biggest tech stack challenge most companies face when becoming more agile is in opening up rigid and siloed systems to allow them to better handshake with other systems.

Operating Model

Content team leaders must consider whether their current operating model is suited to deploy agile content. To gain agility, companies are increasingly shifting from a centralized to a decentralized content production model, where a central team still owns the content strategy and creates standard processes for creation, customization, and storage. Different functions and teams (journey stage leaders, business units, and geographical teams) can then use these standards and guidelines to produce content on their own, while adhering to guidelines and directions from the central team. In this way, each team can create and deliver the custom content they need for digital dialogue far more quickly and with greater relevance to their respective audiences.

Agile content can be a driver of your differentiated interaction. It's on the cusp of technology transformation. Yet it will only benefit your platform if you put in place customer-centric segmentation and journey strategies to support it. Get clear on the role that agile content will play in your platform's success. Prepare to make it part of your investment agenda.

KEY QUESTIONS FOR CONSIDERATION

1. How effective are you across each of the capabilities needed for full-journey agile content? Which ones require the most improvement and investment?

2. Where and how can you advance toward excellence this year in Pre-Market Creation and In-Market Application? How can you extend advances over the next 2–3 years?

3. Which campaigns or initiatives can you use to pilot new content capabilities?

4. What Enabler technology and data investments will you need to support your goals?

5. How suited is your operating model and organization to advance?

6. Which leaders and teams are on point for improvement? How will they measure success?

7. How will you change your relationships with existing vendors or agencies to reflect your new content capabilities? What can be brought in-house versus outsourced?

5.4

ADAPTIVE INNOVATION

British platform company CityMapper, positioned as the "Ultimate Technology for Mobility in Cities," helps urban dwellers get from place to place across complex metro landscapes using paths that combine bus, car-hailing, subway, e-bike, scooter, and foot transportation.[17] CityMapper seamlessly integrates real-time traffic, pricing, sustainability, and service availability into packaged multi-mode options for getting from points A to B. Users swear by CityMapper, whether they are visiting the 119 cities it covers worldwide, exploring their own city beyond their neighborhood, or looking for an air-conditioned London subway route.[18]

In 2017, CityMapper's researchers noted several areas in London that received heavy requests for transportation options but lacked bus service connections. User demand patterns were consistent – therefore predictable. CityMapper's product and development teams launched pop-up bus routes to relieve these underserved areas, at targeted days and times. The service took off! A mapping app had become a bus company based on proprietary user route insights.[19]

CityMapper eventually dropped its bus service to focus on its core business, but it had made a powerful point. Platform providers can spot and act on innovation opportunities through in-market customer analytics. The insights that platform customer visibility provides during use can unlock *adaptive innovation* – that is, new products and services inspired by user insights. This chapter describes how you can turn Use journey customer visibility into an innovation asset that helps you outpace competitors and differentiate on customer interaction in evolving markets.

ADAPTIVE INNOVATION AT SCALE

Using your platform to drive innovation requires new strategic intent, the kind that produces new ways of working. The good news: best practices already exist. Adaptive innovation tactics first emerged among digital marketing and e-commerce teams in the late 1990s and early 2000s in a quest for better results. When smartphone apps took off around 2010, these innovative tactics evolved into "growth hacking" where resource-light, quickly deployed digital tactics helped quickly accelerate audience growth. Now, as platform companies reach for best practices, they are operationalizing adaptive innovation at scale. Three best-practice disciplines form the foundation: Research Ops, Platform Product Ops, and Development Ops. These disciplines empower platform teams to adapt to changing markets, technologies, and audience behaviors at pace – all without disrupting their ongoing delivery of core customer value.

By achieving adaptive innovation excellence across these disciplines, platform companies can compress their innovation cycle times to become a first-to-market innovator, as shown in Fig. 5.4.1. That can yield strategic advantage, as innovation leadership is one of the reasons customers choose one platform over another. It can also differentiate a company on customer experience, as innovation can be designed to incorporate customer interaction.

RESEARCH OPS

Best-practice Research Ops gathers insight signals in a timely, well-structured manner, synthesizes learnings to the point of implications, and tests solutions to inform downstream investment decisions.

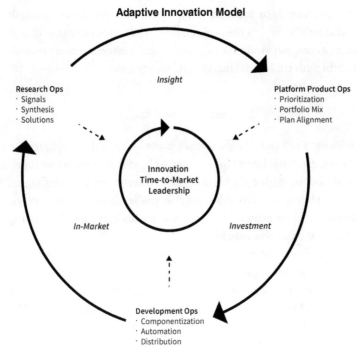

Adaptive Innovation Model

Research Ops
· Signals
· Synthesis
· Solutions

Insight

Platform Product Ops
· Prioritization
· Portfolio Mix
· Plan Alignment

**Innovation
Time-to-Market
Leadership**

In-Market

Investment

Development Ops
· Componentization
· Automation
· Distribution

Fig. 5.4.1

Signal Gathering

Every organization conducts customer research. Platform companies conduct it in new ways, through continuous in-market learning. The best platforms design hooks for signal capture into their code to provide insights – focused on customer and context – as a co-equal objective along with customer functionality and experience.

In-use platform data often shine light on customer intent and indicate if the customer is satisfied or frustrated. These data lead to valuable questions and hypotheses, but they rarely provide root-cause explanations or solutions to questions raised by product marketers or campaign owners. For that, structured customer inquiry is needed. Research Ops teams provide timely, well-administered ways to interact with research respondents – whether they are current, lapsed, or prospective customers. They address "research traffic jam" issues, as the proliferation of data from so many digital sources can put strain on role clarity and customer access coordination with traditional market research teams.

Synthesis to Implications

With data in hand, insight teams extract insights. This includes the "news" from the latest study as well as how that news fits with prior studies to enable the team to spot patterns and trends. Tagging to correlate qualitative ethnographic studies, quantitative surveys, streaming data signals, and external trends can provide a living library of navigable insights.

Research insights are only as valuable as their influence on decisions. Research Ops proactively socializes latest findings among go-to-market teams often in partnership with Platform Product Ops and Marketing to collaboratively extract implications. The same Platform Product Ops team can ideate innovation options in response to findings.

Innovation Test and Learn

After go-to-market stakeholders align on root-cause findings and innovation options, Research Ops can then test innovation options to inform downstream product investment decisions. They can do this with concept testing, pop-up surveys in targeted user journey moments, A/B prototype tests, and even physical trials. If structured with customer experience in mind, this test step can meaningfully involve the customer in sharing their voice with the company, Research Op's data-driven recommendations can then be turned into products and services that have high odds of success.

PLATFORM PRODUCT OPS

Best-practice Platform Product Ops helps translate Research Ops insights into priority investment options, consider those options as a portfolio of growth moves, and facilitate alignment around whether customer inputs are calling for shifts in business plans.

Prioritization of Options

Platform Product Ops translates Research Ops outputs into product investment requirements and potential returns, taking into account competitive context and financial performance trends. If the company innovates to provide what customers are asking for, could it generate ROI through increased adoption, share gains, price increases, or lower churn? Answers to these questions illustrate how real-time platform visibility expands a product leader's mindset from delivering functionality to actively managing business outcomes.

Portfolio Themes

With a view on investment options in hand, Platform Product Ops helps Platform Product Management leadership consider at a meta level how much to invest in one area of opportunity versus another. Platform companies use a mix of bets across markets, customer types, and time horizons to diversify their value drivers and growth. This requires classifying granular investments into broader investment themes and then bringing a perspective on what a balanced growth investment portfolio looks like.

Plan Alignment

Platform Product Ops helps compare the portfolio of investments that Platform Product Management is recommending against medium- and long-term platform goals captured in business plans. They can raise the question of whether in-market learnings should change product portfolio targets and adjust business goals. These discussions and adjustment communications may occur more frequently than annual planning cycles if customer behaviors change, government regulations adjust, or competitors launch new key features and business models.

DEVELOPMENT OPS

Given product innovation decisions, best-practice Development Ops empowers a company to respond quickly by coordinating componentization of tasks, automating standardized processes, and distributing innovations to give all teams access.

Task Componentization

DevOps addresses the fact that many different systems need to change in concert to deliver an end-to-end innovation experience to the customer. For example, a new customer payment step may involve databases, web servers, security applications, payment gateways, and fulfillment processes. In addition, application code updates need to be parallel processed for speed. DevOps addresses this challenge through componentized task design for teams, followed by the integration of cross-team outputs.

Process Automation

DevOps teams put in place processes and tools that standardize and automate the way their new code reaches the market. They transform bureaucratic stage gates and layers of oversight teams by setting tool and methods standards and then automating validation. They also standardize and automate the way that componentized production team outputs will merge with each other and merge into production systems, alleviating concerns about whether new code will work together with legacy systems.

Innovation Distribution

DevOps also facilitates the ability of each development team to access the others' innovations, aiming to speed adaptation with lower cost and effort. Through Application Programming Interfaces (APIs), every database update and newly coded routine can be accessed and used by other teams who need the same data and functionality. The most famous example of transformation was

Jeff Bezos' API Mandate of 2002. It stated that every development team had to do more than write their code well; they also had to write it in such a way that it was internally accessible. This shift was a key contributor to Amazon's innovation growth.

Through adaptive innovation tied to Use journey observation, your platform can become a hotbed of customer and product testing – one that rapidly identifies, experiments, and brings to market innovative offers. By engaging your customers as you find your best innovations, you'll differentiate your customer's journey experience due to the inspiring nature of your interactions.

KEY QUESTIONS FOR CONSIDERATION

1. How effective is your organization at adaptive innovation? How much does it help you arrive first-to-market with innovations?

2. What aspects of your Adaptive Innovation create an advantage? Which requires improvement?

3. Where and how can you advance toward excellence this year in Research, Platform Product, and Development Ops? How can you extend advances over the next 2–3 years?

4. What technology, data, or tool investments will you need to make to reach your improvement goals?

5. How can you interact with your customers during adaptive innovation in a way that it increases their engagement and differentiates your relationship?

6. How suited is your operating model and organization to advance?

7. Which leaders and teams are on point for improvement? How will they measure success?

Part 6

TRANSFORMATION PLAYS

The Interaction Plays we discussed in Part 5 focused on the alignment of technical changes. In Part 6, Transformation Plays, we focus on the alignment of something even more challenging: human change. These plays help you lead people-related transformation to realize your hopes for platform success.

Platforms transform companies on three levels:

- They change the way the entire enterprise operates by making it more interdependent.

- They integrate the go-to-market system, bringing every function into a collaborative state.

- They call for a new function many call Revenue Operations (we prefer Growth Operations).

We provide you a platform play for each of these three transformations.

Enterprise Body, Mind, and Soul (Play 6.1) shares a holistic and human-centric transformation framework that you can apply effectively to your unique platform transformation.

Collaborative Go to Market (Play 6.2) reimagines new go-to-market workflows in a platform era and challenges you to deliver them through cross-functional collaboration.

Growth Operations (*Play 6.3*) outlines new levels of integration that will be needed between your Marketing Ops, Sales Ops, Customer Success Ops, and Product Ops teams.

Our diagram of these plays, shown in Fig. 6.0.1, represents the two "bookends" of transformation, with the most expansive change being expressed through a Body–Mind–Soul visual and the most focused change being expressed through a GrowthOps-related image.

Transformation Plays

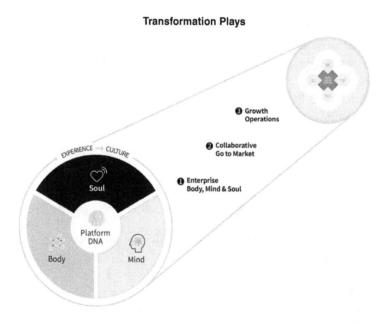

Fig. 6.0.1

6.1

ENTERPRISE BODY, MIND, AND SOUL

How might your company successfully transform to achieve a new level of platform-powered performance and value? For insights, let's look at one of the world's most transformational companies, through the lens of a transformational change model.

First, the company. When Walt Disney created Disneyland, he did more than fulfill his childhood dream.[1] He revolutionized the way that character-rich storytelling could be turned into customer experience and monetization. Mickey Mouse could enhance the consumer's experience of an amusement park, even enhance the experience of a sweatshirt, provided that the consumer had experienced Mickey in a memorable way through story (movie, TV, play, comic book, etc.).[2]

The Walt Disney Company began building on its founder's idea and never looked back.

As it grew in size and value, Disney became famous for three major ways that it innovated and transformed:

- Disney over decades built out *three global monetization vehicles* for its character-rich stories – media entertainment, physical experiences, and consumer products.[3]

- With its monetization system in place, Disney *acquired other character-rich story brands* who could become yet more valuable if Disney owned them (Pixar, Marvel, LucasFilms).

- Disney has made its story content more *globally inclusive*, both to increase relevance in non-US markets and to respond to criticism that its storytelling didn't reflect human diversity.

Given its rich history, it's not surprising that Disney is innovating and transforming again. In this chapter, we'll tell a fourth story. This time, Disney is *digitally enhancing customer experience* and *gaining individual Use journey visibility through platforms*. If successful, Disney's will establish *customer value growth synergies* that rival its story synergies.

DISNEY'S MULTI-PLATFORM TRANSFORMATION

Over the past 10 years, Disney has built platform approaches into all three of its major business units. Because every unit has distinct business models, each unit's platform approach is distinct.

- *Experiences*: Disney's first platform innovation was its theme park accessory, MagicBands. These are bracelets launched in 2013 that enrich, personalize, and simplify guest experiences while creating a data trail of guest movements and activities.[4] With their wireless band, guests can make a pirate's cannon explode, make spell-casting villains appear and recede, or receive photos of their petrified faces as they head down the Mount Everest ride (not to mention enter their hotel room or pay for a meal). In 2018, Disney further enriched its engagement approach via its smartphone app, Play Disney Park, enabling guests to take control of the Millennium Falcon or become role players in a Star Wars battle.

- *Entertainment*: Disney's thunderbolt platform move was the November 2019 launch of the Disney+ streaming media platform, integrating Disney, Pixar, and Marvel media properties. The Disney+ launch team set a goal of 500,000 Day 1 subscribers; they achieved 10 million. Shortly thereafter, Disney launched a new bundled subscription offer combining

Disney+, ESPN+, and Hulu. By spring of 2023, Disney's combined streaming media subscriber bases rivaled Netflix' subscriber base.[5]

- *Products*: Disney has long been committed to a digital "Choose journey"; it launched an online store in 1996 (now shopDisney.com) and in 2021 reduced its self-standing physical store footprint.[6] But Disney's "Use journey" entertainment and experience platforms have given the products group new opportunities. In late 2022, Disney launched a digital storefront embedded within Disney+ so that streaming subscribers can purchase products inspired by stories and characters. The new storefront includes subscriber-only early access and exclusive access products.[7]

Platforms make companies more interdependent by creating more synergy opportunities than ever before. That's true even for a world leader in synergies like Disney. Because each of Disney's three business divisions are now platform-progressive companies, with use journey data that they lacked 10 years ago, Disney is well positioned for new customer synergies. Guest activity history in parks can link to new personalized streaming media and product suggestions. Disney video game designers can craft adventures to be played both online at home and through augmented-reality park experiences. And business analysts reported in 2022 that Disney was exploring a Disney membership, much like Amazon Prime or Uber One, that would provide subscription paying members with discounts and special perks across the breadth of the Disney portfolio.[8]

HUMAN-CENTERED TRANSFORMATION

It's easy to briefly write about a Disney transformation, but in the real world, each change we describe has been a multiyear initiative that has affected the lives of thousands of Disney employees. Every transformation has affected the careers of and required collaborative leadership by real Disney executives. That's where transformations get challenging, whether by Disney or your company. What each one has in common is that they require human change.

We believe that a *Human-centered Transformation* (HCT) model is effective in anticipating and addressing the challenge of transformational change. Its name celebrates the truth that businesses don't change; people change. People create new strategies, build new capabilities, and act in new ways. And when these people change, they change the business. While this model was not developed explicitly for platforms, we've found it applies well.

The human-centered model treats the organization as an exo-system that reflects the dynamics of the many individuals who comprise it. Every organization has DNA, a Body, a Mind, and a Soul. Fig. 6.1.1 illustrates this model. We explore its elements in detail below and illustrate them through Disney's multi-platform transformation.

HCT Model

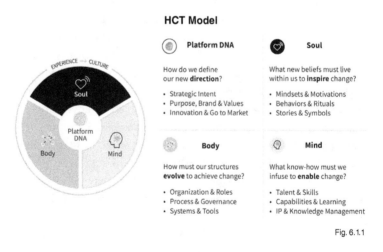

	Platform DNA		Soul
	How do we define our new **direction**?		What new beliefs must live within us to **inspire** change?
	• Strategic Intent • Purpose, Brand & Values • Innovation & Go to Market		• Mindsets & Motivations • Behaviors & Rituals • Stories & Symbols
	Body		**Mind**
	How must our structures **evolve** to achieve change?		What know-how must we infuse to **enable** change?
	• Organization & Roles • Process & Governance • Systems & Tools		• Talent & Skills • Capabilities & Learning • IP & Knowledge Management

Fig. 6.1.1

DNA

The DNA is the instruction set reflecting the strategic direction that the company is following. A DNA transformation draws from a new strategy to provide a modified instruction set.

Disney's new platform DNA carries three strategic priorities. First, enhance the consumer's Disney experience digitally through the latest digital platform and experience technologies. Second, digitally capture the customer's Use journey experience as platform data. Third, integrate all customer knowledge from all customer experiences to determine what to offer the customer next, with the goals of delivering improved customer value, deepening customer relationships, and expanding Disney shareholder value.

Body

The body makes work happen. Body evolution means changing how directive structures should change to achieve new work. Key body elements include the following:

- *Organization and Roles*: how an organization is structured to best create value through work, including formal reporting relationships and role definitions.

- *Process and Governance*: workflows and decision rights, plus KPI/goal setting and oversight of the achievement (or miss) of KPIs/goals.

- *Systems and Tools*: data and technologies plus user interfaces and outputs that are required to carry out digital work.

Disney had a very notable transformation of "Body" through changes it made to incubate and then integrate Disney+ streaming services. Disney+ went through three different Body configurations from pre-launch to post-launch.

- From 2016 to 2022, in order to jumpstart its *Systems and Tools*, Disney progressively acquired BAMTech, a Brooklyn company that provided streaming media services for professional sports leagues.[9] BAMTech gave Disney one of the best content delivery capabilities in the market. Disney+ adopted an incubator-like *Organization and Roles* plus *Process and Governance* in BAMTech's New York City offices, far away and culturally distinct from Disney's Burbank corporate culture.[10] Disney+ was given the kind of *KPIs* associated with a startup

growth company – subscriber-base size and new content creation – rather than profitability. It was a radical departure from
Disney's typical margin and cash flow goals.[11]

- In late 2020, once Disney+ was up and running, Disney's CEO
  Bob Chapek changed the Organization and Roles of the entertainment division to incorporate Disney+. He gave the streaming
  group meaningful influence versus creative studio leaders who
  had for years distributed through theaters. Streaming leadership
  began actively lobbying for control over studio marketing spend,
  causing numerous key creative leaders to threaten to leave[12]
  In addition, concerned investors pressured Disney to focus on
  margins versus high streaming growth.

To resolve tensions, Disney brought back its former CEO. The
day after Bob Iger returned to the CEO role, he announced yet
another *Organization and Roles* decision, with corresponding new
Process and Governance. Iger's new approach would more sensi-
tively balance the influence of the studio creatives and the streaming distribution team in optimizing business decisions.[13] Iger also
signaled Disney's determination to reverse deep Disney+ losses.
Soon after, he took action by reducing content development budgets, planning for ad-revenue supplement models, and raising subscription price hikes with KPIs and goals centered on streaming
profitability by 2024.[14]

Mind

The Mind enables the organization through applied knowledge.
Transforming an organization's Mind means enabling new capabilities. Key Mind elements include the following:

- *Talent and Skills*: the inherent talents and learned skills of the
  company's employees, including recruitment of external talent
  with new skill sets.

- *Learning and Development*: extension of the talent base that
  the company already has through new learning and development programs

- *Intellectual Property and Knowledge Management*: development of a company's patented and unpatented *intellectual capital*, including on-demand information formatted in ways that
  increase employee skills at the point of use.

Disney took several steps to enable Mind-related transformations around Disney+. It selected a streaming unit leader
who had in-depth knowledge of capabilities and content Disney
had acquired for streaming because he played a key role in the
deals (BAMTech, 21st-Century Fox Film, and TV studio cata-
logs).[15] In addition, Disney's acquisition of BAMTech brought
in new talent and skills, including technical streaming and data
science teams who had successfully built streaming platforms
for others, plus performance marketing and customer service
teams who knew how to acquire, retain, and grow subscriber
relationships.

Soul

Core to an organization's Soul are the beliefs that inspire employees to believe in the promise of transformation. Key elements of
Soul include the following:

- *Mindsets and Motivations:* attitudinal traits should be intrinsic
  to the individuals that a company hires – they are the reason a
  firm stresses culture when recruiting. Motivations by contrast
  are shaped by the company's stated priorities and incentives.

- *Behaviors and Rituals:* daily ways of working demonstrate
  a company's collective belief. If they are visibly modeled by
  leadership and cascaded across the firm, they can become a
  sustainable source of organizational belief.

- *Stories and Symbols:* powerful icons reinforce what an organization cares about most. Refreshed stories paired with consistent symbols provide ongoing reminders of shared belief.

Ironically, while much had been made of Disney's successful
launch of Disney+ and the meteoric rise of its subscriber base,

when CEO Iger returned from retirement, he reinforced Disney's long-standing soul. Iger reiterated the company's commitment to story, content, and profit margin management as evergreen value drivers. Iger acknowledged in company wide communications that Disney had just transformed a key element of his business through Disney+. Yet he also made it clear that its streaming platform was now a scale part of its overall media monetization pillar, and would be managed for results as it matured.

YOUR PLATFORM TRANSFORMATION

CEO Bob Iger recently said of Disney, "our ability to endure is going to be solely tied to our ability to transform ourselves."[16] Disney's incorporation of platforms over a 10-year period, including its most recent transformation through Disney+, gives Iger's words real substance.[17,18]

Do you need HCT to succeed in your next evolution as a platform business?

KEY QUESTIONS FOR CONSIDERATION

Pick one or more platform plays that you plan to implement. Focus on those that require significant organizational and cultural transformation to achieve. Use Fig. 6.1.2 template below to guide your answers.

1. What is your *current state* (pre-transformation) DNA, Body, Mind, and Soul? Use the elements from the HCT Model to define key aspects.

2. What is the ideal *future state* (post-transformation) of each of these same elements?

HCT Template

		Current State	→ Transitional State →	Future State
Platform DNA	Strategic Intent			
	Purpose, Brand & Values			
	Innovation & Go to Market			
Body	Organization & Roles			
	Processes & Governance			
	Systems & Tools			
Mind	Talent & Skills			
	IP & Knowlege Management			
	Systems & Tools			
Soul	Mindsets & Motivations			
	Behaviors & Rituals			
	Stories & Symbols			

Fig. 6.1.2

3. Looking at the size of the gap between your current and future states, should there be a *transitional* state for some, or all, of these elements that enables a first round of DNA, Body, Mind, and Soul change?

4. Consider your investment and return on transformation at the element level, plus consider interdependencies of change. Prioritize your investments accordingly.

6.2

COLLABORATIVE GO TO MARKET

The way that most companies divide go-to-market responsibilities is a reflection of staggered technology development from the past, rather than a reflection of their future needs. The go-to-market functions we know today grew up in silos because they launched in different decades (or centuries), each at a point where the emergence of a new technology enabled them to become "the next big thing." Consequently, at their moment of birth, they were not tucked into an existing go-to-market function; they instead fragmented the go-to-market system as they enriched it by adding another valuable function.

Platforms are different. Rather than adding to fragmentation, platforms are a force for uniting go-to-market silos into one integrated system. There are two key platform-related factors pushing in this direction. First, platforms contribute to a 100% digital customer journey. That is now a well-established and growing customer path, creating a homogeneous go-to-market medium and language. Second, the use of platform data to grow value *to* users while growing the value *of* users is a compelling idea that requires full-journey go-to-market collaboration to achieve.

This chapter looks to the future to articulate where we believe platforms are taking modern go-to-market systems. It asks whether your platform company is evolving in this direction at the right pace or hanging on too long to the past. Our goal in raising these uncomfortable questions is to help you be among the first to adopt a higher performing go-to-market system – to help you achieve a key alignment advantage.

A BRIEF HISTORY OF GO-TO-MARKET EVOLUTION

Before we turn to the future ... here's a quick summary of historical go-to-market evolution. We hope it illustrates how technology helped create an amazing but fragmented go-to-market system:

- Distributors emerged first, long ago. They needed basic transportation technology, plus safe-to-travel roads and sea lanes, to bring goods to customers and bring other goods back.

- Company-employed sales reps emerged with the Industrial Revolution in the 1800s. Rail and auto infrastructure of the mid-1800s and early 1900s helped modern sales forces to scale.

- Broadcast marketers came soon after, from the late 1800s through the mid-1900s. They used new communications technology – mass print, radio, and TV – to share pre-sales messages. Retailers built chains to distribute mass advertised goods; modern branding was born.

- Customer service emerged in the second half of the 1900s on the backs of widespread telephone availability, emergence of call center routing, and a faster postal service.

- Customer experience teams sprung up to address the pain points customer service uncovered.

- Direct marketing grew in the second half of the 1900s enabled by corporate computing, databases, analytics software, and remote sales centers.

- Digital marketing and e-commerce grew with the Internet in the 1990s and early 2000s.

- Digital sales prospecting and CRM grew with the Internet in the 1990s and early 2000s.

- Customer growth marketing (under various names), customer success, and digital communities grew from 2005 onward based on cloud computing and smartphone adoption.

- AI/ML, Extended Reality, and Generative AI capabilities grew with growing cloud computing power and software innovations during the 2010s and 2020s.

- Virtual conference and trade show marketing scaled with the COVID pandemic.

REIMAGINING GO-TO-MARKET AS A SINGLE SYSTEM

As the above history implies, go-to-market roles are becoming crowded and overlapping, particularly as everyone digitally transforms. In response, CEOs of platform companies are increasingly putting a dedicated executive in charge of the go-to-market system and its teams. That executive's title may vary; they might be a chief revenue officer, chief growth officer, chief customer officer, EVP of go to market, COO of go to market, or corporate COO. That executive is charged with achieving clearer and more agile go-to-market team integration for greater efficiency and effectiveness. This occurs most frequently in platform companies because of the interdependence and coordination needs that the platform introduces.

These executives often meet resistance to integration because orthodoxy defines go-to-market roles by functions that "own" stages in the customer journey. Marketing owns the top of the purchase funnel, sales owns the bottom, customer success owns post-purchase, and product management owns in-use experience. This thinking is becoming obsolete in the face of new platform requirements and opportunities. How should senior executives rethink go-to-market roles for better outcomes? How would you define a new division of responsibilities if you were in charge of the whiteboard?

A COLLABORATIVE WORKFLOW-COMPETENCY MODEL

We propose a new go-to-market model for the platform company. We believe that over time this could become a best-fit model for most, if not all, companies. Fig. 6.2.1 visualizes the relationships in the Workflow-Competency Model. The axes on this diagram are generic to illustrate the elements. We'll show a populated example later in this chapter.

The model treats three elements as platform go-to-market building blocks:

- Workflows (delivered via functional competencies) – shown as columns.

- Functional competencies (available for workflow duties) – shown as rows.

- Functions (the stewards of functional competencies) – shown as multi-row brackets.

- A dot in a workflow-competence cell represents the traditional role of a competency.

- An arrow in a workflow-competence cell indicates that a competency could add value to a new workflow in the future.

General Workflow-Competency Model

Traditional Role / Platform Role Extension	Competencies	Platform Customer Journey			
		Workflow 1	Workflow 2	Workflow 3	Workflow 4
Function 1	Competency 1	↑	●		
	Competency 2		↑	↑	●
Function 2	Competency 3	●	●		
	Competency 4	↑	↑	↑	●

● Traditional Role
↑ Platform Role Extension

Fig. 6.2.1

Here are tenets of the Workflow–Competency model:

- Go-to-market workflows (not organizational functions) are the most helpful way to define the stages of the platform customer journey. A little over a handful of workflows should describe the entire journey. We favor the six workflows described in the platform playbook's Demand Plays (Part 3): Brand–Demand Lead Engine, Lead-to-Sale Smoothing, Success to Momentum, In-Use Enrichment, Catalytic Community, and Customer Renewal and Expansion. We'll further add two non-stage workflows: Channel Partnership (not addressed in this book due to space limitations) and Adaptive Innovation (Play 5.4).

- Each workflow has a clear owner and goals, clear processes and borders, and clear handoffs to the next workflow. Platform success relies on each workflow operating at best-practice levels. Given the clarity of written workflows, there should be no overlaps or gaps between workflows in covering the full journey, as there are in today's function-defined go-to-market system.

- Each workflow's performance is powered by multiple functional competency teams, working in close collaboration. When we say "functional competency" in the context of this model, we mean a set of activities united by a specific competence such as branding, demand generation, content creation, data analysis, customer support, customer success management, learning, etc. Every workflow has more than one competence, and those competencies come from more than one function. The success of each workflow will be determined by the soundness of its workflow strategy, the quality of its functional competency teams, and the quality of collaboration between those teams.

- Traditional go-to-market functions (Marketing, Sales, Customer Success, etc.) are the stewards of the functional competencies that contribute to each workflow's success. A function can contribute the same competency to the success of multiple workflows. The function's performance is judged by the quality of its competency contributions to every workflow where it has responsibility to contribute.

- The leader of a function (e.g., Chief Marketing Officer) might or might not also be the leader of a workflow (e.g., brand–demand lead engine, catalytic community). Non-function leaders could also serve in the workflow leader role. Most companies will have a mix of dedicated workflow leaders and dual workflow/function leaders.

- Management objectives and key performance indicators will differ between workflow leadership and functional leadership. If the function leader also serves as workflow leader, they will have two or more "multi-hat" responsibilities.

ILLUSTRATIVE WORKFLOW-COMPETENCE EXAMPLES

To be more concrete, let's consider two workflow teams, comprised of the functional experts from which each workflow might draw (excluding established shared services teams):

- The Catalytic Community workflow team may draw on the competencies of:

  o Brand to position the community.

  o Demand generation to recruit community members, attract them to desired activities, and support brand advocacy/community amplification initiatives.

  o Customer success to link community issues raised to success program design.

  o Event management for community and group experience design.

  o Learning and Third-Party Marketplace programs for community member development.

  o Product Management for advisory committee support.

  o E-commerce for community commerce.

  o Social Media for community conversation presence.

  o Analytics for community growth, churn, and shaping insights.

- The Customer Renewal & Expansion workflow team may utilize the competencies of:

  o Analytics for best opportunity, best strategy, and best execution tactics.

  o Customer Success and Account Sales for human intelligence.

  o Brand for cross selling support where the company has less equity.

  o Demand generation for experience blueprint and custom messaging.

  o Analytics for current customer (vs new customer) lead scoring.

  o Product Marketing for marketing/sales assets including demos.

o Inside sales for renewals and expansion qualification.

o External sales for coordinated sales play design and execution.

o Customer Success for technical migration and onboarding support.

Fig. 6.2.2 illustrates these selected combinations.

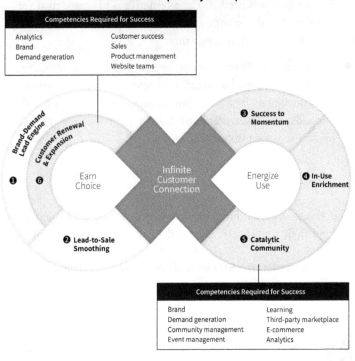

Workflow-Competency Examples

Fig. 6.2.2

ADVANTAGES OF THE WORKFLOW-COMPETENCY SYSTEM

The workflow-competency approach delivers three advantages to companies who adopt:

• *Improved Clarity and Reduced Rivalry.* Documented work-flows will explain full-journey go to market without overlap or gaps, as is the case in today's go-to-market system. Document-ed competencies will explain functional ownership without confusion. As a result, there will be improved clarity and less rivalry. There may still be debates about how much should be in a workflow or a function, but those debates should be more transparent than before.

- *Higher Quality at Lower Cost.* Each competency will have one home only and can be extended nimbly to anywhere in the journey that it is needed. The alternative is to create rival versions of the same competency in traditional functions, leading to excess cost and lower quality.

- *Greater Agility.* When a proactive initiative or a competitive response is required a mature competency can be requested and "imported" by a workflow team. Greater flexibility will also exist year over year at planning time. Traditional go to market is not set up for this agility.

NEW FUNCTION AND COMPETENCY OPPORTUNITIES

Fig. 6.2.3 suggests how key competencies might be extended beyond their traditional functional roles. This time we've filled in

Extending the Relevance of Functional Competencies

● Traditional Role
↑ Platform Role Extension

Competencies	Earn Customer Choice			Energize Customer Use			Channel	Innovation
	Brand-Demand Lead Engine	Customer Renewal & Expansion	Lead-to-Sale Smoothing	Success to Momentum	In-Use Enrichment	Catalytic Community	Channel Partner Preference	Adaptive Innovation
Marketing								
Brand	●	↑		↑		↑		
Content	●	●	●	↑	↑	↑	●	
Demand Gen	●	●	↑	↑	↑	↑	↑	↑
Social Media	●	●	●			↑		
Sales								
Internal Sales / Chat	↑	↑	●		↑		●	
External Sales		●	●	↑			●	
Service								
Success Management		↑		●	↑	↑		
Customer Support				●	↑			
Other								
Learning				●	↑	↑	●	
Product Management			↑	↑	●	●		↑
Analytics	↑	↑	↑	↑	↑	↑	↑	↑

Fig. 6.2.3

the matrix. The platform journey stages are across the x-axis to represent workflows. Common functional competencies and their function stewards are shown on the y-axis. Traditional competency roles are represented by dots; potential platform role extensions by arrows. The volume of arrows we're showing is likely greater than you'll need. We are focused on possibilities and potential needs; you can decide what competency role extensions into what workflows make the sense for your firm.

Each functional competence can view their row on this chart as a potential roadmap for their extended value to the company in a platform environment. To illustrate, here is what two functional competencies might see, followed by the workflows where the competence could contribute:

- Brand can contribute to Brand-Demand Lead Engine, Success to Momentum, Catalytic Community, and Customer Renewal & Expansion.

- Customer Success can contribute to Lead to Sales Smoothing, Success to Momentum, In Use Enrichment, and Catalytic Community.

MOTIVATING ALIGNMENT AND CHANGE

If you adopt a workflow-competence system, you'll need to address several structural enablers. First, gain executive alignment. Next, create a coordinating group (see GrowthOps, Chapter 6.3, for ideas). Third, set up common incentives. Finally, adopt metrics that can measure the positive impact of your new system.

Through our research, we're starting to see signs that traditional siloed operations aren't holding anymore. Increasingly, go-to-market teams are collaborating with each other in more conscious, organized ways. In a 2023 Prophet research study on digital transformation,[19] we found the majority (58%) of sales, service, and marketing departments were sharing customer satisfaction and revenue targets. Don't underestimate a commonly felt need for change.

KEY QUESTIONS FOR CONSIDERATION

1. How are go-to-market responsibilities assigned within your company today?

2. How would your firm benefit by adopting the workflow-competency system described in this chapter? What challenges might you face?

3. What is your company's best configuration of workflows and competency extensions?

4. What team of executives should you convene to discuss?

6.3

GROWTH OPERATIONS

Imagine a dystopian science-fiction movie in which society is debating how best to raise children. On the traditional side of the debate are parents who advocate parenting as we know it today, raising a child from birth until they leave home. On the disruptive side of the debate are experts arguing that four different types of specialist parents should raise each child, taking turns and making handoffs from ages 0–2, 3–6, 7–12, and 13–18.

The disruptive specialists tout the benefits of having child psychology experts do the parenting at each development stage. They'll know exactly what to do, unlike the amateurs in the traditional model. The traditional parents stress the benefits of long-term accumulated knowledge of each unique child. Traditionalists also argue that the child will experience greater stability and bonding by staying with one set of parents. So much context would be lost in the expert system, especially during those handoffs.

These same arguments lie at the heart of modern business debates about a new function called *Revenue Operations* or *RevOps* for short. Using our parenting analogy, in the current state of business, the "child" (the customer relationship) is being raised by four stage-level "parenting specialists" (Marketing Operations, Sales Operations, Customer Success Operations, and Digital Product Operations) who hand off the customer relationship to each other once it leaves their zone of specialized expertise. Nobody on the go-to-market team has holistic knowledge of the "child" (customer) across all contexts, and a lot gets lost in the handoffs. The new Revenue Operations function plays the role of the traditional parent who maintains a constant relationship with the customer throughout their lifecycle, while enabling specialists to solve specific challenges at each stage of the journey.

RevOps is the seamless integration of all go-to-market operations support across the full customer journey. It enables Marketing Ops, Sales Ops, Channel Partner Ops, Customer Success Ops, and Product Ops teams to act as one unit – and perhaps, someday, to become one unit. The idea is taking off in a big way. According to LinkedIn, the Director of RevOps is one of the three fastest-growing job roles in business in 2023.[20]

It's no coincidence that the rise of RevOps is occurring at the same time as the rise of platforms. Platforms inherently call for and incentivize a RevOps approach. Platforms empower your company to get to know your customers *through time*, but your stage-specific operation teams know them *one stage at a time*. Someone in the company should glean longitudinal insights, with an eye toward untapped improvement opportunities. The RevOps team is that someone. When AI and Machine Learning are added, predictive correlations between customer experience or engagement at one part of the journey and customer relational and economic outcomes at another part of the journey become visible, often for the first time. The result is better customer insight (through longitudinal value added) for better relational and commercial growth.

This vision for customer insight extends even further. You can add Innovation Operations insights to expand Revenue Operations into Growth Operations (GrowthOps). That's our recommended scope and team label. GrowthOps gleans opportunity insights and orchestrates action to help your company maximize its engagement growth drivers *and* innovation growth drivers, illustrated by Fig. 6.3.1. There's no reason to compartmentalize growth that occurs from one versus the other. The two produce synergistic insights – innovation creates new reasons for journey interaction, and better journey interaction helps innovation achieve traction. Don't go halfway in benefiting from platform customer insights – get all of the benefits now within your reach.

GrowthOps: New Opportunity Insights and Action Orchestration

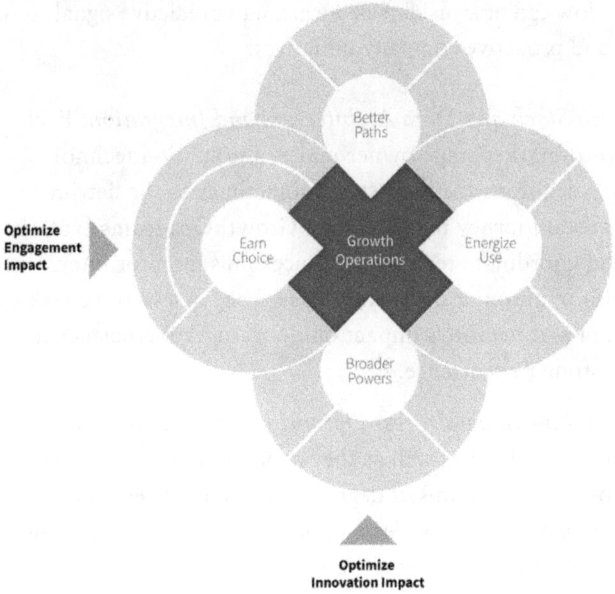

Better
Paths

Optimize
Engagement
Impact

Earn
Choice

Growth
Operations

Energize
Use

Broader
Powers

Optimize
Innovation Impact

Fig. 6.3.1

GROWTHOPs ACTIVITY SCOPE OPTIONS

A GrowthOps function can bring together siloed operations teams
in multiple ways. Here are the most common jobs assigned to
GrowthOps teams. Consider what level of GrowthOps activities
make sense for your company.

- *Longitudinal Customer Opportunity Insights*: GrowthOps
  teams produce journey-wide insights by analyzing three types
  of input data correlated to outcomes data. This analysis is run
  at the customer coalition type, persona, and segment level as
  needed),

  o Input: customer signals and company responses
  o Input: company stimuli and customer responses
  o Input: customer-to-customer activities and responses
  o Outcomes: customer relational and commercial
    advancement

Which patterns produce desired outcomes? Which result in failure? How can new insights be turned into predictive signal recognition and proactive company initiatives?

- *Tech Stack and Data Architecture and Integration*: Each go-to-market stage owner makes automation technology decisions for their stage, sometimes to the detriment of total journey management. GrowthOps teams evaluate and coordinate tech stack choices plus monitor integration of automation technologies. They assess and speak to data architecture's impact on go-to-market efficiency and customer experience.

- *Multifunctional Process Optimization*: When process flows aren't working as well as they could be across two or more go-to-market teams, it degrades customer experience and company outcomes. GrowthOps teams diagnose multifunctional process pain points and missed opportunities, identify their root causes, define better practices, support pilot improvements, drive learning alignment, and train employees on new ways of working.

- *Growth Action Backlog and Orchestration*: GrowthOps teams create growth action backlogs based on the opportunity insights they uncover. This often involves fixing problem areas – places where leads are disappearing, where sales are not converting, where features aren't being adopted, or where churn is unusually high. It may involve upside opportunities as well. GrowthOps team members bring additional value if they can prioritize opportunities by economic impact and orchestrate go-to-market team member responses.

- *Growth Strategy Contributions*: GrowthOps teams are not growth strategy teams – operations are in their name for a reason. That said, some of their insights might lead to strategic initiatives – if, for example, they find an underserved persona in the customer coalition.

GROWTH OPs AUTHORITY OPTIONS

For the next several years, every company's level of go-to-market integration will vary. So will the maturity and authority of every company's GrowthOps team. Fig. 6.3.2 provides a framework that you can use to assess where you currently stand and to determine your best-fit operating model.

Increasing levels of go-to-market integration, expressed generally as GrowthOps team Jobs to be Done, are displayed on the *x*-axis. On the *y*-axis, five operating models are arrayed in increasing formality of organization, seniority of leadership role, and governance authority. Here are profiles of each operating model:

- *Ad Hoc Best Efforts*: There is no formal mechanism for go-to-market coordination, but there is a new mindfulness among leaders about the need to coordinate. They make decentralized best efforts. This will become unsustainable over time as competitors use greater operations integration to improve, but it might fill a stopgap need. Jobs to be done should be focused.

- *Collaboration Council*: Go-to-market leaders establish a Collaboration Council. The council appoints a leader to form task forces that work for the council on a use-case basis, to solve specific pain points and address specific opportunities and then monitor or disband.

GrowthOps: Best-Fit Operating Model Framework

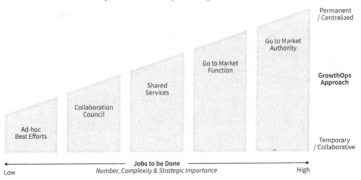

Fig. 6.3.2

- *Shared Service*: The company formalizes GrowthOps as a permanent shared service. The GrowthOps team leader reports to and is guided by the Collaboration Council leader or reports to an executive responsible for go-to-market integration (Chief Growth, Revenue, or Customer Officer; EVP or COO of Go-to-Market; corporate COO).

- *Go-to-Market Function*: The company formalizes GrowthOps as a permanent go-to-market function. The GrowthOps leader is made a lateral peer of other go-to-market leaders, proposing initiatives and budgets the same way they do. All leaders report directly to an executive responsible for go-to-market integration.

- *Go-to-Market Authority*: The company formalizes GrowthOps as a permanent function that provides authoritative go-to-market leadership under an executive responsible for go-to-market integration. GrowthOps acts as a lateral peer of other go-to-market leaders, proposing initiatives and budgets the same way they do, and reviews go-to-market leaders' plans for coherence, evaluating resource allocation across all go-to-market functions to maximize return on investment. The GrowthOps leader is one of the most powerful on the go-to-market team.

There are two last points to call out as you consider what form of GrowthOps is right for you. First, the creation of a GrowthOps team may not require a new headcount. You might be able to build it through the centralization of existing operations support teams. Second, the more you choose a collaborative go-to-market system like the one we described in Chapter 6.2, the more value your GrowthOps team will add through orchestration.

KEY QUESTIONS FOR CONSIDERATION

1. How could a GrowthOps team create value for your company?

2. What is the right scope of activities for your GrowthOps team?

3. What GrowthOps operating model best fits your company's current and future needs?

4. In Fig. 6.3.3, we show the Human-Centered Transformation model introduced in Chapter 6.1. What Body, Mind, and Soul elements need to transform for your GrowthOps to succeed?

Human-Centric Design: GrowthOps Transformation Elements

		Current State →	Transitional State →	Future State
Platform DNA	Strategic Intent			
	Purpose, Brand & Values			
	Innovation & Go to Market			
Body	Organization & Roles			
	Processes & Governance			
	Systems & Tools			
Mind	Talent & Skills			
	IP & Knowlege Management			
	Systems & Tools			
Soul	Mindsets & Motivations			
	Behaviors & Rituals			
	Stories & Symbols			

Fig. 6.3.3

5. If needed, develop a GrowthOps plan based on your answers to Questions 1 through 4, including business case, vision for change, milestone roadmap, and tactics for transition.

LEADING A
PLATFORM BUSINESS

Part 7

CULTURE SHIFTS

Congratulations! You've just immersed in 24 platform plays designed to help you find opportunities for advantage. We hope you prioritized several plays that are immediately valuable. To execute those plays successfully and to gain even deeper advantage, you'll want to develop a company culture that continuously renews your ability to win through platforms when every competitor has one.

The next three chapters focus on powerful cultural attributes you can develop as a leader. These culture shifts support the three kinds of platform advantage you seek:

- To achieve *Strategic Advantage*, you'll need cultural zeal for, and ability to, identify a platform's *kaleidoscopic value* to a coalition of customers.

- To achieve *In-market Advantage*, you'll need cultural commitment to, and creativity in, using customer visibility for *mutualistic gain* versus one-sided gain.

- To achieve *Alignment Advantage*, you'll need cultural attention to, and enthusiasm for, *synchronized performance* as a team sport and performance art.

These shifts to new cultural attributes are born of new values that you instill as a leader. They might first be incubated in a new business team, then become a respected sub-culture, and finally become your company's primary culture. In some scenarios, immediate company-wide cultural adoption may be required to succeed.

In either case, your cultural shifts will be defined by how your talent experiences the importance of new platform-related attributes. If you succeed, your talent will:

- Experience *collective identity and pride* based on organizational excellence at new attributes.

- Experience *personal rewards* for exceptional performance at new attributes (rewards might be psychological, social, professional, and/or financial in nature).

- Experience *prioritization* of new attributes when the business faces constraints.

We have chosen three non-digital stories as analogies for platform culture shift in order to highlight the human-centered nature of the changes you need to instill, plus provide you with a leader's storytelling toolkit. The invention of the kaleidoscope, the idea of symbiosis, and the evolution of synchronized swimming all have valuable lessons to share.

STRATEGIC ADVANTAGE AND THE
VALUE KALEIDOSCOPE

Product line strategy focuses on a product and a customer, one-to-one. Platform strategy and design are built around a many-sided customer coalition, taking into account each customer type's relationship with the company, and with other customer types. This requires a cultural shift to a kaleidoscopic view of value: the ability to see customer benefit, experiential beauty, and economic value from more angles, perspectives, and dimensions than ever before. Like a well-designed kaleidoscope.

A COLORFUL HISTORY

In 1816, a Scottish physicist named David Brewster, who was studying the reflection and absorption of light, added a few small mirrors and tiny pieces of colored glass to the base of a single tube he had built. When Brewster looked through an eyepiece at the other end of the tube, he saw captivating geometric images. Every twist of the base created a new but equally stunning form.

Brewster coined the word "kaleidoscope" to describe his invention. The name came from the Greek words *kalos, eïdos,* and *skopeïn,* which translate into "beautiful," "form," and "look at," respectively.[1] Every viewer sees a unique but beautiful image. Even more riveting to Brewster was the power of recombination and reconfiguration. He calculated that with just 24 glass crystals and 2 mirrors, his kaleidoscope could generate 1,391,724, 288,887, 252,999,425,128,493,402,200 distinct, amazing images.[2]

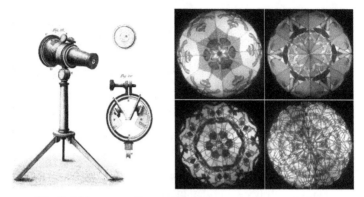

The Kaleidoscope – From a Few Mirrors and Pieces of Glass

Brewster had to settle for fame rather than fortune. He submitted a patent application, but before the government could grant it, a colleague showed a prototype to several opticians in London.[3] Soon, knockoffs were being made all over Europe. The device was wildly successful, selling more than 200,000 units in London and Paris in a few months, but little money ended up in Brewster's pocket.[4] Yet the device he created has evolved and extended; now, kaleidoscopes can be found in forms as diverse as patented liquid and bubble versions, young children's mass market toys, and ceramic objects of fine art. The kaleidoscope continues to inspire the idea of endless possibilities.

NEEDED: KALEIDOSCOPIC VISION

Platforms are value kaleidoscopes, both at the business portfolio and at the customer experience level. That's why those who possess kaleidoscopic vision can achieve advantage when developing them.

Business portfolios are kaleidoscopic because they are the collection of physical assets, business units, brands, customer relationships, and competencies that a company owns. But platforms force leaders to take a new look. They invite executives with kaleidoscopic vision to see how streams of data, connectors, code, algorithms, and ecosystem participants can interconnect, reconfigure, and unlock synergies between newly agile forms of business.

There are myriad ways to produce higher economic value, for all stakeholders. Look from one angle, and you'll see one opportunity. Look from a different angle; you'll see another. The Walt Disney Company is already the world's best at creating business portfolio synergies. Now they're creating many more through platforms. Like an augmented-reality game that players can start in a Disney theme park and continue as a Disney platform game at home. Or a DisneyPlus streaming platform movie that lets audiences order hard-to-find e-commerce merchandise within the movie experience.[5,6]

Customer experience hubs are even more kaleidoscopic as engineering, design, and marketing teams collaborate to develop a new platform with value for the entire customer coalition. Teams with kaleidoscopic vision leave behind their linear value mindsets, where one product serves one customer. They enter a multidimensional world of value where:

- One platform is built for many customer types. Platforms link all of these customer types as a customer coalition, enabling the company to serve them, while enabling them to provide value to each other. Each customer type has unique perspectives and needs to meet. Within each customer type, there are multiple customer personas with more nuanced differences. One platform often serves dozens of personas.

- A platform recombines and reconfigures common platform elements to serve multiple customer experience hubs. These experience hubs might be called apps, clouds, exchanges, or consoles ... but their name doesn't change their role as a customer-centric interface. Instead of common glass beads and mirrors, platform builders develop shared data sets, API connectors, analytical engines, computing code, and algorithms that can be drawn from again and again in unique blends.[7] They create value tailored to the purpose of the experience hub, context, and customer who needs them.

- Each user receives a personalized, beautiful experience. Through subscription choices, feature settings, and signaled preferences, each individual's use is like another twist of the kaleidoscope.

Uber's platform evolution illustrates increasing kaleidoscopic vision. The company launched in 2011 as a black luxury car service priced at 1.5 times that of a taxi, then scaled several years as a multi-tiered ride-sharing service, before building a customer coalition that added corporate transportation buyers, restaurant owners, food delivery drivers, freight shipping companies, truck drivers, and advertisers. Kaleidoscopic vision paid off in Uber's quick revenue rebound during the pandemic and its more profitable growth thereafter.

KALEIDOSCOPIC VISION FOR ALL

For a business to win in crowded markets, kaleidoscopic vision needs to become pervasive. Everyone in the company can learn to see new value-creation opportunities through platforms, for internal and external customers alike.

- Business executives can imagine how the business portfolio might connect and recombine through a platform, plus envision what business pieces might be missing or unnecessary.

- Platform teams can imagine what high-synergy customer coalitions and platform capabilities will differentiate their offerings in the market.

- Software and data teams can develop common digital assets that can be used and reused by application teams in flexible combinations.

- Hub design and experience teams can determine what different customer types and personas would view as compelling within their respective experience journeys.

- Go-to-market teams can imagine new use cases, new customer workflows and lifeflows, and new benefits that make the platform commercially compelling.

- Business support teams can identify ways that the platform enables new business process transformation, creating seamlessness between internal company units and with customers.

A culture that celebrates kaleidoscopic vision will spread an intense empathy for customers. It's already an act of empathy to develop a customer-centric product for one customer. It's a much deeper act of empathy to look at a platform from each customer's perspective so that each coalition member will find their views beautiful. For strategic advantage, as you implement the ideas found in Parts 1 (Portfolio Plays) and 2 (Design Plays) of this book, create a culture that continuously asks what value looks like through each customer's eyes.

IN-MARKET ADVANTAGE
AND THE MUTUALISTIC BEE

In 1879, the German botanist Heinrich Anton de Bary coined a concept as important to the success of your platform culture as it was to microbiology and the natural sciences. De Bary called it *symbiosis*. He defined it as "two or more dissimilar entities living together intimately."[8]

Such a macro idea got its start from a very micro question: How does a fungus reproduce? At the time, two scientific camps were locked in debate. One camp said other organisms were involved; the other camp said fungi reproduced alone. (Turns out both were right; it depends on the fungus.[9])

What fascinated de Bary as he studied lone spores was how they established radically different relationships with their host. Some spores would nourish themselves into adulthood by killing live vegetation. Other spores would beneficially digest dead plant matter.

De Bary's microbial work and follow-on studies of animal behavior established the idea that symbiosis between two entities is not inherently good or bad. It depends on the nature of the relationship. As a result, scientists established a spectrum of symbiotic relationships that range from one-sided and malignant to two sided and mutually beneficial. These relationships – *parasitism, dependence, commensalism,* and *mutualism* – can be found both in the natural world and in the platform world.

The symbiosis spectrum provides a valuable framework for your company's in-market platform culture. Via your platform, your company and your customer will become "two or more dissimilar

293

entities living together intimately." If your culture is right, this coexistence will form a deeply positive customer bond. If your culture is off, coexistence will reveal a dark side that erodes your customer bond.

Here are examples of four types of symbiosis, representing four different in-market cultural ethics that your platform workforce might take on over time. Each is explained through a nature story (we chose insects) and a platform story. Only the last of these four cultural ethics – mutualism – will bring your company in-market advantage.

PARASITISM

In a parasitic relationship, one organism uses another for its advantage, to the negative expense of the exploited organism. For example, one parasitic wasp uses a small insect called an aphid to incubate its eggs. The wasp larvae hatch inside the aphid, eats the aphid's organs, then chews its way out of its mummified aphid host.

Some customers feel platform companies use intimate knowledge about them to take direct advantage of them. For years, customers have complained that airline companies increase their rates if a customer searches for a ticket on multiple occasions.[10] More recently, consumers notice that cell phones listen to their personal conversations and then bring unwanted ads and a creepy feeling of being stalked.[11] Companies who feed on customers' tracked behavior to act in a one-sided manner are engaging in parasitic behavior.

DEPENDENCE

Dependence benefits both organisms, but one more so than the other, with the stronger organism working to keep the weaker one dependent within its grasp. Certain ant species appear to have a mutually beneficial relationship with aphids. They defend aphids from predators – such as parasitic wasps – and they carry aphids into their nests at night and on cold winter days.

Aphids return the favor. They secrete a sugary substance called "honeydew" that serves as a dietary staple for the ants.[12] But the relationship doesn't stay mutually beneficial for long. To ensure a steady supply of honeydew for the colony, ants clip the wings of the aphids so that they can't fly away and then "milk" them for honeydew until they're no longer useful.

Some platform companies create unhealthy dependence in their customers, as ants do with aphids. If social media companies make their platforms intentionally addictive – and if their tactics correlate to the rise of harmful self-images in user groups or social hostility – the relationship becomes unhealthily dependent, even if the customer does receive benefits.[13]

COMMENSALISM

Commensalism benefits one organism while leaving the other organism unaffected. Certain birds benefit from the behavior of army ants.[14] When the ants march across a jungle floor, insects like grasshoppers scramble out of the way of the ravenous militia. The insects who escape the pincers of the ants often end up in the beaks of the birds that follow, scoring the birds a feast, while the ants gain (and lose) nothing.

Many platform companies choose commensalistic relationships with their customers' data. The fine print of a company's privacy statement may reveal that they have permission to collect and sell anonymized customer data. Absent identifying information, the company won't necessarily harm the customer. But it is clearly a one-sided gain with no value-for-data exchange. As societal norms change, commensalist relationships risk being redefined as parasitic.

MUTUALISM

A mutualistic relationship benefits both organisms equally. Honeybees and flowers are a prime example. Bees travel far and wide to gather pollen and nectar from flowers and then feed it to their larvae. As the bees travel from flower to flower, they transmit pollen from one flower to another, cross-pollinating the plants. The seeds of a cross-pollinated plant produce a much healthier second-generation plant by increasing genetic diversity.[15] Both organisms are uplifted in a sustainable, life-giving manner, and there's no downside for either.

There are myriad examples of how platforms can be used to lift and serve their users while also succeeding as a business. Some of these play out at a micro level. When a platform proactively turns children's pictures that a parent took years ago into the home movie they've never had time to make, the parent is grateful (rather than resentful or fearful) of the platform's intimate presence. Part 3 of this book describes ways that your platform can add presence value to your customers through their full choose-and-use journey.

Platform mutualism shows up at a macro level too, lifting every individual who takes part in collective societal improvements. When food companies use platforms to hold themselves transparently accountable for how they treat animals and gain consumer market share for doing so, everyone wins. Part 4 of this book describes ways that your platform can innovatively provide better paths and broader powers for good to your users.

CULTURAL COMMITMENT TO MUTUALISM

Platform companies will gain an in-market advantage by infusing an ethic of mutualism into their cultural values. That ethic will go way beyond what's not permitted. It will inspire employees to brainstorm what they can do next for customers – what new powers they can provide to customers, what new introductions they can facilitate between one customer type and another. This ethic and inspiration should be fueled by a clarity of positive purpose – your purpose in serving customers one-by-one, and your purpose in delivering a broader positive connective impact.

Your company's commitment to mutualism will be tested. You'll have an imbalance of power. You'll be tempted to view customers as resources to be exploited. Win–win relationships may not pay off in the short term. If in these moments your mutualism is just surface "spin" and not core truth, your users will feel it. So will your talent. Unlike the insects in our stories, those customers and that talent can seek better elsewhere.

And the upside is equally true. An authentic purpose rooted in a cultural commitment to mutualism will be felt by your customers and employees. Inspire them and unite them in a common cause. It will make them grateful for the presence of your platform in their lives, yielding advantaged in-market brand relevance, loyalty, and platform use expansion that drives growth.

ALIGNMENT ADVANTAGE AND THE SYNCHRONIZED SWIMMER

When paradigm change occurs, a well-solved puzzle (how a company works) is knocked off the table. It not only scatters the pieces but also breaks each piece into a new shape. How quickly companies build new ways of working to fit a new paradigm puzzle becomes a competitive contest. Alignment advantage goes to the firm who puts the new puzzle pieces together first.

The race to re-sort the puzzle is most dramatic when new technology causes the paradigm shift. In the industrial era, the race was to learn the assembly line to scale low-cost production. In the mass product era, the race was to learn broadcast branding and long-distance logistics to scale retail leadership. In the Internet era, the race was learning digital demand generation and e-commerce to scale on-demand everything.

Companies and their leaders are now scrambling for alignment advantage in the platform era. This time the race is learning to collectively produce a modular platform – made of componentized software code and (at times) connected physical offers – that can be provided to customers through experience hubs that shape shift around their needs.

For leaders in product line companies, this presents a cultural and behavioral challenge. Most leaders have succeeded professionally and risen organizationally by being a *controller of siloed assets* – their product family and its profits. In a platform era, these same leaders need to become a *contributor to shared assets*. Some might contribute their team's code to larger experience hubs and platforms. Others might contribute their team's physical products and services to a larger business model where profitability is driven by platform services. In each scenario, the leader and their team become part of a larger coordinated team.

A similar cultural and behavioral challenge awaits go-to-market leaders when they grow a platform in-market. Leaders of functions like marketing, sales, customer success, and digital service management have traditionally worked in relative silos. Now, full-journey platform customer engagement requires never-before levels of collaboration to turn infinite customer connection into accelerated growth.

There is a theme that runs across these stories. Your alignment advantage opportunity and challenge is to add to your operating model and culture of *smaller-team siloed performance* an operating model and culture of *larger-team synchronized performance.*

It's easy to think that only new corporate adopters of platforms face this challenge, at the moment of company changeover. The truth is that born-as-a-platform companies face a similar challenge. They often grow by collecting entrepreneurial firms through acquisition. Each of the acquired leaders and teams are about strong controllers of siloed success. Furthermore, many platform company hires come from product line firms. As a result, the need to think of synchronized performance as an advantage applies to every platform organization.

NEEDED: SYNCHRONIZED PERFORMANCE ART

Synchronized swimming provides a striking analogy for how platform companies can gain an alignment advantage. The sport, now called Artistic Swimming, can lay claim to being the most challenging of all in the Olympics.[16] It calls on teams to synchronize a deep-water performance by putting together unexpected puzzle pieces: physical strength, technical standards, multilevel mental focus, and artistry.[17]

The sport has been on a long climb toward respectability. It began as entertainment in flooded Roman coliseums under Julius

Caesar, where swimmers formed shapes of tridents and ships.[18] It became a novel European art form in the late 1800s when Berlin swim clubs adopted it as underwater ballet.[19] It gained popular awareness in America through movie extravaganzas in the 1920s.[20]

Now the sport has turned to athleticism and competition. Athletes train between six and eight hours a day doing arduous aerobic routines suspended in deep water. Then comes two hours on land doing weights, cardio, gymnastics, and dance. Yet this individual conditioning only sets the stage for the real challenge – synchronized team performance as art.

Standards-based Excellence

Synchrony starts with alignment on standards. Synchronized swimming routines are composed of formally named and standardized moves. Members of an eight-person team must learn up to 1,000 choreographed motions, carried out in perfect harmony, for a four-minute routine.[21] Standards are a critical teaming aid. Every Artistic Swimmer knows exactly what a Flying Fish Hybrid Spinning 180° means (see below[22]). They'd better, as variation during a routine is failure.

Platform companies compete to impress customers, rather than judges, through interactive experience. They also lean on standards to achieve synchrony. What is each experience hub's visual brand identity and tone of voice? How many named customer personas does the platform serve, and what kind of content should each receive? What do best-practice campaign workflows look like? What single source of data truth should every team member use?

Flying Fish Hybrid Spinning 180°

Artistic Swimming Movement: Flying Fish Hybrid Spinning 180°
From a Submerged Back Pike Position with the legs
perpendicular to the surface, a Thrust is executed to a Vertical
Position and with no loss of height one leg is rapidly lowered to
an airborne Fishtail Position. Without a pause the horizontal leg
is rapidly lifted to a Vertical Position, followed by a rapid 180° Spin.

Part 5, "Interaction Plays," outlines areas where platform teams can align on customer interaction standards to their advantage. Use these plays to synchronize your delivery of always-on, elevated customer experience.

Parallel Attention

A collaborative platform culture is created when employees learn the discipline of parallel attention. They must pay attention at three levels. The first is their individual performance. The next is the small team(s) they work with regularly. The third and new level is the larger platform team throughout the company who is affected by each employee's and small team's performance. While this larger team may be out of sight day to day, they must not be out of mind.

Artistic Swimming again offers a strong parallel and inspiration. Swim team members start with individual concerns. They must hold their breath 1–2 minutes at a time while performing physically challenging acts in nine feet of water, forbidden to touch the pool floor. A neglect of personal performance can be life-threatening.

At the same time, swimmers must pay attention to those right beside them. To achieve higher scores, teams have shrunk the distance between swimmers from feet to inches.[23] Concussions and other injuries result from misalignment with close teammates.

But all the near-in discipline is for nothing unless the swimmer pays attention to the larger team. Each swimmer's ultimate goal is to perfect the artistry of the large group. Teams are scored on overall technical and artistic achievement – even on "the illusion of ease," that is, points are awarded for making complex teamwork feel simple.

The parallel attention that drives success in synchronized swimming is also what will make your platform company successful. Team members must practice individual accountability, precision teamwork with those nearby, and parallel attention to what it takes for the full-platform team to win. Part 6, "Transformation Plays," discusses how to achieve alignment advantage through the kind of collaboration that comes from parallel attention.

Find ways that you can turn synchronization into a dimension of competitive performance so powerful that it becomes an alignment artform – and advantage.

Part 8

TRANSFORMATIVE LEADERSHIP

The final part of our book asks a more personal question: How can you bring transformative leadership to help your company succeed? We'll focus on three types of leadership opportunities: *transforming an entire business, transforming a key business function, and transforming your own personal leadership.*

COMPANY-WIDE LEADERSHIP

Kim, a senior Business Development director, was asked by her CEO several years ago to spearhead the transformation of the company from a labor-based technical services firm to a software-and-labor technical solutions company. She executed extremely well, acquiring over a dozen software firms with lightning speed.

Kim's success drew a second, even more ambitious request: bring together the company's acquired software products into a modular platform that supported a family of experience hubs aimed at serving key customer personas. To prepare for her next initiative, Kim organized a series of workshops designed to produce a platform transformation roadmap. Using our playbook's six types of platform plays as an organizing principle for planning, Kim both distilled her own ideas and gathered inputs from others, one platform play at a time.

Kim classified the company's progress per play in three ways: milestones already achieved, work now underway, and activities to be carried out in the future. The workshops, which took place over several weeks, created thematic inputs that enabled the development of a transformation roadmap for the company.

The process Kim followed is shown above. You'll see one workshop a week, each focused on a different part of the playbook – portfolio, design, demand, innovation, interaction, and transformation plays. The outputs of the workshops were synthesized into a transformation plan with focus areas, workstreams, and work modules. Workstreams and modules could then be mapped and managed to timelines on an agile basis as a transformation program.

When it came time to begin implementing the transformation plan, one helpful leadership aid was a platform transformation gameboard (following figure) that enabled visual communication of what topic the transformation team wanted to focus discussion on at a given moment. The gameboard reflects our playbook but displays plays at varying levels of detail to support discussion topic navigation, rather than strategy and tactic development. The gameboard enables the platform team to keep less-involved executives well oriented. It helps highlight the current discussion topic but also illustrates how that topic might link to another. Strategic issues are on the left, in-market issues are on the right, and transformation issues are on the top and bottom.

Along the bottom of the gameboard are three transformation management topics: "Priorities Management," "Project Management," and "Change Management." These are parts of any transformation but are not platform specific, so they were not covered in the platform playbook. They point to the need for a Transformation Management Office (TMO). A TMO provides each of these three services:

Platform Transformation Roadmap Development

Workshops

WEEK 1	WEEK 2	WEEK 3	WEEK 4	WEEK 5	WEEK 6	WEEK 8
Portfolio Plays	Design Plays	Demand Plays	Performance Plays	Interaction Plays	Transformation Plays	Transformation Roadmap

Strategic Advantage   In-Market Advantage   Alignment Advantage

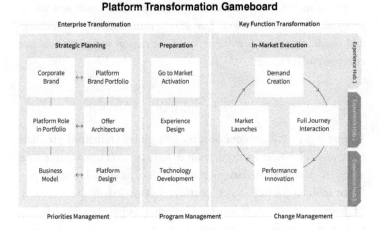

Platform Transformation Gameboard

- Priorities Management:

  o Identification of what should be worked on next and by whom.

  o Translation of lessons learned into adjustments needed.

  o Facilitation of alignment when disagreements arise.

- Program Management:

  o Synthesis of team and overall progress against objectives and timelines.

  o Escalation of issues, troubleshooting strategies, and issue resolution.

  o Communication to stakeholders through updates and on-demand dashboards.

- Change Management:

  o Articulation of strategic destination, rationale, and benefits for all involved.

  o Inspiration to believe in the transformation strategy and the firm's ability to win.

  o Guidance and support of next-step behavioral changes.

The transformation of Kim's company will remain a work in progress for several years, but Kim's transformative leadership and roadmap clarity provide an ongoing reason to believe that her company will succeed.

KEY BUSINESS FUNCTION LEADERSHIP

Joanna is VP of Customer Success at a global industrial products company. Her firm evolved from a hardware manufacturer to a software–hardware-solutions provider that recently launched two Software-as-a-Service (SaaS) platforms. This led to the renaming of Joanna's function (formerly Customer Support) and licensing of customer success technology tools. But so far, the changes to Joanna's group have been more about new labels than new capabilities, ways of working, or value to the firm.

When annual planning approached, Joanna decided to try something new. Rather than propose steady improvement, she proposed transformation. Joanna's steps to success are reflected in the Business Function Transformation framework shown below. Joanna's leadership milestones can be broken down into five key steps: *Vision* (desire to change), *Foundation* (leadership buy-in), *Traction* (budget and enablers), *Results* (pilot and execute), and *Realization* (transformed business function).

This framework differs from transforming an entire business (as in Kim's story) because Joanna can't assume that her function's transformation is an investment priority. She'll need to earn transformative investment in her Vision, Foundation, and Traction steps. She'll need to remake her case annually based on Results until Realization, given ongoing business changes.

Here's a step-by-step overview of Joanna's transformative leadership.

Vision: Why, What, and Who

Joanna won the CEO's approval to spend time on a transformation plan by explaining *why* transformation was needed – profiling the root cause of unsatisfactory customer subscription churn. She also described *what* steps similar firms in other SaaS markets had taken to achieve better renewal results. She asked for the CEO's sponsorship to invite three neighboring executives – the Chief Marketing Officer, Chief Sales Officer, and Head of Customer Analytics – to join three of her own leaders as the *who* of the transformation planning team. She left the CEO's office with a shared *vision of transformation* and *desire to change*, with agreement on next steps.

Foundation: Plan, Persuasion, and Pitch

Joanna's transformation leadership team aligned on a five-point *plan*, inspired in part by plays in the platform playbook:

- Customer Success Team Upskilling: Joanna's leaders would receive advanced training on customer success (Play 3.3).

- Customer Momentum Marketing: Digital Marketing would deliver user-centric messaging to help achieve Customer Success' momentum objectives (Play 3.3).

- In-use Enrichment: Customer Success teams would contribute to new in-use support and learning links (Play 3.5).

- Predictive Relationship Analytics: Customer Analytics would create predictive account churn or expansion propensities so that proactive measures could be taken (Play 3.6).

- Renewal and Expansion Selling Role: Customer Success reps would partner with Renewal Marketing and Sales to improve results (Play 3.6).

Joanna capped her plan by rewriting her function's value proposition to the company. She pledged that Customer Success would become a customer-base growth engine.

The CEO was impressed by the *plan's* outcome-oriented focus and collaborative spirit. Additional *persuasion* discussions with powerful C-suite members proved fruitful. There was ample support in the room when Joanna made her formal C-suite *pitch*. Approval of her plan became her *foundation* as a transformer.

Business Function Transformation

Traction: Resources, Reinforcements, and Roles

Joanna was now on the clock to come back to the C-suite with an actionable, detailed plan. She needed to go through budgeting for special initiatives to gain adequate *resources*. Upskilling training was expensive, as were third-party churn specialists and analytical software for propensities. In addition, Joanna needed *reinforcements* in the form of a TMO. Finally, she wanted to shift *roles* to give her two strongest managers new responsibilities for key transformation outcomes. Joanna's budget and enablers convinced skeptics in her department that she had, in fact, gained real traction.

Results: Act, Analyze, and Amplify

Joanna felt her first payoff when several transformation teams, organized by the TMO and led by the trusted managers she had put in charge, began to achieve *results* by changing how the company did business. Teams *acted* in two-week sprints, first to prepare for pilots and then to carry out pilots. Each pilot's impact was analyzed, leading to adjustments and re-piloting until objectives were achieved. The TMO then *amplified* the news to remaining Customer Success team members, scaling new practices via on-demand training, support desk help, and interventions where needed.

Realization: Report, Re-adjust, and Re-recruit

Joanna was mindful that the C-Suite might lose focus on Customer Success. To *realize* a full transformation despite the twists and turns of corporate support, she *reported* through dashboards that made self-service inquiries easy, plus she sent communications highlighting what was being piloted, learned, scaled, including *re-adjustments*. Joanna continuously *re-recruited* the C-Suite by highlighting the emerging impact of transformed Customer Success until she achieved her goals.

One day Joanna called her friend Marc, the Chief Marketing Officer at another platform company. She found him leading a transformation initiative, too. His change agenda was different: It involved migrating to platform brand architecture, opening an e-commerce channel, launching a series of AR/VR experiences, and building a new user community. Yet despite their different agendas, Joanna was struck by how similar their process had been as transformative leaders of key business functions. It reaffirmed that her five-step framework could work for others, too.

YOUR PERSONAL TRANSFORMATION

How could platform transformation have the side-effect of transforming your own leadership skills and approach?

You might be called on as a leader to transform a small or mid-sized team, versus the key business function or company-wide changes we've discussed. Regardless of your scope, the leadership skills you'll develop and the impact you'll make in others' lives will be significant. Here are three reasons to be excited.

First you'll sharpen your leadership thinking. Like Kim, you'll need to diagnose your situation, identify the platform plays relevant to your needs, and visualize your roadmap to help communicate it to others. Like Johanna, you'll need to cast a vision that others believe in, make a case for resources amidst competing priorities, and earn your team's trust that you'll deliver.

Second, you'll expand your ability to inspire. You'll clearly describe to your team the platform plays they need to implement, and how those plays fit into larger platform-related change. You'll learn and share a handful of platform company stories that serve as analogies to your own firm's trajectory and needs. You'll plant the seeds of culture shift, then nurture them until they take root.

Finally, you'll personally model the change you'll want to see in your teams. You'll find ways to display kaleidoscopic vision, an ethic of mutualism, and a commitment to synchronized performance. You'll openly share with your teams the lessons you are learning along the way. You'll maintain optimism, generosity, and persistence in the face of challenges.

In short, being a transformative leader in the platform era's mainstream years will help you transform, personally and professionally. You'll develop a reputation, inside your industry and out, as someone who knows how to reshape a business for a relevant, advantaged future.

It's our hope that "winning through platforms" will describe more than a successful outcome for your firm. We hope it will also describe a richly rewarding outcome for you.

REFERENCES

INTRODUCTION

1. Hepeng, J. (2006, July 26). He asked for the moon – and got it. *China Daily.* http://www.chinadaily.com.cn/cndy/2006-07/26/content_649325.htm

2. Day, D. A. (2007, March 5). Death throes and grand delusions. *The Space Review.* https://www.thespacereview.com/article/824/1

3. Foust, J. (2020, November 5). New report outlines international approach to lunar exploration. *SpaceNews.* https://spacenews.com/new-report-outlines-international-approach-to-lunar-exploration/

4. Schmitt, H. (2004). Mining the moon. *Popular Mechanics.* https://www.popularmechanics.com/space/moon-mars/a235/1283056/

5. Sourced from Malone, M. S. (2014). *The Intel trinity* (pp. 143–157). Harper Collins.

6. Crunchbase. (2022). *Crunchbase database query of "SaaS" companies founded between 2010 and 2021.* Crunchbase. https://www.crunchbase.com/

7. Brand Relevance Index®: Top brands of 2021 | Prophet. Prophet Brand Relevance Index 2014–2021. (2021, March 3). *Brand and marketing consultancy | Prophet.* https://relevantbrands-2021.prophet.com/

8. Financial technology, data, and expertise. (2022). Graph constructed using MSCI World Technology Index data and MSCI World Index data, provided by Refinitiv. Cumulative average growth rates (CAGR) calculated over the data range: 1 January 2010 to 1 January 2020. @Refinitiv. https://www.refinitiv.com/

9. Statista. (2022b, April 22). *Number of Netflix paid subscribers worldwide from 1st quarter 2013 to 3rd quarter 2022.* https://www.statista.com/statistics/250934/quarterly-number-of-netflix-streaming-subscribers-worldwide/

10. Top stocks of the 2010s. (2018). Yahoo Entertainment. https://www.yahoo.com/entertainment/top-stocks-2010s-212909732.html

11. Graphic is illustrative of the messaging key competitors shared during the period.

12. Dellatto, M. (2023, February 17). Paramount gains subscribers as Disney+ reports losses: Where all the major streaming services stand. *Forbes.* https://www.forbes.com/sites/marisadellatto/2023/02/16/paramount-gains-subscribers-as-disney-reports-losses-where-all-the-major-streaming-services-stand/?sh=223c4d4dc4ac

13. Maas, J. (2023, February 23). HBO max subscribers, Discovery+ reach 96 million. *Variety.* https://variety.com/2023/tv/news/hbo-max-subscribers-discovery-plus-q4-2022-1235533690/

14. Statista. (2021, November 23). *Number of paying Amazon Prime members worldwide from 2015 to 2020.* https://www.statista.com/statistics/829113/number-of-paying-amazon-prime-members/

15. Statista. (2022a). *Global users of Apple TV Plus 2022.* https://www.statista.com/statistics/1136261/number-of-apple-tv-plus-subscribers-us/

16. Wise, J. (2022, June 7). *How many videos are on YouTube in 2022?* EarthWeb. https://earthweb.com/how-many-videos-are-on-youtube/#:%7E:text=As%20of%202022%20data%2C%20YouTube,its%20over%202%20billion%20users

17. Cook, S. (2022, April 13). *50+ Netflix statistics & facts that define the company's dominance in 2022.* Comparitech. https://www.comparitech.com/blog/vpn-privacy/netflix-statistics-facts-figures/#:%7E:text=Netflix%20has%20over%2017%2C000%20titles,it%20offered%20in%20January%202018

18. Coen, B. (2019, December 10). *7 of Amazon's biggest acquisitions before the blockbuster Whole Foods deal.* TheStreet. https://www.thestreet.com/technology/as-a-slack-quisition-looms-here-are-amazon-s-7-biggest-purchases-html

19. Filmmaking, A. (2014). *Curious refuge*. https://curiousrefuge.com/ai-filmmaking

20. Sperling, N. (2022, April 19). Netflix loses subscribers for the first time in 10 years. *The New York Times*. https://www.nytimes.com/2022/04/19/business/ netflix-earnings-q1.html

21. Dellatto, M. (2023, February 17). Paramount gains subscribers as Disney+ reports losses: Where all the major streaming services stand. *Forbes*. https://www.forbes.com/sites/marisadellatto/2023/02/16/paramount-gains-subscribers-as-disney-reports-losses-where-all-the-major-streaming-services-stand/?sh=223c4d4dc4ac

PART 1: PORTFOLIO PLAYS

1. ICEF Monitor. (2019, July 17). *OECD: Number of degree-holders worldwide will reach 300 million by 2030*. ICEF Monitor – Market Intelligence for International Student Recruitment. https://monitor.icef.com/2019/07/oecd-number-of-degree-holders-worldwide-will-reach-300-million-by-2030/

2. Spangler, T. (2022, January 27). Apple powers to record $124 billion year-end 2021 quarter, services revenue soars 24%. *Variety*. https://variety.com/2022/digital/news/apple-record-quarter-year-end-2021-services-1235165383/

3. When consumers went smart phone shopping in 2022, they could compare the iPhone's 2.2 million premium app lineup, including only-on-Apple apps, against Samsung/Android's broader 3.5 million apps, Windows' 0.7 million apps, and Amazon's 0.5 million. Even if app attraction doesn't make or break an Apple-or-Samsung decision, it can distinguish both heavyweights from follower brands, and it clearly creates hurdles for would-be entrants.

4. Statista. (2023). *Revenue from services as a share of Apple's total global revenue from 3rd quarter 2015 to 1st quarter 2023*. https://www.statista.com/statistics/1101212/services-revenue-as-share-of-apples-total-revenue/

5. Mogg, T. (2023, January 11). *Guess how much Apple has paid App Store developers – You won't even be close*. Digital Trends.

https://www.digitaltrends.com/mobile/apple-reveals-developer-app-store-revenue-total

6. In 2023, Apple reported paying a cumulative $320 billion to app developers. Developers receive an estimated 75–80% of the total paid by consumers – we assumed 80%.

7. Behance. (2022). *Behance Blog | Boost your creative career with Behance.* Behance.net. https://www.behance.net/blog/adobe-max-2022-behance-updates

8. Metz, C. (2015, August 10). A new company called Alphabet now owns Google. *Wired.* https://www.wired.com/2015/08/new-company-called-alphabet-owns-google/

9. Rushe, D., & Thielman, S. (2015, August 11). Inside Alphabet: Why Google rebranded itself and what happens next. *The Guardian.* https://www.theguardian.com/technology/2015/aug/11/alphabet-google-rebranding-what-happens-next

10. Zillow Group investor presentation. (2022). https://s24.q4cdn.com/723050407/files/doc_financials/2021/q4/Zillow-Investor-Strategy-Presentation-(February-2022)-ZG.pdf

11. Zillow Group investor presentation. (2022). https://s24.q4cdn.com/723050407/files/doc_financials/2021/q4/Zillow-Investor-Strategy-Presentation-(February-2022)-ZG.pdf

12. Ingram, L. (2023, August 14). *How Peloton Just Ride run workout work.* Real Sophisticated Consumer. https://www.leahingram.com/peloton-Just-Ride-run-workout/

13. AWS. (2020). *Breaking the banking mould: How Starling Bank is disrupting the banking industry.* https://aws.amazon.com/solutions/case-studies/starling-bank-case-study/#:~:text=Starling%20Bank%20Builds%20a%20Successful,on%20AWS%20(3%3A3A29)

14. Google Cloud. (n.d.). *Starling Bank: Enhancing data-driven decision-making with BigQuery.* https://cloud.google.com/customers/starling-bank

15. PYMNTS. (2022, July 21). *5 Things to know about Starling's banking-as-a-service product. Engine.* https://www.pymnts.com/

news/banking/2022/5-things-to-know-about-starlings-banking-as-a-
service-product-engine/

16. Warnock, E. (2022, July 21). *Starling posts first annual profit as
    revenues rise 93%*. Sifted. https://sifted.eu/articles/starling-2022-
    financials/

PART 2: DESIGN PLAYS

1. The concept of business design was first outlined by Adrian
   Slywotzky in his books *Value Migration* and *The Profit Zone*.

2. Blyston, D. (2023, April 18). *The story of Uber*. Investopedia.
   https://www.investopedia.com/articles/personal-finance/111015/
   story-uber.asp

3. Campbell, H. (2021, February 24). *Lyft & Uber driver survey 2020:
   Uber driver satisfaction takes a big hit*. The Rideshare Guy. https://
   therideshareguy.com/uber-driver-survey/

4. Crunchbase. (2023). *Crunchbase*. https://www.crunchbase.com/
   organization/uber

5. Kirby, W. C. (2016, August 2). The real reason Uber is giving
   up in China. *Harvard Business Review*. https://hbr.org/2016/08/
   the-real-reason-uber-is-giving-up-in-china

6. Russell, J. (2018, March 26). *It's official: Uber sells Southeast Asia
   business to Grab*. TechCrunch. https://techcrunch.com/2018/03/25/
   gruber-official/

7. Lahoti, N. (2019, January 2). *Uber business model explained: From
   start to finish*. Mobisoft Infotech. https://mobisoftinfotech.com/
   resources/blog/uber-business-model-explained/

8. Uber investor day presentation. (2022, February 10). Uber. https://
   s23.q4cdn.com/407969754/files/doc_presentations/2022/Uber-
   Investor-Day-2022.pdf

9. Littman, J. (2021, December 14). *Lyft, Olo partner to offer restaurant
   delivery*. Restaurant Dive. https://www.restaurantdive.com/news/lyft-
   olo-partner-to-offer-restaurant-delivery/611486/#:~:text=Lyft%20

has%20partnered%20with%20Olo,through%20their%20
websites%20and%20apps

10. Uber investor day presentation. (2022, February 10). Uber. https://
    s23.q4cdn.com/407969754/files/doc_presentations/2022/Uber-
    Investor-Day-2022.pdf

11. Campbell, H. (2022, November). *How many Uber drivers are
    there in 2023?* The Rideshare Guy. https://therideshareguy.com/
    how-many-uber-drivers-are-there/

12. Uber investor day presentation. (2022, February 10). Uber. https://
    s23.q4cdn.com/407969754/files/doc_presentations/2022/Uber-
    Investor-Day-2022.pdf

13. Ride with Uber | request rides 24/7 | Official Uber site. (2023). Uber.
    https://www.uber.com/us/en/ride/

14. Picaro, E. B. (2019, May 16). *Uber adds a Quiet Mode so you can
    politely tell your driver to shut it.* Pocket-Lint. https://www.pocket-
    lint.com/apps/news/uber/148082-uber-adds-a-quiet-mode-so-you-
    can-politely-tell-your-driver-to-shut-it/?newsletter_popup=1

15. S-1. (2019). *Sec.gov.* https://www.sec.gov/Archives/edgar/data/
    1543151/000119312519103850/d647752ds1.htm

16. 2019 One-stop shopping consumer preferences. (2019). https://
    narfocus.com/billdatabase/clientfiles/172/21/3444.pdf. Platform
    innovators raised customer expectations and empowered a shift
    in customer behavior toward use of a one-stop-shop model. In
    2008, roughly 29% of home buyers surveyed told the US National
    Association of Realtors that they used a one-stop-shop model; in
    2019, over 50% reported one-stop-shop model use.

17. Lebowitz, S. (2017, November 2). *How one genius product feature
    got 1 million people to check out Zillow the day it launched – Now
    it's a $7 billion company (ZG).* Yahoo Life. https://www.yahoo.com/
    lifestyle/one-genius-product-feature-got-123100465.html

18. Fontinelle, A. (2021, December 22). *How Zillow makes money.*
    Investopedia. https://www.investopedia.com/articles/personal-
    finance/110615/why-zillow-free-and-how-it-makes-money.asp

19. Zillow Group investor presentation. (2022). https://s24.q4cdn.
    com/723050407/files/doc_financials/2021/q4/Zillow-Investor-
    Strategy-Presentation-(February-2022)-ZG.pdf. *Note*: The $300
    billion addressable market for real estate services that Zillow cites
    excludes the market for "I-buying" that Zillow started and then
    stopped. That initiative tapped into in the $2 trillion market of
    acquiring and reselling real estate properties.

20. We've provided a table of the most common platform features
    and benefits as an ideation resource at the end of this chapter. We
    cover these features and benefits in greater depth in Chapter 4.1,
    "Reimagined Flows."

21. Real, Z. (2022, December 29). *Zillow: Real estate, apartments,
    mortgages & home values*. Zillow. https://www.zillow.com/

22. *Note*: If you'd like to explore these features and benefits in greater
    depth, see Chapter 4.1, "Reimagined Flows."

23. Our story. (2021, November 2). Zillow Group. https://www.
    zillowgroup.com/about-us/story/

24. Lienhard, J. H. (2003). *Inventing modern: Growing up with x-rays,
    skyscrapers, and tailfins* (p. 204). Oxford University Press.

25. Kassinger, R. (2002). *Build a better mousetrap* (p. 128). John Wiley &
    Sons.

26. Google Search vs Google Maps: Where are your users?/Beyond Blue
    Media. (2021, February 4). Beyond Blue Media. https://beyondbluemedia.
    com/blog/marketing/google-search-vs-google-maps-where-are-your-users/

27. The algorithm – How YouTube search & discovery works. (2022).
    Tubics.com. https://www.tubics.com/blog/youtube-2nd-biggest-
    search-engine

28. LinkedIn. (2023). *Linkedin.com*. https://www.linkedin.com/pulse/
    google-makes-massive-investments-chatgpt-competitor-anthony-castrio/

29. Automating data classification and mapping to embed data context.
    (2023). Onetrust.com. https://www.onetrust.com/blog/automatingdata-
    classification-and-mapping-to-embed-data-context-intooperations/

30. Cyber risk management solutions. (2023). Bitsight.com. https://www.
    bitsight.com/

31. Wong, K. (2022, October 10). *AU 2022: Setting up industry-focused
    clouds*. Digital Engineering. https://www.digitalengineering247.
    com/article/au-2022-reflecting-on-industrial-transformation-setting-up-
    the-cloud-trinity/design

32. About Zebra Technologies Corporation. (2022, February 20). Zebra
    Technologies. https://www.zebra.com/us/en/about-zebra.html

33. Hood, D. (2015, November 5). Thomson Reuters launches Onvio
    platform. *Accounting Today*. https://www.accountingtoday.com/
    news/thomson-reuters-launches-onvio-platform

34. Hood, D. (2015, November 5). Thomson Reuters launches Onvio
    platform. *Accounting Today*. https://www.accountingtoday.com/
    news/thomson-reuters-launches-onvio-platform

35. Bonner, P. (2020, September). 2020 Tax software survey. *Journal of
    Accountancy*. https://www.journalofaccountancy.com/issues/2020/
    sep/tax-software-survey.html

36. Intuit excels with smaller businesses (through its TurboTax and
    QuickBooks products), while Wolters Kluwer has strength with
    larger businesses (through its CCH product).

37. Checkpoint learning CPE for CPAs | Your online resource for
    CPA CPE. (2022). Thomsonreuters.com. https://checkpointlearning.
    thomsonreuters.com/

38. GRC World Forums. (2022). *Kabir Barday, CEO of the fastest
    growing company in America, OneTrust in conversation for
    GRCTV*. GRC World Forums. https://www.grcworldforums.
    com/data-protection-and-privacy/kabir-barday-ceo-of-the-fastest-
    growing-company-in-america-onetrust-in-conversation-for-
    grctv/2234.article

39. Crunchbase. (2022). *Crunchbase – OneTrust company financials*.
    https://www.crunchbase.com/organization/onetrust/company_
    financials

40. OneTrust. (2023, February 21). *OneTrust Cloud Solutions | Trust Intelligence | OneTrust.* https://www.onetrust.com/

41. Garin, C. (2020, September 15). *How did MasterClass start? The history of MasterClass.* Medium; Brand Origins. https://medium.com/brand-origins/how-did-masterclass-start-a5cffd7644d9

42. Garin, C. (2020, September 15). *How did MasterClass start? The history of MasterClass.* Medium; Brand Origins. https://medium.com/brand-origins/how-did-masterclass-start-a5cffd7644d9

43. Qadri, M. (2022, July 31). *Whatisthebusinessmodelof.com.* https://whatisthebusinessmodelof.com/business-models/masterclass-business-model/

44. Cooke, C. (2020, April 11). *MasterClass review – 8 pros & cons to consider in 2023.* Upskillwise. https://upskillwise.com/reviews/masterclass/

45. Friend, T. (2021, October 15). Can MasterClass teach you everything? *The New Yorker.* https://www.newyorker.com/magazine/2021/10/25/can-masterclass-teach-you-everything

PART 3: DEMAND PLAYS

1. Strong, E. K., Jr. (1925). *The psychology of selling and advertising* (pp. 9&349). McGraw-Hill. E. Saint Elmo Lewis created the "Sales Funnel" in 1898 which later evolved into the Purchase Funnel. It's considered the first formal theory of marketing. When the *Psychology of Selling and Advertising* by Edward K. Strong, Jr was published, it became commonplace to attribute the authorship of the AIDA model to Lewis. According to Strong, Lewis in 1989 formulated the acronym AID: attract Attention, maintain Interest, create Desire in 1898. Strong then added the final "A" – get Action.

2. Kotler, P. (1965). *Marketing management: Analysis, planning, and control.* Prentice Hall.

3. Select Comfort changes name to Sleep Number. (2017, November 1).
    Sleepnumber.com. https://ir.sleepnumber.com/news/news-details/2017/
    Select-Comfort-Changes-Name-to-Sleep-Number/default.aspx.
    Founded in 1987, the company called itself "Select Comfort." For its
    first 30 years. In 2017, the same year that it launched the Smart 360
    platform bed, the company changed its name to Sleep Number – a
    move that supported the brand promise transformation we
    discuss here.

4. Ballistocardiography science & technology – Sleep Number.
    (2022). Sleepnumber.com. https://www.sleepnumber.com/pages/
    sleep-science-smart-sensing

5. Sleep science – Sleep Number. (2022). Sleepnumber.com. https://
    www.sleepnumber.com/pages/sleep-science

6. Joffrion, E. F. (2018, July 10). The designer who changed Airbnb's
    entire strategy. *Forbes*. https://www.forbes.com/sites/emilyjoffrion/
    2018/07/09/the-designer-who-changed-airbnbs-entire-strategy/

7. Aydin, R. (2019, September 20). *The history of Airbnb, from air
    mattresses to $31 billion company*. Business Insider. https://www.
    businessinsider.com/how-airbnb-was-founded-a-visual-history-2016-
    2#since-2016-airbnb-has-been-expanding-its-services-through-a-series-
    of-high-end-and-acquisitions-adjacent-to-its-main-service-28
    Ting, D. (2019, April 30). *Airbnb says its tours and activities
    gamble is winning*. Skift. https://skift.com/2019/04/30/
    airbnb-says-its-tours-and-activities-gamble-is-winning/

8. Zelaya, I. (2020, April 13). Airbnb debuts online experiences
    with unique activities. *Adweek*.com. https://www.adweek.com/
    brand-marketing/airbnb-debuts-online-experiences-with-
    unique-activities/

9. Asai, H. (2021, March 30). *Made possible by hosts*. Airbnb
    Newsroom. https://news.airbnb.com/made-possible-by-hosts-2/

10. Userpilot Content Team. (2022, April 12). *MQL vs SQL: What's
    the difference?* Thoughts About Product Adoption, User
    Onboarding and Good UX | Userpilot Blog. https://userpilot.com/
    blog/mql-vs-sql/

11. Snapshot® test drive terms and conditions. (2023). Progressive.com. https://www.progressive.com/auto/discounts/snapshot/snapshot-test-drive-terms-conditions/

12. Parker, W. (2019). *Warby Parker*. https://www.warbyparker.com/app

13. Houghton, B. (2023, April 25). *Spotify reports solid growth as monthly users top 515M, margins improve*. Hypebot. https://www.hypebot.com/hypebot/2023/04/spotify-reports-solid-growth-as-monthly-users-top-515m.html

14. Sabon. (2019, June 24). *Case study: How Spotify achieves astonishing 46% conversion rate from free to paid*. GrowRevenue.io. https://growrevenue.io/spotify-free-to-paid-case-study/

15. Dropbox. (2023). *Dropbox*. https://www.dropbox.com/basic

16. What is elasticsearch? (2019). Elastic. https://www.elastic.co/what-is/elasticsearch

17. Atlassian. (2023). *Free cloud software plans*. https://www.atlassian.com/software/free

18. Rao, V. (2020, August 12). *Dropbox referral program – A story of 3900% growth in just 15 months*. Linkedin.com. https://www.linkedin.com/pulse/dropbox-referral-program-story-3900-growth-just-15-months-rao/

19. Wassel, B. (2019, March 27). *AI-powered digital mirror "reads" Sephora shoppers' look*. Retail TouchPoints. https://www.retailtouchpoints.com/topics/customer-experience/ai-powered-digital-mirror-reads-sephora-shoppers-look

20. Bain, M. (2021, May 3). *Prime has never been more important to Amazon*. Quartz. https://qz.com/2004369/the-pandemic-made-prime-even-more-valuable-to-amazon

21. Ellevest Team. (2022, March 7). *19 Money wins from the Ellevest community*. Ellevest. https://www.ellevest.com/magazine/elle-raisers/elle-raisers-money-wins

22. Johnson, E. (2017, March 6). *Steve Jobs's first reaction to the Genius Bar: "That's so idiotic! It'll never work!"* Vox.

https://www.vox.com/2017/3/6/14823460/apple-store-steve-jobs-genius-bar-ron-johnson-recode-podcast

23. Aaker, D. (2012, January 5). The genius bar – Branding the innovation. *Harvard Business Review*. https://hbr.org/2012/01/the-genius-bar-branding-the-in?registration=success

24. Apple services enrich peoples' lives throughout the year. (2022, January 10). Apple Newsroom (United Kingdom). https://www.apple.com/uk/newsroom/2022/01/apple-services-enrich-peoples-lives-throughout-the-year/

25. Wong, P. (2022, May 12). *Exploring Apple's retail strategy that fueled its $3 trillion valuation*. Headless E-Commerce Platform | Fabric. https://fabric.inc/blog/apple-retail-strategy/

26. Brand Relevance Index®: Top brands of 2021 | Prophet. Prophet Brand Relevance Index 2015–2021. (2021, March 3). *Brand and marketing consultancy | Prophet*. https://relevantbrands-2021.prophet.com/

27. The team at Into the Gloss, Inc. launches Glossier, the first digital beauty brand. (2014, October 6). https://assets.ctfassets.net/p3w8f4s vwgcg/5BF1GSuh9YQOOGUGgeomIk/9cd9e783ee364173de8ae34 62eab5e5d/GlossierLaunchPressRelease_10-6-14.pdf

28. Lorincz, N. (2022, August 2). *Glossier marketing breakdown: How this beauty brand became a $1.2 billion company*. OptiMonk – Personalize, monetize, optimize. https://www.optimonk.com/glossier-marketing-breakdown

29. Chitrakorn, K. (2022, July 15). *Glossier's new CEO on why she's backing influencers, ending the DTC era and opening stores*. Vogue Business. https://www.voguebusiness.com/beauty/glossier-new-ceo-on-why-shes-backing-influencers-ending-the-dtc-era-and-opening-stores?status=verified

30. Behance. (2022). *Behance Blog | boost your creative career with Behance*. Behance.net. https://www.behance.net/blog/adobe-max-2022-behance-updates

31. Sanne, A. (2021, March 26). *Atlassian community 2020 year in review*. Atlassian Community. https://community.atlassian.com/t5/

Watercooler-articles/Atlassian-Community-2020-Year-in-Review/
ba-p/1648429

32. Sanne, A. (2021, March 26). *Atlassian community 2020 year in review*. Atlassian Community. https://community.atlassian.com/t5/ Watercooler-articles/Atlassian-Community-2020-Year-in-Review/ ba-p/1648429

33. Company History. (2016). *Schwab brokerage*. https://www. aboutschwab.com/history. Schwab had $7.6 billion in Assets under Management (AUM) in 1985, a year after it launched its Mutual Fund Marketplace – the precursor to Schwab One Source in 1993 and Schwab ETF OneSource in 2013. On December 31, 2022, Schwab's parent company's AUM was $1.85 trillion: Charles Schwab's $552 billion plus TD Ameritrade's $1.3 trillion (Schwab acquired TD Ameritrade in 2020).

PART 4: INNOVATION PLAYS

1. DayDayNews. (2020, November 21). *Let 10,000 families eat peking duck again, Haier refrigerator lane change scene is effective*. Daydaynews.cc. https://daydaynews.cc/en/technology/930419.html

2. Haier corporate facts – Haier. (2018). Haier.com. https://smart-home.haier.com/en/gsgk/?id=KeyFigures&spm=inverstor.31579_ pc.irheader_20200506_1.5. Haier 2020 operating revenue of CNY 210 billion converted to USD at exchange rate 0.15268 USD = 1 CNY.

3. Haier corporate facts – Haier. (2018). Haier.com. https:// smart-home.haier.com/en/gsgk/?id=KeyFigures&spm=inverst or.31579_pc.irheader_20200506_1.5.

4. Haier investor relations – Haier. (2023). *Haier Smart Home Co., Ltd. annual report 2020* (p. 34). Haier.com. https://smart-home.haier. com/en/gpxx/iv/P020210429639454409151.pdf

5. Haier investor relations – Haier. (2023). *Haier Smart Home Co., Ltd. annual report 2020* (p. 34). Haier.com. https://smart-home.haier. com/en/gpxx/iv/P020210429639454409151.pdf

6. Minnaar, J. (2021, May 8). *The next management model ... is from China?* Corporate Rebels. https://www.corporate-rebels.com/blog/next-influential-management-model-of-the-world

7. Gu, C. (2021, September 12). *Haier: Transforming the ecosystem and searching for the next phase of growth*. Warc.com. https://www.warc.com/newsandopinion/opinion/haier-transforming-the-ecosystem-and-searching-for-the-next-phase-of-growth/en-gb/5537

8. Haier investor relations – Haier. (2023). *Haier Smart Home Co., Ltd. annual reports*.

9. Stone, B. (2021, May 11). The secret origins of Amazon's Alexa. *Wired*. https://www.wired.com/story/how-amazon-made-alexa-smarter/

10. Brustein, J. (2016, April 19). *The real story of how Amazon built the Echo*. Bloomberg.com. https://www.bloomberg.com/features/2016-amazon-echo/

11. Stone, B. (2021, May 11). The secret origins of Amazon's Alexa. *Wired*. https://www.wired.com/story/how-amazon-made-alexa-smarter/

12. Stone, B. (2021, May 11). The secret origins of Amazon's Alexa. *Wired*. https://www.wired.com/story/how-amazon-made-alexa-smarter/

13. Introducing more than 50 features to build ambient experiences, drive growth with Alexa. (2021). Alexa-Blog. https://developer.amazon.com/en-US/blogs/alexa/alexa-skills-kit/2021/07/more-than-50-features-to-build-ambient-experiences

14. Ribeiro, C., & Martins, D. (2021, September 20). *What Fire TV says about Amazon's strategy*. Amazon Maven. https://www.thestreet.com/amazon/media/what-fire-tv-says-about-amazons-strategy

15. Cain, Á. (2022, August 29). *The history of Amazon and whole foods' rocky 5-year marriage*. Business Insider. https://www.businessinsider.com/amazon-whole-foods-market-history-2022-8

16. https://www.popsci.com/technology/amazon-alexa-lose-money/#:~:text=Business%20Insider%20claims%20Alexa%20is,Assistant%20(81.5%20million%20users)

17. Introducing the Amazon Advertising Partner Network. (2021). Amazon Advertising Blog. https://advertising.amazon.com/blog/introducing-partner-network

18. Matter debuts at Amsterdam launch event. (2022, November 3). CSA-IOT. https://csa-iot.org/newsroom/matter-the-new-global-standard-for-the-smart-home-debuts-at-amsterdam-launch-event/

19. Haier offers smart home solutions. (2022). Chinadaily.com.cn. http://qingdao.chinadaily.com.cn/2022-09/10/c_810567.htm

20. Boehm, J., Grennan, L., Singla, A., & Smaje, K. (2022, September 12). *Why digital trust truly matters*. McKinsey & Company. https://www.mckinsey.com/capabilities/quantumblack/our-insights/why-digital-trust-truly-matters

21. Komnenic, M. (2023, February 28). *98 Biggest data breaches, hacks, and exposures [2023 update]. Counted through end of 2022*. Termly. https://termly.io/resources/articles/biggest-data-breaches/#biggest-data-breaches-in-2022

22. Data protection and privacy legislation worldwide. (2023). UNCTAD. https://unctad.org/page/data-protection-and-privacy-legislation-worldwide

23. The new cascade of influence 2022 Edelman trust barometer special report. (2022). https://www.edelman.com/sites/g/files/aatuss191/files/2022-06/2022%20Edelman%20Trust%20Barometer%20Special%20Report%20The%20New%20Cascade%20of%20Influence%20FINAL.pdf

24. GRC World Forums. (2022). *Kabir Barday, CEO of the fastest growing company in America, OneTrust in conversation for GRCTV*. GRC World Forums. https://www.grcworldforums.com/data-protection-and-privacy/kabir-barday-ceo-of-the-fastest-growing-company-in-america-onetrust-in-conversation-for-grctv/2234.article

25. Transform personalized experiences with preference management. (2023). Onetrust.com. https://www.onetrust.com/blog/transform-personalized-experiences-with-preference-management/

26. The state of personalization 2022. (n.d.). https://segment.com/pdfs/State-of-Personalization-Report-Twilio-Segment-2022.pdf

27. Schreiber, D. (2017). *Lemonade sets a new world record.* Lemonade Blog. https://www.lemonade.com/blog/lemonade-sets-new-world-record

28. Welcome to Snapshot by Progressive Insurance. (2023). Progressive.com. https://www.progressive.com/auto/discounts/snapshot/

29. Washington, D. (n.d.). *United States Securities and Exchange Commission.* Retrieved May 28, 2023, from https://d18rn0p25nwr6d.cloudfront.net/CIK-0000080661/c567f587-57f7-402c-85eb-a926c3a57bdd.pdf

30. Turing, A. M. (1950). *Computing machinery and intelligence* (pp. 433–460). Aberdeen University Press. The Turing Test goes like this. A human judge asks questions of both a computer and another human (each in separate rooms and unknown to the judge). The computer tries to sound human in substance and style. If the judge can't tell which responses are from the human, the computer wins The Imitation Game.

31. Anyoha, R. (2017, August 28). *The history of artificial intelligence.* Science in the News. https://sitn.hms.harvard.edu/flash/2017/history-artificial-intelligence/

32. Turing, A., & Copeland, B. J. (2004). *The essential Turing: Seminal writings in computing, logic, philosophy, artificial intelligence, and artificial life, plus the secrets of Enigma.* Clarendon Press.

33. Aaker, D. (2018). *Creating signature stories.* Morgan James Publishing.

34. Aaker, D. (2022). *The future of purpose-driven branding.* Morgan James Publishing.

35. Gill, T. (2020, May 28). *Niantic's upcoming feature will make your Pokémon react to its surroundings.* Mashable SEA. https://sea.mashable.com/tech/10764/niantic-is-releasing-a-new-feature-thatll-make-your-pokemon-more-lifelike

36. John, L. (2021, November 12). *Reimagining Paris with the help of an urban digital twin*. Unity Blog. https://blog.unity.com/industry/reimagining-paris-with-the-help-of-an-urban-digital-twin

37. Lovejoy, B. (2022, June 22). *Next-generation Ikea augmented reality app lets you delete your existing furniture*. 9to5Mac. https://9to5mac.com/2022/06/22/ikea-augmented-reality-app

38. AccuVein to display market leading vein visualization technology at AVA 2018. (2018, September 6). AccuVein, Inc. https://www.accuvein.com/accuvein-to-display-market-leading-vein-visualization-technology-at-ava-2018/

39. Edelman trust barometer. (2023). Edelman. https://www.edelman.com/trust/trust-barometer

40. Global Report. (n.d.). https://www.edelman.com/sites/g/files/aatuss191/files/2023-02/2023%20Edelman%20Trust%20Barometer%20Global%20Report.pdf

41. The new cascade of influence 2022 Edelman trust barometer special report. (2022). https://www.edelman.com/sites/g/files/aatuss191/files/2022-06/2022%20Edelman%20Trust%20Barometer%20Special%20Report%20The%20New%20Cascade%20of%20Influence%20FINAL.pdf

42. The new cascade of influence 2022 Edelman trust barometer special report. (2022). https://www.edelman.com/sites/g/files/aatuss191/files/2022-06/2022%20Edelman%20Trust%20Barometer%20Special%20Report%20The%20New%20Cascade%20of%20Influence%20FINAL.pdf

43. Provenance founder speaks on transparency. (2019, June 4). Provenance.org. https://www.provenance.org/news-insights/the-next-web-keynote-provenance-founder-speaks-on-transparency-circularity-and-the-future-of-commerce

44. Askew, K. (2020, September 21). *Princes adopts blockchain as part of its "proactive approach" to illegal labour in Italian agriculture*. Foodnavigator.com. https://www.foodnavigator.com/Article/2020/09/21/Princes-adopts-blockchain-as-part-of-its-proactive-approach-to-illegal-labour-in-Italian-agriculture

45. Patagonia action works – The Shorty Awards. (2023).
    Shortyawards.com. https://shortyawards.com/3rd-socialgood/
    patagonia-action-works

46. Yvon Chouinard donates Patagonia to fight climate crisis. (2014).
    Patagonia.com. https://www.patagonia.com/ownership/

47. S7428A. (2022, November 18). *NY State Senate bill S7428A*. NY
    State Senate. https://www.nysenate.gov/legislation/bills/2021/S7428

PART 5: INTERACTION PLAYS

1. Nike launches new Nike+ Run Club App. (2016, August 22).
   Businesswire.com. https://www.businesswire.com/news/
   home/20160822005972/en/NIKE-Launches-New-Nike-Run-Club-
   App. In 2009, the Nike+ Run Club and Training Club apps first
   launched. In 2016, a major upgrade launched featuring adaptive
   coaching, inspiration, and community linkages.

2. Nike launches SNKRS App – SneakerNews.com. (2015, February 11).
   Sneaker News. https://sneakernews.com/2015/02/11/nike-launches-
   snkrs-app/

3. Engelhardt, F. (2020, February 10). *NikePlus: "more personal at
   scale."* Medium; Incentive X. https://blog.spaaza.com/deep-dive-
   nikeplus-and-being-more-personal-at-scale-3020259a4a32. In 2016,
   Nike launched its Nike+ membership, a single account that provides
   a gateway to all Nike Apps. It is free but requires account login.
   Nike+ connects members to Nike's Experience activities & event
   calendar.

4. Cheng, A. (2019, May 9). Nike unveils "a game-changing
   innovation": A fit feature to fix shoe sizing online and in-store.
   Forbes. https://www.forbes.com/sites/andriacheng/2019/05/09/this-
   new-nike-fit-feature-could-be-a-game-changer/?sh=568fde622473

5. Nike Virtual View on FinishLine.com lets you "try on" apparel.
   (2020). 8th Wall. https://www.8thwall.com/blog/post/56019017301/
   nike-virtual-view-on-finishline.com-lets-you-try-on-apparel. In 2020
   Nike launched "Virtual View" to let the shopper see Nike apparel on
   hologram models.

6. Lawler, R. (2021, December 14). *Nike just bought a virtual shoe company that makes NFTs and sneakers "for the metaverse."* The Verge. https://www.theverge.com/22833369/nike-rtfkt-nft-sneaker-shoe-metaverse-company

7. Nike's digital transformation gains speed in midst of COVID-19 pandemic. (2023). Warc.com. https://www.warc.com/content/paywall/article/warc-exclusive/nikes-digital-transformation-gains-speed-in-midst-of-covid-19-pandemic/en-GB/134131?

8. Nike's digital transformation gains speed in midst of COVID-19 pandemic. (2023). Warc.com. https://www.warc.com/content/paywall/article/warc-exclusive/nikes-digital-transformation-gains-speed-in-midst-of-covid-19-pandemic/en-GB/134131?

9. Acronyms stand for Data Management Platforms (DMP), Customer Relationship Management Platforms (CRM), and Customer Demand Platforms (CDP). These labels use the word "platform" to mean databases rather than a type of business; we will use the term "database" to avoid confusion with our book's use of the word.

10. Waxman, O. (2015, July 31). *The number of ways you can put together 6 Lego bricks will astound you.* Time.com. https://time.com/3977789/lego-brickumentary-math-professor-combinations/

11. Higgin, C. (2017, February 12). How many combinations are possible using 6 LEGO bricks? *Mental Floss.* https://www.mentalfloss.com/article/92127/how-many-combinations-are-possible-using-6-lego-bricks

12. In 2015, a Copenhagen-based math professor wrote a computer program that corrected the Lego engineers. They hadn't thought of all structure types. They focused on only 6-high vertical towers, not shorter horizontal ones. The correct answer was 915 million combinations.

13. Shipley, K. (2019, April). *How to personalize your creative at scale.* Think With Google. https://www.thinkwithgoogle.com/marketing-strategies/video/personalized-advertising-machine-learning/

14. Faull, J. (2018, November 16). *Lexus reveals ad 'created by AI'. Is it a gimmick? No. Will it win any awards? Probably not.* The Drum. https://www.thedrum.com/news/2018/11/16/lexus-reveals-ad-created-ai-it-gimmick-no-will-it-win-any-awards-probably-not

15. Case Study. (2022, February). *Citizens Bank success story.* Aprimo. https://wpapi.aprimo.com/wp-content/uploads/2022/02/SS_CB_Original-file.pdf

16. Case Study. *Use location to personalize the drive-thru and kiosk experience for anonymous customers.* XP2 by Dynamic Yield. https://www.dynamicyield.com/use-case/drive-thru-and-kiosk-location-personalization/

17. About Citymapper. (2017). Citymapper. https://citymapper.com/company

18. Alexander, T. (2022, July 15). *I tried Citymapper's new air conditioned route mapper that helps you stay cool.* MyLondon. https://www.mylondon.news/whats-on/reviews/london-underground-i-tried-citymappers-24500898

19. Etherington, D. (2017, July 20). *Citymapper will offer actual paid bus service in London this year.* TechCrunch. https://techcrunch.com/2017/07/20/citymapper-will-offer-actual-paid-bus-service-in-london-this-year/

PART 6: TRANSFORMATION PLAYS

1. American Experience. (2017, March 16). *Reinventing the American Amusement Park.* Pbs.org. https://www.pbs.org/wgbh/americanexperience/features/reinventing-american-amusement-park/55. *Note*: Synergies abounded even before Disneyland construction started. ABC funded the Disney Brothers' construction of the Disneyland in return for a weekly one-hour Disneyland TV show.

2. American Experience. (2017, March 16). *Reinventing the American Amusement Park.* Pbs.org. https://www.pbs.org/wgbh/americanexperience/features/reinventing-american-amusement-park/55.

3. Disney's organization structure and financial reporting is slightly more granular – media entertainment is broken into media networks, studio content, and media products – but for our story telling we'll keep things aggregated.

4. Sylt, C. (2021, January 11). Inside Disney's Internet of Things. *Forbes*. https://www.forbes.com/sites/csylt/2020/06/06/inside-disneys-internet-of-things/?sh=8664e9a75459

5. Disney's three streaming service subscriber bases and Netflix's subscriber base were just over 230 million.

6. Tyko, K. (2021, September 15). Disney store closings: More locations are closing but here's the list of stores staying open – for now. *USA Today*. https://www.usatoday.com/story/money/shopping/2021/09/14/disney-store-closings-list-stores-open-september-2021-liquidation-sale/8324369002/

7. Perez, S. (2022, November). *Disney+ expands into e-commerce with an exclusive merch shop for subscribers*. TechCrunch. https://techcrunch.com/2022/11/01/disney-expands-into-e-commerce-with-an-exclusive-merch-shop-for-subscribers/

8. Toonkel, J., & Krouse, S. (2022, August 31). Disney explores membership program like Amazon Prime to offer discounts and perks. *The Wall Street Journal*. https://www.wsj.com/articles/disney-explores-amazon-prime-like-membership-program-to-offer-discounts-and-perks-11661978329?mod=djemalertNEWS

9. Fletcher, B. (2022, November 30). *Disney buys MLB's remaining stake in BAMTech for $900M*. Fierce Video. https://www.fiercevideo.com/video/disney-buys-mlbs-remaining-stake-bamtech-900m. *Note*: Disney took a stake in BAMTech in 2016 bought majority shares in 2017 and completed the buyout in 2022. It began using BAMTech for ESPN+ as a part owner and then took operational control in advance of the Disney+ launch.

10. Faughnder, R., & James, M. (2019, November 12). Disney's massive streaming gamble has arrived. It may change the TV industry forever. *Los Angeles Times*. https://www.latimes.com/entertainment-arts/business/story/2019-11-12/disney-plus-streaming

11. Goldsmith, J. (2022, November 29). *Disney says restructuring could squeeze financials, buys in BamTech*. Deadline. https://deadline.com/2022/11/disney-bob-iger-bob-chapek-dmed-bamtech-1235184428/

12. Faughnder, R., & James, M. (2022, December 2). The rise and fall of Disney executive Kareem Daniel. *Los Angeles Times*. https://www.latimes.com/entertainment-arts/business/story/2022-12-02/kareem-daniel-and-the-rise-and-fall-of-the-disney-executive-who-helped-define-the-bob-chapek-era

13. Fischer, S. (2022, November 22). *Bob Iger announces restructuring at Disney, top media exec to depart*. Axios. https://www.axios.com/2022/11/22/bob-iger-announces-restructuring-at-disney-top-media-exec-to-depart

14. Sherman, A. (2022, November 8). *Disney wants you to focus on revenue and profit instead of streaming subscribers – just not this quarter*. CNBC. https://www.cnbc.com/2022/11/08/disney-gets-hit-by-media-worlds-shift-to-emphasize-profit-and-revenue-over-subscriber-growth-.html

15. Franck, T. (2019, April 12). *Iger says Disney bought Fox because of value it adds to streaming service: "The light bulb went off."* CNBC. https://www.cnbc.com/2019/04/12/disney-wouldnt-have-bought-fox-assets-without-streaming-plans-iger-says.html

16. Hough, J. (2019, January 4). Disney's Bob Iger talks streaming, park plans and learning from Kodak. *Barron's*. https://www.barrons.com/articles/disneys-bob-iger-talks-streaming-park-plans-and-learning-from-kodak-51546599600?mod=article_inline

17. Palmer, R. (2015). *Bob Iger explains why Disney has to transform for streaming*. Whatsondisneyplus.com. https://whatsondisneyplus.com/bob-iger-explains-why-disney-has-to-transform-for-streaming/

18. Littleton, C. (2019, January 29). Disney Plus: Inside the ambitious plans for the streaming service. *Variety*. https://variety.com/2019/biz/features/disney-plus-streaming-plans-bob-iger-1203120734/

19. Akhtar, O. (2023, March). *The 2023 state of digital transformation.* Prophet. https://prophet.com/2023/03/download-the-2023-state-of-digital-transformation/

20. Smith, M. (2023, January 19). *The 10 fastest-growing jobs in the U.S. right now – Many pay over $100,000 a year.* CNBC. https://www.cnbc.com/2023/01/18/the-10-fastest-growing-jobs-in-the-us-right-now-many-pay-over-100000.html.

PART 7: CULTURE SHIFTS

1. Bellis, M. (2018, March 16). *The history of the kaleidoscope and David Brewster.* ThoughtCo. https://www.thoughtco.com/history-of-the-kaleidoscope-1992035

2. Brewster, D. (1816). *The kaleidoscope: History, theory, and construction.* Van Cort.

3. Sack, H. (2021, July 10). *David Brewster and the invention of the kaleidoscope.* SciHi Blog. http://scihi.org/david-brewster-kaleidoscope/

4. The Kaleidoscope Online Book. (n.d.). *Kaleidoscope history.* http://www.thekaleidoscopebook.com/thescopebook/scope-resources/kaleidoscope-history?showall=&start=2

5. Perez, S. (2022, November). *Disney+ expands into e-commerce with an exclusive merch shop for subscribers.* TechCrunch. https://techcrunch.com/2022/11/01/disney-expands-into-e-commerce-with-an-exclusive-merch-shop-for-subscribers/

6. Sylt, C. (2021, January 11). Inside Disney's Internet of Things. *Forbes.* https://www.forbes.com/sites/csylt/2020/06/06/inside-disneys-internet-of-things/?sh=8664e9a75459

7. *Note*: This engineering approach is called Service Oriented Architecture (SOA) and when data or code is called for, it's considered an internal digital "service" when the platform delivers it.

8. De Bary, A. (1879). *Die erscheinung der symbiose.* Verlag von Karl J. Trubner.

9. Gaines, J. M. (2022, April 20). This fungus has more than 17,000 sexes. *The Scientist Magazine*. https://www.the-scientist.com/news-opinion/this-fungus-has-more-than-17-000-sexes-69930

10. Shen, L. (2017, September 18). *The truth about whether airlines jack up prices if you keep searching the same flight*. Time.com. https://time.com/4899508/flight-search-history-price/

11. On Bareckas, K. (2023, March 7). *Is my phone listening to me? How to stop it*. NordVPN. https://nordvpn.com/blog/is-my-phone-listening-to-me/

12. McVean, A. (2017, August 16). *Farmer ants and their aphid herds*. McGill. https://www.mcgill.ca/oss/article/did-you-know/farmer-ants-and-their-aphid-herds

13. Hoge, E., Bickham, D., & Cantor, J. (2017, November 1). *American Academy of Pediatrics*. https://publications.aap.org/pediatrics/article/140/Supplement_2/S76/34184/Digital-Media-Anxiety-and-Depression-in-Children

14. Brumfield, R. (2007, June 1). *Birds follow army ants to find prey*. National Science Foundation. https://beta.nsf.gov/news/birds-follow-army-ants-find-prey

15. Stainbrook, K. (2020, February 21). *Discover why plant pollination is anything but random*. UWM Report. https://uwm.edu/news/where-the-bees-are/

16. Gelineau, K. (2021, August). *Brutal beauty: Is artistic swimming Tokyo's toughest sport?* AP News. https://apnews.com/article/2020-tokyo-olympics-sports-health-australia-olympic-team-artistic-swimming-16808d0730d0f91f802d593da3c19999

17. English, A. (2021, August). What is the difference between synchronized swimming and artistic swimming? *Diario AS*. https://en.as.com/en/2021/08/01/olympic_games/1627845508_487283.html

18. Valosik, V. (2021, July 2). *Artistic swimming: Ancient Roman spectacle to modern Olympic sport*. https://www.swimmingworldmagazine.com/news/artistic-swimming-ancient-roman-spectacle-to-modern-olympic-sport/

19. Bennett, P. (2011, December 2). *Curious about ... synchronized swimming. Chronicles: Musing on meaning.*

20. Valosik, V. (2016, August 12). Synchronized swimming has a history that dates back to ancient Rome. *Smithsonian Magazine.* https://www.smithsonianmag.com/history/synchronized-swimming-has-history-dates-back-ancient-rome-180960108/

21. Joe, H. (2019, July 26). *10 Interesting facts about synchronized swimming.* Njswim. https://njswim.com/10-interesting-facts-about-synchronized-swimming/

22. Technical required elements: Team. (2022, October 21). Inside Synchro. https://insidesynchro.org/technical-required-elements-team/

23. What is artistic swimming? Why the sport's name changed from synchronized swimming. (2021, August 2). NBC Chicago. https://www.nbcchicago.com/news/sports/tokyo-summer-olympics/what-is-artistic-swimming-why-the-sports-name-changed-from-synchronized-swimming/2576787/

PART 8: TRANSFORMATIVE LEADERSHIP

N/A

INDEX

PERSONAL THANKS

To Nicole for our life's journey together
and for encouraging, engaging, and enduring me during this project
To Lakin and Eléonore for the joy you've brought
and your courage to build the future
To Lorraine and Art for the many ways you have given life.

– Ted

To my mum Catherine, Gwendoline, and Jessica
for inspiring me to believe that anything is possible.
To everyone reading this book, I hope it inspires you to make a
difference.

– Charlotte

To my wife Tamsi for supporting me, encouraging me, talking me
off the ledge and holding down the fort when I disappeared into
my many writing holes.
To my children Rami, Kian, and Maya, whose
love and demands for playtime made me write more efficiently.
To my parents who believed I was a writer from Day 1,
and never wavered from that belief, even when I occasionally did.

– Omar

CONTRIBUTORS

This book benefited greatly from many contributors. While our brief mentions won't do justice to each person's activities, we share them as signs of our gratitude.

DEVELOPMENT CONTRIBUTIONS

Thanks to the American Marketing Association, and to AMA board member Bernie Jaworski, for inviting Ted to participate in its seven-book series on modern marketing. Ted also thanks his former partner and co-author Adrian Slywotzky for years of thought leadership role modelling and inspiration.

Michael Dunn, Prophet's Chief Executive Officer, provided invaluable encouragement and leadership support for this book's development, displaying the same business IQ and human values with which he leads the firm. Jesse Smith contributed always-on legal support, Amy Silverstein enabled well-justified investment, and Amanda Nizzere and Alexis Thomas provided critical marketing support. Special thanks to David Aaker for idea sharing lunches along the way and for investing time and thought to write this book's foreword.

Genoveva Llosa, Olivia Peluso, and Jeremy Herman each provided distinctly valuable editing services. Additionally, Aubrey Littleton, Olivia Mayeda, and Chad Nichols provided very helpful copy support. Jacqui Liu, Harrison Freemyer, Maggie Royce, and Davinci Lam worked to ensure that this book's insights can be communicated well to clients and colleagues. Josh Feldmuth, Jorge Aguilar, and Jeff Gourdji invited their clients into early-stage conversations that helped to evolve our thinking.

Major thanks to Charlotte Maiorana, Nick Wallwork, Thomas Creighton, Kathy Robson, S. Rajachitra and Pavithra Muthu of Emerald Books for their patience in awaiting the manuscript and for their publishing support thereafter.

CONTENT CONTRIBUTIONS

Introduction

David Novak was an early and influential thought partner on the modern customer journey and various dimensions of marketing transformation that underpin this book. Mike Leiser provided a valuable sounding board on the evolving role of marketing. Christine Brandt Jones advocated customer centricity throughout, while Chris Burzminski and Michael Puff provided Brand Relevance Index data and analytical support that enabled us to express the customer's voice through longitudinal data. Nate Borchers supported the streaming media example through research. Darcy Muñoz, Isabella Courtenay-Morris, and Claire Akkan helpfully generated playbook-related names.

Portfolio and Design Plays

Jacqui Liu, Sarah Mier, Jarrett Fein, and Kim Roffey did client work and codified insights that contributed significantly to the design plays that appear in four chapters: "Magnetic Architecture," "Platform-Wide Differentiators," "Pivotal Persona Value," and "Customer Coalition Edge." Aubrey Littleton supported Optimal Platform Role archetypes through his research. Chan Su and Charles Gariepy developed views on convergent competition that proved a helpful stimulant. Gordon Smith contributed expert perspective on new ways platforms are being used in financial services.

Demand and Innovation Plays

Research and client work by Mat Zucker, David Novak, Marisa Mulvihill, Sarah Mier, Thomas Anderson, and Hanif Perry contributed to Brand–Demand Lead Engine thinking. Michael Puff, Evan Rowe, Jenneva Vargas, and Melissa Goldner helped generate Lead-to-Sales Smoothing ideas. Jacqui Liu, Nate Borchers, Kristen Groh, Tobias Bärschneider, and Jessica Holdcroft provided helpful Success to Momentum and In-Use Enrichment examples. Eunice Shin contributed DTC advocacy and key Catalytic Community concepts. John Ellett, Angie Getter, and Mason Adams enriched Customer Renewal and Expansion through their account-based marketing and customer lifetime value management approaches.

Thanks to Alan Casey, Jacqueline Alexis Thung, Cecilia Huang, Tom (Yixi) Zhang, Elaine Fok, Nuttorn Vongsurawat, and Lily Wen for Reimagined Flows and Extended Ecosystem examples and support. Christian Cortes and Darrell Ross contributed to Better Data Deal constructs. Darcy Muñoz' client work and perspectives enriched Brands Get a Brain, while Tali Krakowsky Apel's original thinking on living brands was influential on our perspective. Danny Pomerantz and Mat Zucker contributed their thinking to Reality Shifts. Larry Reed, Richard Leftley, Joseph Oliver, Dan Truman, and Kristen Groh supported ideas and example development on Visibility for Good.

Interaction and Transformation Plays

Digital engagement practitioners Ashleigh Smith, Maria Seaver, Ron Surfield, Alex Whittaker, and Evan Rowe contributed insights to Full-Journey Engagement. Customer insights and analytics experts Andrew Marcum and Kyle Manlove provided valuable inputs to Dynamic Segmentation. Amy Laskin's content expertise helped shape Agile Content. Alex Moseman made a particularly helpful contribution by drafting Adaptive Innovation.

Tony Fross drafted key sections of Enterprise Body, Mind, and Soul. The Human-Centered Transformation model reflected thought leadership of Tony Fross, Helen Rosethorn, Michael Welch, and Paul Teuton. Paul Lambert and Michael Lopez contributed new thinking, including how platforms can be used to allocate internal team resources.

DESIGN CONTRIBUTIONS

Diagrams throughout this book were designed by the authors and then refined and made consistent through the design services of Alexandra Wong and VSNRY. The principles for the cover design of this book and the AMA book series were contributed by Spencer Seligman, Alejandro Largo, and Craig Stout. The final cover design for this book was developed by VSNRY.

ABOUT THE AUTHORS

 **Ted Moser** is a Senior Partner at Prophet, a growth and transformation consultancy. He helps leading technology-based companies to anticipate customer and market evolution, craft distinctive value growth strategies, and realize their ambitions.

He holds an MBA with highest honors in marketing and strategy from the Wharton Business School, following a BS in Political Science from Wheaton College. Based in San Francisco, he has lived and worked extensively in Europe, Latin America, and Asia.

His published thought leadership focuses on pattern recognition that helps companies thrive in the face of change. He previously co-authored *Profit Patterns* to identify how profit pools would shift with Internet business model innovation. In recent years, his extensive consulting work with global platform leaders and with companies transforming to platforms inspired him to write *Winning Through Platforms*.

Ted supports global microfinance development as a lifelong avocation. He has helped to scale the Opportunity International microfinance network, which has served over 250 million of the world's poor and is developing innovative platforms to better serve poor farmers, schools, and microentrepreneurs. He served on program boards of CGAP, the World Bank-affiliated multilateral research group, to help extend the boundaries of global digital financial inclusion.

Charlotte Bloom is the CEO of VSNRY, a strategic consulting firm where she works with visionary leaders to identify and bring to market industry-defining business strategies and innovations. Her clients have successfully launched new businesses, rebranded, pivoted to more lucrative business models, launched digital and platform transformations, been acquired, and IPO'd.

Recognized as an international thought leader on personal and business growth, she is a regular contributor to leading business publications such as *Inc.*, *Entrepreneur*, *Forbes*, and *Bloomberg* and a recipient of titles such as Chartered Fellow for the *Chartered Management Institute*. Also a Serial Entrepreneur and Advocate for carbon negativity/climate positivity and women's opportunities, she has garnered awards from *HSBC*, *Enactus*, and *The Prince's Trust* for her nonprofit work.

Born and raised in the UK, Charlotte graduated with a first-class honors BSc in business and finance. She first worked in M&A and restructuring at *Lazard* and then in corporate strategy at the UK's largest energy company. She now lives and works internationally, divides her time between London and the USA, all while inspiring and driving positive change.

Omar Akhtar conducts research and advises companies on best practices in data, technology, and go-to-market excellence. He is the Research Director and an Associate Partner at Prophet, a growth and transformation consultancy. His research publications include digital practice benchmarks, maturity models, guides for developing strategies, and frameworks for evaluating people, processes, and technologies.

As a Technology Expert, he has provided Commentary for prominent media outlets, including *The Associated Press*, *National Public Radio*, *Forbes*, *TechCrunch*, and *Yahoo News*.

A graduate of Columbia University's Journalism School, Omar has covered tech and finance for *Fortune* and was the editor-in-chief of the business tech blog *The Hub*, where he was one of the first writers to cover marketing cloud technology. He lives in the San Francisco Bay Area with his wife and three children, with a vigilant eye on where the next tech disruption will come from.

Printed in the USA
CPSIA information can be obtained
at www.ICGtesting.com
JSHW010655101123
51857JS00002B/2